To the ozone community,
whose deep connections and moral courage saved humanity.

To my parents (Mary and Bob), my in-laws (Nancy and Jim),
and my husband (Chris) for their unconditional love.

This book is filled with collective wisdom from people who have
built deep, meaningful connections that have changed their lives and the
lives of so many others for the better. With great thanks to them for their
honesty, love, laughter, and wonder. They are the true authors of the
wisdom in this book (although any mistakes are all mine).

This book is a celebration of co-creation. It would not exist without
a collective who believed in the idea and who worked alongside me for
years. The mentions of "I" in this book are really the "we" of this group.
With great thanks for their wondrous partnership: Andrea Brenninkmeijer,
Joann McPike, Ellie Kanner, Kelly Hallman, John Stares, Shannon
Sedgwick Davis, Cindy Mercer, Todd Holcomb, Keith Yamashita,
Mich Ahern, and Lisa Weeks Valiant.

Contents

Introduction   *xi*

ONE
Six Degrees of Connection   *1*

TWO
Something Bigger   *13*

THREE
All-In   *37*

FOUR
The Ecosystem   *67*

FIVE
Magnetic Moments   *115*

SIX

Celebrate Friction   *149*

SEVEN

Collective Connections   *173*

EIGHT

Interconnected   *203*

Gratitude   *213*

Plus Wonder Partnerships   *219*

Six Degrees of Connection Shorthand   *227*

Words of Wisdom and
Collaborative Resources   *231*

Six Degrees of Connection Images   *269*

Notes   *271*

Photo Credits   *281*

Index   *283*

Join Our Plus Wonder Community   *295*

Letter from Simon Sinek

The vision is clear: to build a world in which the vast majority of people wake up every single morning inspired, feel safe wherever they are, and end the day fulfilled by the work that they do. And the best way for us to advance toward this vision is together. But there's a problem . . .

Most people already know the importance of teamwork, cooperation, and "building strong working relationships" to get things done (and there have been countless books and articles written that drive home the point and teach us the skills to do those things). But there is another kind of relationship that gets less attention. A kind of relationship that is essential to advance any cause of value. A kind of relationship that goes much deeper than even some of the highest functioning teams and the most productive working relationships. That of the partnership.

I hesitate to even call these magical unions "partnerships" because the word actually does these relationships a disservice. A "partnership" is a noun, a thing. Two people may *have* a partnership or *be in* one, but for a partnership to reap the true benefits of the dynamic, it must be active. It must be a verb. A daily practice. To advance something greater than ourselves we must learn to *partner*.

Partnering is an exploration of these deeper, more enduring kinds of relationships. Many of them look more like marriages than professional relationships (and some of them are marriages). What they all have in common, however, is the willingness of both parties to completely open up themselves to their partner and to invest in deepening their relationship. This is why they not only last, but why they work.

As Jean Oelwang's life progressed, she kept meeting and getting the chance to work with some of these remarkable partners. She saw, firsthand, the remarkable math that takes place when these partnerships work. It wasn't the tired $1 + 1 = 3$, it was more profound. It was more like $1 + 1 =$ millions. The power these partnerships produced inspired businesses, social movements, radical change, and the countless people who helped.

Jean became more than fascinated by these unique relationships and what made them different from other partnerships. She learned that there were discernible patterns among all these partnerships. Patterns that we could practice. In other words, every one of us has the ability to partner. This is a big deal. And this is why I asked Jean to write a book for Optimism Press. If more of us can learn to partner like the people in this book, then we become better equipped to advance big things and enjoy the deep safety and confidence that comes from knowing that there is someone by our side that will never, ever leave.

Partner on!
Simon Sinek

Introduction

Who has loved you into being?

—Mr. Rogers

On October 24, 2006, I jumped into a taxi along with my boss, Richard Branson, the founder of the Virgin Group, and a friend, Nicola Elliott. We made our way to Houghton, a leafy green suburb of Johannesburg, South Africa. Each of us carefully clutched a three-ring binder filled with hundreds of precious pages. When we arrived, we hopped out of the car and were greeted by Nelson Mandela's wife, Graça Machel. Her combination of authentic warmth, formidable wisdom, and radiant generosity quickly made us feel like we had known her for a lifetime. She had been the education minister of Mozambique, had been a freedom fighter, and now had become a fierce international advocate for women and children.

We settled into their living room and Nelson Mandela soon came to join us, dressed in one of his signature silk shirts with a detailed print, untucked at the waist. His towering stature, bright smile, and quick wit immediately lit up the room with joy and laughter. We started to go through the binders page by page. They were filled with the rich biographies of inspired global leaders, all potential candidates to become one of the twelve Elders, a collective created by Graça and Mandela in partnership with Richard and his close friend, the brilliant musician Peter Gabriel, to work on conflict resolution and other seemingly intractable issues facing humanity. I had the good fortune (alongside a wonderful set of partners) to work with them to make the idea a reality.

For hours, we alternated between roars of laughter and tears as Mandela shared story after story about people like Archbishop Tutu, former UN secretary-general Kofi Annan, former president of the United States Jimmy Carter, and former president of Ireland Mary Robinson. The love, respect, and depth of connection he had with each one of these great leaders was clear. These relationships had helped make Mandela who he was in this world and had given all of them enormous support toward creating something much bigger than themselves.

Beyond Mandela's electric energy, the other thing that filled the room was Graça and Mandela's love for each other, an ever-present reminder of the power of a deep relationship. It was a romantic love, of course, but their relationship went well beyond that. The two were so deeply connected that you could see and feel their bond in even their most trivial interactions. Each was always looking out for the other's welfare, quick to praise the other, and constantly lifting the other up with a quiet glance, a gentle smile, or the touch of a hand. Their shared love and respect radiated to all of us in the room. I had never felt such a strong degree of loving presence, curiosity, and purpose.

It was in that moment of listening to Graça and Mandela talk about their friends that I realized that the path to living a meaningful life is through the Deep Connections we nurture with each other.

These Deep Connections are relationships of purpose that make us who we are. They are the enduring "got your back" friendships found in all aspects of our lives. These relationships help us become our best selves and multiply the impact we make in the world.

That realization sparked a fifteen-year exploration of Deep Connections and their role in architecting collaborative initiatives, beginning with The Elders, then The B Team, a group of business leaders working toward a better way of doing business, and about a dozen more initiatives that emerged from my work with Virgin Unite, the charitable arm of the Virgin Group. Over the years I spent working with many legendary collaborators, it has become clear to me that none of them achieved their legacies of impact alone. They each became who they are through the meaningful relationships they built along the way.

Once I became attuned to Deep Connections, I saw them at the heart of every major initiative, every key innovation, every well-lived life. I've learned that the only way we are really going to solve humanity's biggest, most complicated problems is by forging meaningful partnerships and then using those relationships as catalysts to drive even larger collaborations and social movements: Archbishop and Leah Tutu working with a group of friends to help take down apartheid in South Africa. José María and Christiana Figueres, siblings who have dedicated their lives to stopping climate change, as demonstrated by Christiana's collaborative leadership of the Paris Agreement, a global agreement to reduce greenhouse gas emissions. Business partners like Ben Cohen and Jerry Greenfield, of Ben & Jerry's, long at the forefront of the movement to change business for the better.

These remarkable agitators and innovators don't dominate. They collaborate. They listen. They lift each other (and many others) up.

Deep Connection, I've come to believe, doesn't just make us happy, it is fundamental to our continued existence. Mastering the skills of partnering is the first step to building the collaborations necessary to tackle our toughest challenges. Understanding the skills required to build Deep Connections will redefine how you think about leadership. This isn't easy. Over my years of research since that October day, I've learned how powerfully we are programmed to prioritize individual accomplishment over the Deep Connections and partnerships that truly make a difference.

I've also realized how profoundly that programming has impacted my own life.

Close to twenty years before that moment in South Africa, I was fresh out of college and just starting a role at a large telecommunications company, where I'd been sent off for "leadership training." Nervously cradling a glass of water, I started talking to one of the more senior executives at the event. Success on my mind, I boldly asked him what he'd done to achieve his own.

"You need to bleed blue," he replied matter-of-factly, nodding to the company color. "You need to give everything you've got to the job. You need to make sure you shine above everyone else." After I survived the training and started my job, my well-intentioned first boss gifted me two books. A copy of *The Art of War*, a 2,500-year-old book of military strategy long embraced by business leaders looking for an edge over their competitors. Message received. Business was a battle. Also, a copy of *The Joy of Cooking*. Second message received. Most women don't survive the battle.

Determined to prove that I could be a successful female leader without relying on military tactics, I set out on a journey to work hard and to smash as many glass ceilings as possible. Over a two-decade career, I helped start and grow mobile phone companies on six continents before launching a global foundation, Virgin Unite. In my personal life, I was a serial monogamist, changing partners every time I changed countries, eight countries in twenty years. My fly-by visits to my parents, wedged in uneasily during my near-constant travels, always left them feeling like a whirling dervish had momentarily whisked through their lives. Work colleagues were carefully placed into "work boxes," and friendships were squeezed into "taxi calls" at all hours from all over the world. Yet along the way I believed I had built significant partnerships in all aspects of my life, nurturing truly loving relationships. But the truth was that most of my partnerships were built on fleeting in-between moments. They were far from deep, lifetime connections.

When I had the chance to learn from the great partnerships you will meet in this book, the curtains of glorified individualism were pulled back. It struck me that in my quest for "success," I had not properly invested in the most important part of life: building meaningful, enduring relationships that make the world a better place. These extraordinary partnerships showed me that we don't "win" by scrambling to the top of whatever ladder we're climbing. We win by nurturing Deep Connections that accomplish so much more than any of us could ever do on our own.

Of course, who could blame any of us for thinking differently? From a young age, we're pushed to compete, to win at all costs. As we grow, we're encouraged to build a large network of shallow connections to help achieve society's warped vision of success. This mentality leaves us disconnected from each other and from a meaning-ful life of purpose. Ultimately, it even stifles organizations. This was clear in a 2021 Gallup poll that found that 64 percent of people in the United States feel disengaged at work, and 80 percent globally feel disengaged. Interestingly, the 36 percent of employees in the United States who do feel engaged used words like *cooperative, collaborative, warm relationships, family,* and *teamwork* to describe their companies.

I believe the glorification of hyperindividualism has plunged us into a crisis of loneliness. We fear difference instead of celebrating it. We respond to leadership through domination rather than coopera-tion. We forget basic civility. Prioritizing individualism perpetuates racism, climate change, and inequality as people get so lost in them-selves and their own interests that they repeatedly miss the opportu-nity for achieving greater collective good. A 2020 study from the Pew Research Center revealed that 57 percent of Americans think that most of the time, people would just look out for themselves, not try and help others.

"When we liberated the individual from the collective, that was a sociological equivalent of splitting the atom," explains renowned anthropologist Wade Davis, "and we suddenly, in doing so, cast the individual adrift into a world that could be quite lonely." Digital tech-nology and the loss of physical community gathering spaces have often amplified this disconnection. Wade sums up the impact of these new social norms by imagining life on Earth as seen through the eyes of a Martian anthropologist: "If the measure of success was technological achievement, we would shine like a diamond," he concedes. "But if they looked at our social structures, they'd ask a few obvious questions. Hey, you know, you guys love marriage, but half your marriages end in divorce. . . . You love your families, but you have this weird slogan, '24/7,' implying total dedication to the workplace. . . ."

We spend massive amounts of time working, finding ourselves, keeping fit, and building the breadth of our connections. Yet we invest very little effort in increasing the depth of our connections with the people who mean the most to us. We take those relationships for granted, living under the misconception that we somehow make ourselves who we are. In reality, it is the people we surround ourselves with who make us.

The world needs a relationship reset.

This reset begins with an understanding of how to build Deep Connections in all aspects of our lives. These are the foundations that allow for exponential impact. Since that moment in Graça and Mandela's living room, I have been consumed with the question that eventually led to the writing of this book: How do you find, build, and cultivate meaningful, lasting relationships that will help you become the best possible version of yourself in order to have the greatest positive impact on others?

To answer this question, I have appealed directly to the source: long-lasting partnerships that made a much bigger difference in the world together than they could ever have on their own, starting with some of The Elders. Talking with each of them, I asked them some crucial questions: How do you build trust? What happens when trust breaks? How do you disagree about something that's important to you without destroying the relationship? How do you stay connected over the years?

Soon enough, I found recurring patterns. Though the partners came from wildly disparate backgrounds and had made positive impacts in different areas, there were fundamental similarities in the way they related to each other and to the outside world. I saw these patterns once more when I did a deep dive into what had worked and what had not across the more than a dozen collaborations we have incubated over the past fifteen years at Virgin Unite.

Curious, I began plastering the walls of my home with printed snippets from the interviews in an attempt to arrange them according to these emerging patterns. Soon, the walls proved insufficient to the task, so I became more systematic, coding and organizing hundreds of pages of transcripts, all in an effort to home in on the remarkable similarities that emerged from very different worlds. I saw how naive it was to think that a few conversations would crack the secrets of Deep Connection. Ten interviews became twenty, then thirty, then sixty—and still counting. What rose to the surface over the course of all this exploration was an elegant set of principles, six beautiful aspects of true connection that I found to be consistent across all the types of relationships I explored: friends and family members, romantic and business partners. This investigation into human connection bloomed into Plus Wonder, a not-for-profit initiative focused on inspiring people to nurture Deep Connections that matter in their own lives and the lives of others. Plus Wonder has evolved into many beautiful things, including, now, this book.

Over the past fifteen years I've interviewed entrepreneurs, friends, siblings, romantic partners, social activists, public servants, religious leaders, philanthropic leaders, journalists, cultural icons, and digital pioneers. Some of these partnerships are well known; others you'll be delighted to meet for the first time. I've been on a journey with this great group of partners to explore how we can spark a relationship reset, for ourselves and for the world.

The more absorbed I became in the over fifteen hundred years of collective wisdom of the partnerships I interviewed, the more I realized that this is not simply about building great relationships in your life. It's about fundamentally changing the way we connect with one another. Each of the relationships profiled in this book has a handful of lifelong, deep connections (including each other) that have helped multiply their impact. These few close relationships serve as "connection labs" where partners can safely practice and evolve the six patterns of connection. The benefits of mastering these patterns then extend to all the people they connect with, even in their most fleeting of relationships. I've called these interconnected patterns the **Six Degrees of Connection**. As you practice each one in your most important relationships, you increase the depth you can achieve in all your relationships.

Subsequent chapters delve into each of the Six Degrees through the profound and refreshingly honest stories of the over sixty partnerships. You'll see how they lift each other's purpose, how they stay all-in for the long run, how they build unbreakable bonds, and how they gracefully manage conflict.

Throughout the book, I also explore some of the greatest collective efforts of our time and the Deep Connections at the hearts of these achievements. The citizens who collaborated to protect the ozone layer and literally saved all our lives. The friends who ultimately ended the cruel apartheid regime in South Africa and transformed the lives of millions. We'll uncover the collaborative design principles that led to the success of these and other extraordinary collective achievements. These insights will help us respond to the existential threats we face today.

For most of my life, I believed that building meaningful relationships in work and life came down to simply waiting for the universe to bring me the right partners. The partners in this book opened my eyes to an opportunity I'd never seen. They were successful together not thanks to fate or luck but because they'd worked hard to invest deeply in each other. They each helped the other do something much bigger in life than they ever could have done alone. Instinctively, they'd each come to understand the six patterns at the heart of this book. Most of us spend our whole lives wondering idly why our most important relationships never become as close or as meaningful as we hoped. It's tragic. We are taught only a tiny sliver of what it takes to build great relationships.

The world was shut down by the coronavirus pandemic in 2020, during the completion of this book. During that difficult time, there was one thing that was universally missed: human connection. Isolation, social distancing, and quarantine made it clear how irrelevant all the shiny things we chase—power, money, fame, material goods— really are. We paused our 24/7 lives and simply craved being with one another. As we watched loved ones die from the other side of a window or on a Zoom call, unable to even hold their hand, we realized that the only things that really matter, the only true measure of success, are the Deep Connections we build with the people who matter to us.

When Warren Buffett was asked about success and the meaning of life, he posed a simple question: "Do the people you care about love you back?" As someone who has achieved the pinnacle of financial gain, he realizes that the true measure of success is the depth and meaning of our relationships. The importance of measuring success this way became so clear to me a few years after my initial meeting with Graça and Mandela. We were gathered in a hotel in Johannesburg for an anything but ordinary lunch. The meal was punctuated by laughter, love, and intense discussion about the state of the world as The Elders celebrated Nelson Mandela's ninetieth birthday.

When Mandela stood up to leave, he looked around the table one last time, his welcoming smile like a burst of sunshine. It would be one of the last times The Elders were all together with him before he passed away. His smile said a million things about his gratitude to his friends and his understanding that his legacy of change would live on through them. Mandela then turned to his left and gently slipped his hand into Graça's. They gracefully left the room. As he watched them go, Archbishop Tutu, in a rare moment of intense seriousness, said, "My, how we are all prisoners of hope."

Mandela stayed hopeful even as he weathered the unthinkable, becoming one of the most successful leaders of our time in large part because he surrounded himself with greatness, people whose love and shared commitment to ending apartheid and to a better world lifted him and so many others.

As I glanced at the people around the lunch table, I saw past presidents, formidable human rights activists, business leaders, and artists, and realized that they all shared what made Mandela so successful. They had forged enduring partnerships of meaning that helped them change the world for the better.

They were who they were because of their Deep Connections.

A few years after that lunch, Mary Robinson, former president of Ireland and now the chair of The Elders, summed it up beautifully in a tribute to Mandela at his funeral: "We can honor him best by giving of ourselves to others."

At that first meeting with Graça and Mandela, I thought that perhaps the realm of meaningful connections was out of my reach, reserved for leaders like The Elders. What I've learned on this journey is that it's anything but. Any one of us can build deep, lasting, and purposeful relationships in our lives. Like anything meaningful, though, it's hard work. Nobody enters, maintains, and grows partnerships perfectly.

You might have heard the proverb, "If you want to go fast, go alone; if you want to go far, go together." But what has become clear to me through these interviews is that the only way we can go both *fast and far* is *together*. What's been missing is the *how*. It's not about shoving a group of people together and hoping for the best. It's about building the Deep Connections that act as scaffolding for larger-scale collaborations.

The roots of Deep Connection aren't complicated. But they are profound, and they go against society's training. That's why I've written *Partnering*: to help readers everywhere understand the six principles that will transform all their most meaningful relationships. This has not been a rigorous, scientific endeavor, but an in-depth exploration grown from a belief that the world needs these principles now more than ever. My work with these partners has been to channel and synthesize their collective wisdom. I am incredibly humbled to have been welcomed into their inner lives.

I hope the wisdom they shared with me will affect your life as deeply as it has mine.

PARTNERING

CHAPTER ONE

Six Degrees of Connection

Life turns on good relationships. All of life.

—Lord Hastings
of Scarisbrick CBE

On June 28, 2015, André Borschberg and Bertrand Piccard had to make the most difficult decision of their lives.

André was alone in the cramped cockpit of a plane called Solar Impulse, built to fly around the world using only the power of the sun collected in its seventeen thousand solar panels. Pasted above the controls was a picture of his beloved wife, Yasemin, and their three children. André was only a few hours into a treacherous five-day flight over the Pacific from Nagoya, Japan, to Hawaii. Bertrand was in the control center in Monaco with their world-class team of engineers and scientists, monitoring every aspect of the weather, pilot health, and safety of the plane.

Though Solar Impulse was a technological marvel, it had a light frame, like the bones of a bird, and a power output only slightly greater than that of the Wright Brothers' first plane. There was little room for error. One mistake would be the end of the plane, and likely the end of André.

André, an entrepreneur, fighter pilot, and engineer, and Bertrand, a psychiatrist, explorer, and aviator, had dedicated the past twelve years of their lives to a shared mission of showing the world the possibilities of renewable energy by circumnavigating the globe in this plane powered only by solar energy. Since meeting in 2003, they'd bonded over a love of adventure and commitment to clean energy. Now the two friends were taking turns piloting each of the twelve legs of the flight, with André at the controls of this particularly long and difficult stretch to Hawaii.

Suddenly, André heard the beeping of the emergency alert system. Something was wrong.

The team quickly huddled in the control center to investigate. Identifying an electrical malfunction, they strongly recommended that André turn the plane around and return to Japan rather than risk the five-day flight. They knew that beyond the technical risks, André was already going to be pushing the limits of human endurance by sleeping in twenty-minute bursts, or about three hours a day. The constant emergency beeping would endanger even that.

After a month stuck in China, an unexpected stop in Japan due to weather, and two previous attempts to cross the Pacific thwarted by storms, André and Bertrand were concerned. They knew that turning around now would likely signal the end of their shared mission to help propel the world toward solar energy.

The two friends got on the satellite phone and went through all the potential risks. Their trust in and respect for each other, built over years of working together, and their belief in the quality of the plane that had been lovingly built by their team, had prepared them for this difficult moment. They calmly talked through the risks in a safe space, knowing they had each other's backs.

Despite Bertrand and André's calm, the rest of the team's tension in the control room was palpable as they waited for the outcome.

Bertrand hung up the phone and announced their decision: "Let's go. Let's cross the Pacific."

Five days later, André successfully landed in Hawaii. His was the first solar flight to make the Pacific crossing and the longest ever solo flight in the history of humanity.

Yet they still had 8,765 miles to go and many more challenges to tackle. They continued to take turns piloting the plane for the next year to complete their global mission. On July 26, 2016, Bertrand completed the final leg and landed in Abu Dhabi, where he opened the cockpit of the plane and embraced André. They were on the same runway where, sixteen months earlier, Bertrand had waved him off at the start of their journey with the words, "Have a good flight, André, my friend, my solar brother."

Over twelve years, they'd endured challenge after challenge—together. Neither of them could have done it alone, as each man readily admits.

Not that building their relationship wasn't hard work itself. They had to learn how to share credit, how to turn disagreements into what they called the "sparkles" of learning something new (see chapter six), and how to work together for extended periods in high-stakes situations.

This hard work has paid off, not just in the success of Solar Impulse and the promotion of renewable energy but also in a meaningful, deep relationship that has changed them both for the better.

The stories in this book—the first solar flight to circumnavigate the globe, closing the ozone hole, creating businesses like Airbnb and Ben & Jerry's, lifelong relationships—have something important in common: a crystal-clear framework for building meaningful partnerships. This framework, which I've called the Six Degrees of Connection, is the result of fifteen years of researching, coding, and synthesizing hundreds of pages of interviews to capture more than fifteen hundred years of collective wisdom and experience from more than sixty successful partnerships and collaborations.

Here is a quick overview of the framework that will unfold through the partnership stories in this book:

- **First Degree: Something Bigger**—Lift your purpose through meaningful partnerships. Deepen your connection by becoming part of something bigger.

- **Second Degree: All-In**—Feel safe in the relationship and know you 100 percent have each other's backs for the long run. This gives you the freedom and confidence to do something bigger.

- **Third Degree: The Ecosystem**—Stay all-in through a moral ecosystem, alive with the daily practice of six essential virtues. These are Enduring Trust, Unshakable Mutual Respect, United Belief, Shared Humility, Nurturing Generosity, and Compassionate Empathy. Over time, they become reflexive responses, creating an environment of kindness, grace, and unconditional love.

- **Fourth Degree: Magnetic Moments**—Keep connected and strengthen your ecosystem through intentional practices, rituals, and traditions that keep curiosity and wonder alive, create space for honest communication, spark unlimited joy, and build a wider supportive community.

- **Fifth Degree: Celebrate Friction**—Take the heat out of conflict and turn it into a learning opportunity. Ignite sparks of creative combustion for shared solutions and greater connection, staying all-in and focused on something bigger.

- **Sixth Degree: Collective Connections**—A framework of design principles to scale collaborations, with Deep Connections at the center as role models, hubs of momentum, and connective tissue.

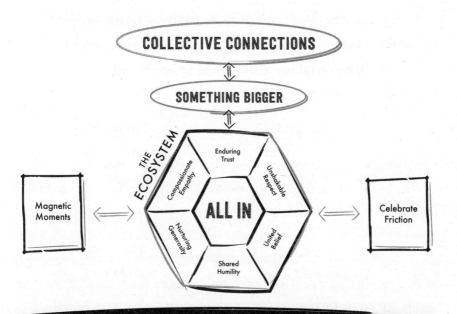

SIX DEGREES OF CONNECTION™ FRAMEWORK FOR DEEP CONNECTIONS

All Six Degrees are interconnected, so mastering one will indeed help you master the others and deepen your relationships. However, if you master one yet ignore another, you put your partnership at risk. Of course, even with this framework, we will all make mistakes—no relationship is ever perfect. The key is having the insight to course correct and the courage to embrace each other's mistakes.

The relationships in this book are hardly the stuff of fairy tales. They are messy and complicated, and they have their own disagreements and pain. They have required patience, acceptance, trust, and hard work. Mindful perseverance has paid off, though, because the people in these life- and world-changing partnerships have learned how to gracefully celebrate their differences and navigate conflict, in large part because their relationships are firmly anchored in meaningful purpose.

When I interviewed President and Mrs. Carter, they calmly told me how very close they had come to getting a divorce (they couldn't even use that word during our conversation, out of respect for each other), ironically when they were writing a book about sharing the rest of their lives together. One of the most beautiful parts of this interview was watching the Carters lovingly and honestly discuss this painful period in their seven-decades-long marriage. They've navigated the hard times and kept their bond strong, as you'll see in chapter three.

This book is filled with rich insights from deeply connected people like the Carters, but it's not about identifying the perfect partner through a carefully developed list of attributes or algorithms, nor is it about finding the silver-bullet fix for partnerships. It does, however, offer profound practical and personal insights from some of the best and most enduring combinations in the world.

Ultimately, the goal is to help you build Deep Connections of your own in all aspects of your life. These are the relationships that define who you are and multiply your positive impact in the world.

I know that embracing, internalizing, and practicing some of the partnership behaviors shared in the Six Degrees of Connection framework won't be easy. Making the change to a partnership mentality is like leaving an Olympic team as an established solo gymnast and joining a troupe of high-wire acrobats who must trust each other with their lives.

Right up front I want to share some of the common mistakes people make when trying to nurture deeper relationships.

The Pitfalls

There is no such thing as a perfect, fairy-tale relationship in which nothing ever goes wrong. We must begin by unlearning much of what we've been told. Starting in childhood, we are taught to search for our Prince or Princess Charming, with whom we fit like a glove, so we can live happily ever after. In school we are encouraged to search for friends who look and act like us, who will entertain us, follow us on social media, and make us feel part of the in-crowd. In work we're taught to find the people and companies with the best ideas, the winning products, the largest compensation packages—the next unicorns. Very little energy is put into teaching us how to find and build diverse relationships across all aspects of our lives, with those who are different from us and will challenge us to become better people—who will support us, and whom we will support in return—on our way toward achieving a bigger mission.

As we invest in deeper relationships, we also need to keep an eye out for the opposite of Deep Connections—the relationships that drag us down, taking us away from our mission in life. Watch out for the people who make you lose your confidence, put their own interests above everything else, erode your ability to trust others, crush your dreams, and stoke your fears. All of us have been stuck in the quicksand of negative relationships that subtract from the precious time we have in this world to make a difference for others.

Drawing from the insights of business coaches, psychologists, and other relationship experts, I identified the following five pitfalls that keep us from creating Deep Connections. Not surprisingly, they broadly correlate to the Six Degrees of Connection:

1. **Lack of shared meaning**—The number one thing that derails relationships is an inability to find shared meaning.

2. **Imbalance of commitment**—When one partner seems absent from the relationship, or someone feels like they are putting in more time and energy than the other, connection suffers.

3. **Mismatched values**—Lack of shared values can end a relationship before it really begins.

4. **Roller coaster of conflict**—Nothing saps more positive energy from a partnership than repetitive drama.

5. **Superhero syndrome**—We are so programmed to be individual leaders that others often simply check out if

they feel like we are not in it *with* them. With that retreat comes a shift in commitment, a lack of accountability, and the end of any attempt to collaborate.

There is no perfect answer to where you can find meaningful connections. The good news is that opportunities exist everywhere, but only if we take the time to slow down, connect, and be present when we meet new people. Many of the partnerships in this book met randomly—in school, at work, on a blind date, in a poetry slam class, in an art gallery, in a courtroom, in the African bush, in their own families, and, if you happen to be as fortunate as President and Mrs. Carter, as neighbors at birth.

What's important is thoughtfully investing time in identifying and nurturing a diverse group of Deep Connections and deepening those important relationships. Richard Reed, cofounder of Innocent Drinks, whom you'll learn more about in chapter five, says, "The most important decision you're ever going to make is who you choose to spend your life with, personal or professional. We are nothing other than the summation of our relationships. So, choose wisely."

Deep Connections also help you define your purpose. They keep you on track when the going gets tough, and in turn they create far more resilient and meaningful relationships. While purpose and partnerships constantly reinforce each other, they often have the added benefit of bringing down the flawed barriers we put up between work and life. As Beverly Joubert, cofounder of Big Cats Initiative, told me, "When you find your core passion, it becomes a part of your life—not just 'work' that separates you from the rest of life."

We've created a false myth that work and personal relationships must be kept separate. When you step back and reflect on this idea, it makes no sense whatsoever. We spend over 33 percent of our lives at work; if we fail to invest in Deep Connections that can bring greater meaning to a third of our life and beyond, we're missing a major opportunity.

When we apply the same skills we use in building friendships to a work setting, our connections at work transform from being transactional and goal driven to having true depth and purpose. Ultimately, these Deep Connections will create better businesses as well. Richard Reed started his business with his three best mates, and eighteen years later, they are still best friends. Yet he still gets asked whether it is weird doing business with his friends. He always replies, "Isn't it weird *not* doing business with your friends?"

Creating Deep Connections increases the opportunity for diverse thinking and more robust approaches to whatever challenges we decide to take on. Of course, there is no set number, shape, or size of Deep Connections. The breadth of partnerships I've studied has shown me that the skills to build a strong relationship are consistent, whether in a friendship, business partnership, or romantic partnership (or, in some cases, all three in one).

Some people have one Deep Connection, while others have a handful—the number is not important; the depth is. There is also a depth continuum across relationships: some at one end as your deepest connections and others at the opposite end, those with whom you might have a fleeting relationship. Nurturing your Deep Connections will help make all your relationships as meaningful as possible, approaching every interaction with trust, respect, and curiosity as second nature.

Our Deep Connections bring us meaning, love, and got-your-back friendships—a chance to become the best possible version of ourselves and to create significant positive impact.

They are also the key to many of the collaborations that have changed the shape of our world for the better.

CHAPTER TWO

Something Bigger

First Degree of Connection

There isn't a single superhero; no individual
is strong enough alone.

—Jim Roth, cofounder of
LeapFrog Investments

Professor Frank Sherwood Rowland walked in the front door. His
wife, Joan, still remembers how he responded when she asked how
work had been. "It's going really well," he told her. "The only trouble
is, I think it's the end of the world."

Professor Rowland started the chemistry program at the University
of California, Irvine, in 1964. He was building a family and deeply in
love with Joan. At six feet five inches, he had played basketball at
Ohio Wesleyan. His humor and good-natured affability had long ago
earned him the nickname "Sherry." He was widely admired by the
chemistry students who came to UCI to work with him. One of these

students was Mario Molina, from Mexico City, who joined Sherry's postdoctoral program in 1973 and with whom Sherry would discover what did indeed feel like the end of the world.

I never had the chance to meet Sherry, but I was fortunate to have a video interview with Mario from his home in Mexico just months before he died in 2020. Warm and soft-spoken, Mario had an obvious overflowing affection and deep respect for Sherry. He was a dedicated academic scientist with a laser-like focus. In contrast to Mario's understated demeanor, Sherry, while somewhat shy, had a confident personality that matched his physical stature. Yet despite their different dispositions, their futures would soon become entwined in ways neither could have imagined. "We had very different personalities, but we became very close friends," Mario shared with me.

When he arrived in the UCI chemistry department, Mario was looking for a challenge, and together, he and Sherry decided he would focus on atmospheric chemistry, tackling the question of what happens to chlorofluorocarbons in the environment. Chlorofluorocarbons, or CFCs, were in everything from refrigerators to pesticides to air conditioners to deodorant and hair spray. Sherry's interest in CFCs had been sparked when he'd learned about the work of British chemist James Lovelock, the first to conclude that CFCs remained in the atmosphere, drifting around the planet, for far longer than anyone had previously imagined.

Suspecting there might be more to the story, Mario spent months poring over the published data, running calculations, and conferring with Sherry. Before long, the two scientists knew they were onto something, yet what they discovered was almost too hard to believe: CFCs were carried by wind currents to the stratosphere, where they were catalytically breaking down the earth's protective ozone layer.

Without this invisible shield in place, the destructive force of ultraviolet radiation from the sun would cause a significant increase in skin cancer and cataracts, compromise the human immune system, destroy ecosystems, and wreak havoc on agriculture. "My first reaction was there must be some mistake," Mario told me. He was stunned that CFCs could be the source of such catastrophic damage. As scientific breakthroughs go, this one was huge. Nothing less than the future of humanity and life on Earth was at stake.

Sherry and Mario had found their shared "something bigger," which was so important that they felt an urgent need to raise the alarm. In 1974, they published their first article about CFCs in the scientific journal *Nature*. In it, they hypothesized that CFCs stay in the atmosphere for 40 to 150 years. They warned that when CFCs reach the stratosphere, ultraviolet radiation from the sun causes them to decompose and release chlorine, which in turn causes a chain reaction that destroys the ozone layer at an alarming rate. They expected that the journal article would spur the world to immediately mobilize to save humanity.

Instead, almost nobody wanted to believe them.

While most scientists may have published their results and stepped back, Sherry and Mario realized that too much was at stake; they could not remain silent, so they went in the opposite direction: they began using their scientific data to mobilize politicians, business leaders, the media, and the public to take action. As expected, they were attacked by the companies who were benefiting from the multibillion-dollar CFC industry. Executives discounted Sherry and Mario's findings and accused them of being publicity seekers. What they did not expect was the assault by their fellow scientists, who considered it improper for academic scientists to take a position and advocate for change.

But they weren't deterred. "What's the use of having developed a science well enough to make predictions if, in the end, all we're willing to do is stand around and wait for them to come true?" Sherry said to a *Newsday* reporter. As scientists, Sherry and Mario were bound by their joint discovery. As humans, they'd found a deep, lifelong connection to each other and to a bigger mission to alert the world to the danger of CFCs to save humanity and the planet.

Bigger Than Us

I have often mistaken purpose as a solo endeavor, but the most meaningful things happen when people come together, like small streams merging into a powerful river. Sometimes, this might just lead to something bigger for the world, as it did with Mario and Sherry, two scientists who shared something bigger that saved humanity.

Purpose multiplies through our relationships and deepens our connections, but only if we are able to stop asking what we can get out of our relationships and start asking what we can give to the world through them. In doing so, individuals shape and grow into something bigger together—whether that's a personal mission, a shared one, or a bit of both.

I knew when I started interviewing partners for this book that they had a bias toward positive impact. After all, I had selected them because their relationships have allowed them to make a bigger difference in the world than they ever could have on their own. So, I was not surprised that purpose featured in the interviews; what blew me away was that it not only featured, it *dominated*.

People used different language to describe purpose: "an audacious goal," "a mission," "a North Star." But over and over again, I heard them say that they reached to achieve something bigger, an outcome that went beyond themselves, their partnerships, and their organizations.

As I started to peel back the layers of "something bigger," it was clear that purpose was also a central factor in the longevity and depth of the interviewees' relationships. Their experiences show how goals that are bigger than a partnership's individual members broaden the focus beyond surface conflicts and into a realm of Deep Connection. A desire for collective success ultimately helps relationships weather inevitable ups and downs. In turn, the people in these solid, long-term relationships can supercharge their shared or individual impact by holding each other accountable and supporting one another.

As you will see in the stories from these partnerships, "something bigger" acts as the foundation for a flourishing, enduring relationship—and a meaningful life for yourself and others. These stories also help us understand that this is not a stagnant, perfectly packaged end goal. It is an ongoing evolution that takes shape over time, that your partnerships can help you discover and fine-tune. It also does not have to be world changing. Every individual needs to find the path that will bring them meaning and that leverages their unique gifts.

An Unstoppable Shared Purpose

For decades, the ruthless South African government's apartheid system controlled the country's Black majority through racist legislation that institutionalized white supremacist policies. Black people had to carry a passbook at all times, they did not have access to quality education, they could live only in certain areas, and they were not allowed to marry white people. Segregation was woven throughout every aspect of life; these atrocious policies, and hundreds more, exploited Black people and held them in trauma and poverty.

In October 1963, the Rivonia Trial kicked off as an attempt to convict and imprison the anti-apartheid movement's core leaders, including Nelson Mandela. The government wanted to stifle the growing global movement and quiet its loudest voices, but in the end, the opposite happened. During the trial, Mandela gave a moving three-hour speech about his commitment to a free society, finishing with the words: "If it needs be, it is an ideal for which I am prepared to die."

By the early 1990s, the brutal regime was ended by a collective global force. At the center of this force was a group of friends who had forged unbreakable Deep Connections over decades of atrocities and loss. This group included leaders like Walter Sisulu, Albertina Sisulu, Oliver Tambo, Ahmed Kathrada, Nelson Mandela, Archbishop Tutu, Leah Tutu, and many others. They had inspired a distributed network of resistance movements that formed a growing national and global force, led by students, trade unions, religious groups, and many more diverse collectives. It grew into one of the best examples the world has ever seen of a collective of connections that shared one common purpose: to end apartheid.

Shortly after Nelson Mandela's death in December 2013, I witnessed the enduring love and strength of the core group of friends when I attended a celebration of Mandela's life, hosted by the Nelson Mandela Foundation in South Africa. Hundreds of people crammed into a tiny tent, and despite the pouring rain that flowed on our heads and soaked the grass beneath our feet, there was an explosion of joy in the crowd. One after the other, the remaining anti-apartheid heroes—now mostly in their seventies, eighties, and nineties—got up on the stage to pay their respects and offer tributes to an extraordinary man.

They glowed with love for one another as they came off the stage and embraced. I turned to one of their family members sitting next to me and asked how these heroes could still be so positive and connected after all the pain inflicted upon them by the apartheid regime.

The woman didn't hesitate. "They had two things that allowed them to bring down apartheid," she said. "And both these things kept them bonded for life. One was a clear purpose. And the other was a deep respect and love for one another." She went on to say, "Any one of them could have played the role of Mandela, but instead, they each played the role that the wider collective needed them to play."

Archbishop Tutu was one of the heroes—a member of that group of friends—who climbed onto the rickety, slippery stage that evening, in his long purple robe, to share a tribute. As usual, the Archbishop moved the room to tears with his combination of humor and fiery compassion.

Archbishop Tutu's accomplishments are deservedly well known: he stood up again and again against the tyranny of apartheid, and he led the heart-wrenching, courageous Truth and Reconciliation Commission. What we have not heard enough about is the Deep Connection that kept him going through all of it, the force of nature who was his rock when he faltered, his partner in life and in bringing down apartheid—the wonderful Leah Tutu. In July 2021, they celebrated their sixty-sixth wedding anniversary and a lifetime of lifting each other up.

From the moment I sat down to interview the Tutus, they were joking, laughing, and teasing each other. The room was crowded and noisy, yet everything fell into the background. The love between these two great human beings was wondrous as they spoke about how they met, how they'd suffered together under the cruel regime, and how their love kept them going.

Then suddenly, Archbishop Tutu went silent. He turned to Leah and said, "At one time, one of the apartheid government ministers said, 'The problem with Desmond Tutu is that he talks too much,' and so when I got home that day, I said to Leah, 'Do you want me to keep quiet or what? Do you think I talk too much?' She said she would much rather I be [captive and] happy on Robben Island than free and quiet outside."

He then went on to talk about how he didn't really care about who else respected him. All he cared about was what Leah thought of him. "I mean, I might make a speech and get a standing ovation, I don't know why," he said, "but until Leah says, 'Oh, that was not so bad,' I am on edge."

Then they both burst into giggles.

Leah and Arch, as many who know him call him, were able to keep on fighting during the apartheid years because of their Deep Connection. When one was down, the other lifted them back up. Together they were, and remain, a force of unconditional love, joy, and compassion.

They are the first to admit their relationship is a constant work in progress and that romance is not automatic. They constantly affirm each other with kind words, small gifts, and "treating each other gently." They also fiercely protect their time together. When they first got married, a date was to go out and share one cup of coffee. Then they could afford two cups of coffee, and then they stepped up to fish and chips. During one of their many fits of giggles, they shared that they love to bring each other joy, but sometimes miss the mark. They then end up disappointing each other and have to remember to turn it into a "growing point."

They've created mutuality over sixty-six years as their lives have gone through the stages of growing a family, moving, and changing jobs, all while maintaining their spirit of ubuntu, as the Archbishop loves to say. The African saying means "I am because you are."

Their shared purpose, which started with ending apartheid, has evolved into striving for every human being to have the chance to live a life of dignity. And they live true to this purpose in every human connection and interaction, even in the most mundane moments, like when they are driving and see a stranger struggling to walk up a steep hill. Leah will shout out, "Oh, just stop and give her a lift to the top." I'll never forget being at the airport with the Archbishop one time. When a group of officials tried to whisk him to the front of the security line, he politely refused, joking that he didn't want to jump the queue as it might interfere with his chances in the more important queue to heaven.

At every gathering, instead of concerning themselves with so-called important people, the Archbishop and Leah focus on acknowledging and celebrating the people serving the meals, cleaning the rooms, and preparing for the meetings. They are always aware of, and present with, everyone around them, especially when it comes to those whose voices might not be regularly heard. If someone needs a kind word or a helping hand, the Archbishop and Leah are the first to be there for them. This generosity of spirit lifts their partnership and everyone around them. It is a living embodiment of their shared something bigger.

Arch and Leah's partnership is based on cooperation, affirmation, and contagious laughter, which was only strengthened by the hardness and misery of the apartheid years. Leah shared what she called the

"unsureness" of never knowing whether Arch was coming home, or if
he had been arrested, or if he was in some kind of trouble. Each time
he walked through the door, she said there was this sense of lightness,
deep appreciation for each other, and a strengthening of their commitment to end apartheid.

Their affirmation of each other was even more important when
they were under brutal government attack. They took it in turns,
standing up for each other and strengthening their resolve to keep
going. They also extended that strength to others. Leah became a
steel backbone for their community in the face of police brutality,
as well as a great source of comfort for Arch after soul-wrenching
days leading the Truth and Reconciliation Commission. Day after
day, he listened to horrendous stories of torture and cruelty, but he
told me that the process of forgiveness was liberating for everyone.

Through all this difficulty they always kept joy and love front and
center. A quote I love from the Arch is, "We are made for loving. If we
don't love, we will be like plants without water."

1 + 1 = millions

Your purpose does not have to be as earth shattering as ending apartheid or closing the ozone hole. It must be simply something bigger than
yourself, something that will make a difference in others' lives. Maybe
that's raising your children to be the best possible human beings, or
building satellites to connect people all over the world, or making your
company a great place to work. All such endeavors are important.

Of course, something bigger must be authentic; it cannot be about
ego, power, or money. It must focus on a legacy of change that fits

with who you are and the unique skills you and your partner can bring to making a positive difference in this world.

In the conversations I had with successful partners, I often heard that a commitment to something bigger had emerged from the celebration and importance of service as part of a family's DNA. This spirit of service and purpose is an important gift that parents, teachers, or any of us can give to young people. One of my favorite moments was when José María Figueres, the former president of Costa Rica, joked with his sister Christiana about having "service for breakfast, lunch, and dinner" when they were growing up.

The author Uzodinma (Uzo) Iweala talked about how both of his parents were devoted to service, but in different ways. "My parents were very much in partnership with each other," Uzo says. "We saw a very equal set of behaviors. For me, just watching that modeled from both of them was extremely important, but also, watching and learning from my mother what it means to be a strong woman in the world has been extremely important." His father, Dr. Ikemba Iweala, is focused on changing an individual's life. His mother, Ngozi, is focused on systems change and global service—first as the Nigerian finance minister, then in key roles in the World Bank, and now as the first woman and the first African to hold the position of director-general of the World Trade Organization (WTO). Neither of them would have succeeded in their missions without each other. Breaking through the ceiling of the WTO, a seventy-five-year-old male-led organization, was not easy. Ngozi credits her husband as an important factor in her success, as he consistently stood by her side and gave her moral support during the toughest moments. As a doctor, author, and now the head of the Africa Centre, Uzo is a hybrid of his extraordinary parents.

You can't choose your parents, but you can choose whom you

surround yourself with. Achieving something bigger in the world begins with the handful of Deep Connections you nurture in your life. Choose carefully to surround yourself with greatness, people who will challenge you to move out of your comfort zone, pull you back when you are out on a limb, and stretch your thinking—not hold you back and limit your dreams.

There are lots of great resources to help you identify your personal purpose, like Simon Sinek's book *Find Your Why*. Your Deep Connections can help you exponentially lift your personal purpose. They act as a mirror to help you better understand your strengths and weaknesses. They hold you accountable and encourage you to keep going. Sometimes, simply having a partner to be a sounding board is all you need to take that next step toward something audacious that you might not have the courage to consider on your own.

Building a shared purpose with a partner, or a collective, can be one of life's most fulfilling experiences. It often starts with finding someone whose skills complement rather than compete with your own skills. Many successful partnerships are made up of radically different people, which often feels counterintuitive. Your values and work ethic also need to be aligned, as you will see throughout this book.

Here are **five insights** to consider as you leverage your Deep Connections for greater purpose, either on a shared mission or in supporting each other's individual purposes.

Light Your Heart and Soul on Fire

The concept of something bigger is much more than an empty statement. Amory Lovins, cofounder of RMI (Rocky Mountain Institute), calls it "applied hope." Sangu Delle, who builds socially impactful businesses across Africa with his brothers, says it's "almost like a religion that gets you out of bed each morning."

Finding and building a purpose can seem like a daunting task, one that is only compounded when shaping a shared purpose for a partnership or organization. We often get tangled up in thinking our mission has to be perfect. We mistakenly think that our mission is one thing that we'll discover and then chisel in stone. But our purpose constantly evolves—it must be *perfectly imperfect* so it has space to grow. What is most important is that it continues to light our hearts and souls on fire. As the poet David Whyte once said, "Anything or anyone that does not bring you alive, is too small for you."

Simplicity is also important in shaping our purpose. A "something bigger" mission statement that is short, clear, and authentic will be far more motivational than one that is so complicated and long that even you struggle to remember it. You want a mission that is going to get you out of bed every morning, not put you back to sleep. Write down your mission to keep as a motivator and a reference point. Here are a few examples of simple missions you'll hear more about in this book:

- **Spreading the power of optimism,** John and Bert Jacobs, Life is Good

- **Making healthier lives accessible through nutritious vegan food that appeals to everyone,** Erika Boyd and Kirsten Ussery, Detroit Vegan Soul

- **Ending the death penalty,** Anthony Ray Hinton and Lester Bailey

- **Providing financial services and healthcare to low-income individuals**, Andy Kuper and Jim Roth, LeapFrog Investments

Yours, Mine, Ours

Some partnerships will have a shared purpose, some will support each other with individual purposes, and some will have a combination of both. What's important, as Caskey Ebeling of Not Impossible Labs shared, is that you find a path that is authentic to you and "a partner who lets you live your truth."

Acclaimed couples therapist John Gottman says a sense of shared meaning and purpose is critical to a relationship. He explains, "My own calling is science and my wife's is healing." Though they have different callings, John and his wife respect each other's.

Chris Anderson, founder of TED, and Jacqueline Novogratz, founder of Acumen, are a great example of a couple with both individual and shared purposes. How do Chris and Jacqueline think about the latter? Simply and elegantly. "It's about human dignity," explains Jacqueline. "We won't have dignity as a human species until all of us have dignity."

"We aren't always doing the same thing at the same time," says Chris, "but we are passionately interested in sharing each other's work." He continues, "Sometimes, it feels like we're part of a joint mission, and sometimes it doesn't. But it always feels like we're living for something bigger than we are. I think that's the core of much of our relationship."

Recognizing the delicate balance between achieving "something bigger" goals separately and as a couple, Chris found his commitment to support Jacqueline tested when she traveled to Pakistan on her own to visit a housing development her organization had helped fund. All of a sudden, there was a shootout, and Jacqueline was caught in the crossfire. "It was really terrifying," she recalls. "And when I called Chris after, there was so much strength on the other side of the phone. It wasn't, 'Come home right now.' It wasn't, 'Why did you put yourself in this danger?' It was, 'I'm really proud of you. I'll be waiting for you with open arms.' And so, what resonated for me was that Chris was basically saying, I'll hold you, and I'll also let you go to the places that you need to go in the way that you need to go. That's incredibly empowering when you're out in the world trying to create change."

Many years later, Chris and Jacqueline took a much-needed vacation together. On the first night, Jacqueline got an emergency call informing her of floods in Pakistan. She had to pick up and go. She woke Chris up at three in the morning to tell him. He immediately volunteered to travel to Pakistan with her so he could help out in the disaster zone. "It wasn't a vacation," says Chris, "but it was probably one of the most connective weeks we'd ever had as a couple. It was just amazing what we were able to do together."

As Chris was growing up, his family mantra was "Don't live for yourself, live for other people," which had a lasting, indelible effect on him: "My whole life, I was told that things don't really take off until you start looking beyond yourself. And this is where the biggest, deepest joy is."

Jacqueline had a similar upbringing in that sense. "It was, 'To whom much is given, much is expected,'" she says. "I was told that we had to give back more than we took in this world."

Chris and Jacqueline's sense of service was instilled in both of them through their parents and then constantly recognized and affirmed by each other. This made it simple to do things like cancel a holiday and go to Pakistan together. Each time they made choices aligned with their purpose, their love and respect for each other deepened.

Shared Audacity

Getting to something bigger is much easier if you are not attempting it alone. Partners push each other toward audacious goals and hold each other accountable to reach them. A Deep Connection is like a renewable energy source that keeps you going, even in the midst of challenges. Audacity is not only defined by the size of your mission— it is also defined by your willingness to take risks, to do something bigger than yourself and your partnership. Your Deep Connections will give you the safe space to do this.

Of course, you can't just come up with your mission statement and claim success. Audacity, and staying true to your purpose, takes hard work. The everyday grind toward something bigger can be grueling. Many of the partners I interviewed talked about how important it is to create achievable steps and goals along the way, rather than shooting for something so big that you constantly get disheartened and feel like you are failing. This also gives you the chance to keep up the momentum by celebrating wins along the way, or course correcting quickly if something is not working.

Mark Kelly, a NASA astronaut and US senator, and Gabby Giffords, a former US representative, have a shared something bigger in their service to America. When they first combined their lives, it was like bringing together two fast-moving trains, both on their own paths of purpose—one using space to make a difference on Earth, and the other determined to show that politics could be a force for good.

Four years after their wedding, on Saturday, January 8, 2011, Mark was preparing for his next space flight while Gabby was doing what she loved most: talking to people in the community she represented in Congress. This "Congress on Your Corner" session was being held in a Safeway parking lot in Tucson, Arizona. In a split second, it turned into a nightmare when a gunman shot Gabby in the head and then opened fire on the community, killing six people, including a nine-year-old girl.

Mark soon retired from the navy and his job at NASA to support Gabby in her long path to recovery. Ninety percent of people never recover from a serious brain injury like Gabby's, so they knew that they were fighting against all odds, but their Deep Connection gave them the hope and determination to keep fighting. Gabby kept putting one foot in front of the other and struggling with every word. Through persistent effort, her speech and mobility slowly started to return. Along the way, Mark and Gabby learned to pause and simply be in the moment to celebrate Gabby's small wins toward recovery, making them both stronger and deepening their connection with each other.

The couple continued their lifelong mission of public service, despite this tragedy.

Today, Gabby's organization, Giffords, is leading the fight to make communities safer and end gun violence in America. It brings together Americans of all stripes, uniting youth, veterans, law enforcement officials, gun owners, and faith leaders to find actionable solutions.

In August 2020, nine and a half years after Gabby was shot in the head, she gave an 84-second, 155-word speech at the Democratic National Convention, all in a single take. Nothing short of a miracle. After her speech, Joe Biden was inspired to tweet, "Our nation's gun violence epidemic is really a cowardice problem."

On November 4, 2020, Mark Kelly was elected as a US senator for Arizona. During his campaign, he committed himself to working with Republicans and Democrats in service to Arizona, much like Gabby did during her time serving in the US House of Representatives. He won with a platform of unification and peace rather than division. "It becomes pretty obvious pretty early that when you get into space," he said, "we're all kind of in this together."

Almost exactly ten years after Gabby was shot, Mark was locked down inside the US Capitol while a mob attacked the building. When Gabby learned he was safe, she tweeted, "I couldn't stop thinking about what you must have gone through 10 years ago this week. I'm so glad you and your staff are safe. I love you, sweetie."

That evening, Mark was back on the Senate floor protecting American democracy.

Mark and Gabby's shared something bigger is built on a deep commitment to service, shared values, and audacious possibilities. Gabby summed up their partnership journey perfectly: "Together you can get through the darkest days and continue to fight, fight, fight."

One step and one word at a time.

A Grounding Force

As something bigger grows beyond a partnership to a wider community in your company, in your neighborhood, or in the world, it is even more important to have clarity on the mission. Your clear something bigger can be a grounding force to always bring you back to what's important and keep you on track when you hit resistance.

Erika Boyd and Kirsten Ussery started the Detroit Vegan Soul restaurants to make good, healthy food accessible to everyone in their community and break the cycle of diet-related diseases. Erika and Kirsten launched their business after Erika's father died, a horribly tragic event made even more painful because Erika realized her father's poor diet had contributed to his death. Kirsten saw similar health issues in her own family and felt the same calling as Erika did to help members of their community.

Helping the community to get healthier became their shared mission.

Getting people to accept their vision wasn't always easy. When you're trying to audaciously change deeply entrenched and embedded behaviors, like unhealthy eating, you're going to experience significant resistance and pushback. Indeed, Erika and Kirsten told me story after story about how people would immediately hold their noses when confronted with the concept of soul food turned healthy, vegan, and sugar- and fat-free. In response, the partners just dug down deeper and worked harder to keep their dream alive.

"We heard people say, 'You've got to be kidding,'" recounts Kirsten. "They also threw in a few other choice words along the way, too." At times this pushback made Kirsten and Erika question their audacious vision. Luckily this often came in waves and when one of them was down, the other one picked her up and they both kept going. The benefit of these setbacks was innovation. They started to think about how they could create dishes that were familiar to people. Like a

Trojan horse that got people to at least taste the healthier food before dismissing it.

They stuck with their vision and continued to focus on serving life-changing, comforting meals to reduce obesity, diabetes, and heart problems. Once the community started sampling Detroit Vegan Soul's menu—including dishes like Catfish Tofu, Sea Vegetable Hush Puppies, and Hoppin' John without pork—the lingering skepticism and hostility started to melt away, along with the pounds.

"Detroit Vegan Soul has become way deeper than just Erika and myself," says Kirsten. "It's really all about strengthening the community we serve. . . . If we've made an impact in Detroit, and helped both the city and its people survive, then that's even more fulfilling."

Millions of Moments

Less than a decade ago, the investment community scoffed at the importance of purpose. I clearly remember sitting at many larger-than-life boardroom tables with seas of well-suited people. Whenever I brought up the imperative of positive social and environmental impact, faces would glaze over. When leaving the room, I'd hear the inevitable hushed whispers of "tree hugger" or "swampy," as they call environmentalists in the UK.

We've come a long way. The public now holds corporations accountable for a better way of doing business. Investors rush to put their money into companies with a mission to do something more than just make profit, often led by people like those whose stories we share in this book.

But achieving something bigger isn't up to just founders and CEOs.

It's also up to us in how we choose to live every moment of our lives, and how we partner with everyone we have the chance to connect with.

When my father was nearing the end of his life, he opened up to me about how, throughout his life, he struggled with balancing work, family, and purpose. This was understandable, as he had a thirty-two-year career at Sears, Roebuck and Co., a sixty-seven-year marriage, and four children.

Amid the loud beeps, blinding lights, plastic-covered beds, and smell of ICU cleaning fluid, my father opened his eyes and smiled. We thought we had lost him, but here he was, back again and as joyful and sharp as if the past forty-eight hours of emergency hospital interventions were all some type of bad dream.

I asked him what he was looking forward to, and he immediately said, "I want to spend the next one hundred years of my life helping people." He went on to talk about how, throughout his life, he always felt there was a trade-off between working hard to support his family, ensuring we did not experience the poverty he had growing up, and spending time helping others in his community.

I reminded him of the big, beautiful, brown leather book I found in his office a few years earlier, a gift from the people who partnered with him when he was the manager of the Burlington, Massachusetts, Sears store. On the cover, in gold handwriting, it read, "Robert C. Oelwang, Sears Burlington, 1968–1978." Inside the cover were the beautiful opening words, "A retail store is nothing but a pile of concrete and glass . . . until people breathe life and spirit into it."

Page after page held moving tributes to my father thanking him for breathing life into the store. As we read through it together, he shared countless stories about the people he worked with and the experiences he'd had that made all those years worthwhile. What was most heartwarming was that in all the comments and his stories, people thanked him for building relationships—a family, not just a successful store (which it was):

"Thanks for taking the time to remember us as working moms and getting us flowers on Mother's Day."

"Thanks for giving me a second chance after I made a big mistake and stole from the store."

"Thanks for helping me get into rehabilitation to get healthy again."

"Thanks for letting me date (and later marry) my co-worker (wife)."

The admiration went on and on.

My dad was a successful business leader because he focused on relationships and community, not just the balance sheet.

Amid the chaos of the ICU, we spoke about how he actually hadn't made a trade-off at all: he had not only supported his family, giving us every opportunity possible, but he had also changed the lives of everyone he came into contact with for the better, including all those who helped him breathe life into that store in Burlington.

In the years after returning home from the ICU in 2014, my father witnessed his beloved Sears collapse, a once-great company that had lost its something bigger. Built over a span of one hundred years, Sears had become the world's largest retailer, ensuring all Americans had access to good products at reasonable prices. They did this by focusing on their people, which was why my father loved and was so loyal to them. For him, Sears was like family—he could barely watch the company's painful death.

In 2018, Sears filed for bankruptcy. Individual interests linked to short-term profit had strangled all the life out of it, leaving it a shell of its former self. The company became trapped in a vicious cycle of greed, focused on monetizing assets rather than investing in its people and its purpose to provide exceptional service and quality products at affordable prices.

On September 4, 2019, my wonderful father passed away. Two days before, the whole family celebrated my parents' sixty-seventh wedding anniversary. They had the chance to renew their vows in the hospital. My parents laughed like teenagers when the priest told them it was time for their honeymoon. As I left the hospital that night, I smiled, realizing what a meaningful life my father had lived. His something bigger—to bring joy and love to everyone he connected with—permeated all his relationships, at work and at home.

Sometimes purpose and partnership feel like a faraway goal to aspire to, when, as my father showed, it can be lived every day. Our purpose is achieved simply by being 100 percent there for our Deep Connections—providing trust, respect, and belief in one another and helping each other reach our something bigger. This daily practice inevitably extends to every life we touch, making all our connections and our lives meaningful.

I'll never forget asking some people from across the Virgin Group about what they believed made the company's culture so human. One of them stood up and said, "Culture is ours to win or lose in every single interaction. We can choose to be human and loving a million times a day, or we can do the opposite and destroy our culture." Our Deep Connections help us understand and practice purpose in every action, word, and connection we make with others, building a way of being that becomes the foundation for our lives and our legacy of positive change.

CHAPTER THREE

All-In

Second Degree of Connection

We are nothing other than the summation of our relationships.

—Richard Reed, Cofounder of Innocent Drinks and JamJar Investments

After their groundbreaking paper about CFCs came out in *Nature* in 1974, Sherry Rowland and Mario Molina found themselves out on a limb and taking a beating from industry, politicians, and even peers. Most fellow scientists were harshly critical that they were advocating for change based on their academic research. Over the next decade, Sherry's invitations to speak at conferences were quietly withdrawn, and others never came at all. Postdoc chemistry students stopped coming to his lab for fellowships. "That really hurt his feelings," his wife, Joan, said, in the PBS documentary *Ozone Hole: How We Saved the Planet*. "But what are you going to do, stop? No."

The discovery that CFCs were depleting the ozone layer would deepen Sherry and Mario's relationship and alter the course of their lives. Although they hadn't signed up for life in the public eye, there was now no turning back, despite the incredible odds against them. They knew that they had to jump all-in together to get people to listen, but they never dreamed how difficult this would be.

By that time, worldwide production of CFCs, at 900,000 tons a year, had come to represent an $8 billion slice of the chemical industry. The industry, especially US company DuPont and UK company Imperial Chemical Industries (ICI), as large producers of CFCs, was not ready to give in. Corporate executives, customers, and industry associations attacked Sherry and Mario's hypothesis and attacked their character. The chemicals were safe, they said. Sherry and Mario had no proof. DuPont took out a full-page ad questioning the legitimacy of the research. A chemical trade magazine accused the two scientists of being Soviet spies.

"They were taking potshots—it was bad," said Donald Blake, then a young atmospheric chemist whom Sherry had taken under his wing. Don would go on to work with Sherry at UC Irvine for thirty-four years, having arrived in the chemistry department as a doctoral student in 1978. "But Sherry would tell me to calm down," Don said. "He had thick skin, and he never got mad." He fiercely protected his team, too. "He would be the one out front taking whatever he got from the industry or anybody else," his son, Jeffrey, told me.

What critics didn't understand was that Sherry and Mario didn't want to be right. They'd much rather have continued their lives as academics than as frontline warriors. But the scientific facts were in front of them and they wanted the public and policy makers to understand how important this was for humanity's survival. "When it came down to testifying in Congress, Sherry had no trouble going to the Senate and telling them what they needed to hear," said Don. Mario also spoke out, and he was particularly successful in building a group of allies with other scientists, like Ralph Cicerone, Richard Stolarski, Harold Johnson, and Paul Crutzen (whose work in the early 1970s was crucial in highlighting the dangers of CFCs).

Even consumers didn't believe CFCs were a risk. In 1980, the Environmental Protection Agency requested public feedback on potential CFC restrictions. They received an overwhelming response of 2,300 letters. Only 4 supported restrictions, the other 2,296 fiercely opposed them.

Despite the challenges, Sherry and Mario remained undeterred. Their trust, respect, and belief in each other and their findings never wavered. The strength of their Deep Connection gave them the resilience they needed to stay focused on their goal. Together, they were able to weather the criticism because they knew something had be done. "If not now, when? If not us, who?" Mario recalls Sherry saying.

They struggled to get the media to pay attention to their published findings, but they kept speaking out, politely answering even the simplest questions. They presented their findings to the government, NASA, and countless scientific and industrial organizations. They stayed committed to their shared mission by being all-in together, knowing they had each other's backs. They worked hard together to perfect their communication about the science of the ozone layer so that when they did have a chance to raise the issue, every word counted. When their work was attacked, they stayed open. They would publicly announce the challenge to their data and then share the progress as they reviewed it. They realized that they were up against difficult odds. "It looks and sounds like science fiction," Sherry said.

"I'm sure there were some who thought it was an elaborate joke on our part."

They were on a clear mission to do everything they could to mobilize the world to protect the ozone layer. And fortunately for all of us, they had such a deep belief in each other and the scientific data that they never gave up.

Sherry and Mario, and other scientists, like Paul, were beacons for the next generation of scientists. They turned the scientific world upside down when they went all-in and acted on their findings rather than simply publishing them. They sparked a movement of scientists who are not confined to their labs. They took a global approach and partnered with government, business, media, and environmental organizations, and with the public—anyone who would help them protect the ozone. "Rowland invented a new kind of science, and we will never look at the world the same way again," said Susan Trumbore, an Earth science professor at the University of California, Irvine, where she met Sherry. "Because of Rowland and a few others like him, globalism is a natural concept to scientists of my generation."

Still, these were particularly rough times for Sherry. He paid a high price for standing up, putting both his successful career and his hard-earned reputation at risk. Yet he always knew that his family was there for him no matter what. Sherry and Joan shared an integrity that never wavered, and Joan grew angry whenever Sherry came under fire from the chemical industry. "Everybody knew not to mess with her," their daughter, Ingrid, told me. Joan was all-in for her husband every step of the way, helping him stay committed to what he knew was right. When the industry sent hecklers to disrupt a presentation Sherry was giving, he would simply ignore them. "He was so big and so dignified, and he'd just look, and sometimes he'd laugh," Ingrid said.

Don described Sherry and Joan's relationship as a "role model for married life." He credited Joan with helping Sherry keep going and achieve far greater impact than he would have without her. Her support gave him a safe place to come back to as he weathered personal abuse and the undermining of his scientific work. And it went both ways: Sherry supported and respected Joan, encouraging her quest to lift the voices of female scientists. Joan became deeply engaged with the general scientific aspects of ozone depletion, and as Sherry wrote in his biography for the Nobel Prize, "she has been a knowledgeable and trusted confidante through all of the last two decades of ozone research." In a US Senate hearing in 1986, Sherry was asked what he would do "if he were king." His response was that he would ask the queen, Joan of course.

He may have enjoyed science, but he loved Joan more. "His first love was his wife and his family, and his second love was chemistry," said Jeffrey. Sherry was always all-in for Joan and for his children. When Jeffrey got into a horrible car accident, Sherry immediately took a leave of absence from his job, even though it was during a critical moment for his work. He stayed in the hospital with Jeffrey every day for five months.

Finally, more than ten years after publishing their findings and making an all-in commitment to keep fighting, Sherry and Mario received the validation they needed. Research by a team of British scientists working near the South Pole revealed a "hole" in the ozone layer over the Antarctic. Soon other studies would confirm that the protective shield was disappearing at a startling rate.

But these new discoveries were only the beginning. The world now needed to come together to rid the atmosphere of CFCs, a goal that might have appeared next to impossible if not for the loyalty and trust Sherry and Mario shared. They never wavered from their all-in commitment to each other and to inspiring what neither one of them could have achieved alone: getting the world to listen.

A Commitment to the Commitment

Committing yourself to something bigger prepares you for going all-in, allowing you to feel safe in the relationship and know you 100 percent have each other's backs. All-in commitment gives you the freedom to do something bigger, shifting your gaze outward, beyond yourself.

An all-in relationship is a conscious decision to be there for each other and your mission, no matter what. Jacqueline Novogratz calls it "making a commitment to the commitment." It's a home to come back to, a place where you are safe to be vulnerable and take risks because you know someone is there to catch you.

Ultimately, being all-in is about giving 100 percent through unconditional love. The author Gregory David Roberts once told me, "Love is a passionate search for a truth other than your own." Yet we are bombarded with advice on a self-centered, conditional approach to love—how you can get love and what it can give you, rather than how to give unconditional love to others and learn from their truth. You will also be hard-pressed to find any insights on the role of love in healthy businesses and friendships.

Jacqueline Novogratz's mother used to say you never should ask if someone loves you. The question should always be, *"Am I loving enough?"* I've found this simple question to be a beautiful tool to test whether we are giving ourselves fully to all our relationships—

business, friendships, and romantic alike. Holding back even a little to protect ourselves will eventually undermine the relationship. It will never reach the all-in depths of the Tutus, Mario and Sherry, Gabby and Mark—as well as the other extraordinary Deep Connections in this book.

Becoming all-in is not an automatic way of being or an end state, nor is it as simple as popping on a glass slipper. It takes courage and hard work. It takes patience and creative approaches to conflict.

Fortunately, the benefits are more than worth it.

Back to the Center

I had practiced the questions in my hotel room. I'd even tried them out with the taxi driver on the way to Atlanta. Yet I was still scared to death when I crossed the threshold of the Carter Center. This was one of the first interviews I would be conducting for this book, and I'd be interviewing one of my lifelong heroes. Embarrassingly, I had dressed as a peanut in first grade to campaign for his presidency. Though I had worked with President Carter for ten years in connection with The Elders, this was different. This conversation was going to be an exploration of his personal partnership with his wife, Rosalynn.

We set up for the interview in a slightly stuffy conference room with no windows, American flags as a backdrop. President and Mrs. Carter entered the room and sat down a bit stiffly, side by side. His first words to me were, "You have thirty minutes."

Rosalynn whispered in reply, "Shush, Jimmy, don't be so rushed."

They started with the story of how they met and fell in love. That took up the allocated thirty minutes. They became so immersed in their honest stories from their all-in seven decades that I thought we might talk well into the evening. One of the most touching reflections was the number of times President Carter credited Rosalynn as the most important person in the White House during his presidency, his eyes and ears across America and the rest of the world.

Their story started in the small town of Plains, Georgia, in 1927, the year Rosalynn was born. President Carter was three years old and lived in the house next door. Their romance sparked some fifteen years later on their first date, when he was home one weekend from the US Naval Academy.

The morning after their first date, President Carter's mother was cooking breakfast, and she asked him what he'd done the previous night. He told her, "I went to a movie with a girl." She asked who. When he said, "Rosalynn Smith," and his mother replied, "What do you think about Rosalynn?" Without hesitating, he told her, "She's the one I am going to marry."

The next day, he was catching the midnight train back to the Naval Academy. His mother encouraged Rosalynn to wait for him at the train station to say goodbye. She did, and he kissed her. Seventy-five years, four children, twelve grandchildren, and fourteen great-grandchildren later, they now hold the record for the longest-lasting marriage of any US president.

What was most striking to me was their honesty, especially about how bumpy the road can be. They never go a day without a disagreement, but every night they talk through any differences before they go to sleep. Their openness about failure was refreshing. One of their toughest times in their marriage was when they "lost the White House." They got home and were questioning what to do for the decades ahead of them, thrown into a situation where for the first time in their marriage they were home all day, every day, together—a radical change from their days as America's first couple.

Struggling with what was next, they decided to write a book together, *Everything to Gain: Making the Most of the Rest of Your Life*. Only there was a little glitch: they could not agree on the details of some of the historic stories that comprised their life.

"One of the worst things that we ever tried to do was write a book together," Rosalynn said. "We wrote it, but that was the closest that we ever came to . . ." She let her words trail, and I knew she was avoiding the word *divorce*. "It really endangered our marriage," she finished, and went quiet.

President Carter added, "We almost broke up over that darn book."

During the writing, they stopped talking to each other, communicating only via a single computer on the kitchen table. President Carter would type a message on the screen and then, after he left, Rosalynn would type a response. (This was long before the internet.) This arrangement continued for some time until they reached out to their editor, asking him to mediate the dispute. The editor came up with the idea that Rosalynn would have her version of the story with an *R* next to the paragraph and Jimmy would have his with a *J* next to it. Whether or not this small editorial innovation saved their marriage, it created a safe space for them to talk rather than type, and helped them to learn how to weather difficulties and stay all-in together.

"Well, usually when we fail it's a common failure, it's something that both of us have failed to do," President Carter said. "If we fail, we just do the best that we can, and we learn from that experience. The common failure comes because we are in it together from the very beginning."

Part of their secret to staying all-in was giving each other space and cultivating shared interests like jogging, skiing (for the first time in their fifties), fly-fishing, and bird-watching. And they of course continued their tireless fight together for peace and human rights through the Carter Center.

Even though they sat stiffly side by side during the interview, rather than facing each other, the atmosphere between them was anything but formal. They joked, laughed, made faces, and simply shone with their love for and belief in each other. What connects them goes beyond their shared experiences in the White House, their work in the Carter Center, and their four children. Their Deep Connection doesn't mean they have a perfect relationship, but they share a level of commitment that can withstand anything. Being all-in means that you can grow in your own directions but always come back to the center, to each other.

President Carter's final words to me that day were, "As you can tell, we have a good life."

Rosalynn agreed. "Yes, it's a good life."

Strength in Opposing Forces

The Carters' relationship is grounded in their similar backgrounds, yet some of the strongest all-in connections I studied emerged across deep divides. One partnership story is so striking that it feels like it couldn't possibly be true.

In 1995, Azim Khamisa's only son, Tariq, a twenty-year-old college student, was delivering a pizza in San Diego. After knocking on many doors with no response, he returned to his car. As he climbed into the driver's seat to leave, he was shot and killed by fourteen-year-old Tony Hicks as part of a gang initiation.

What happened that day was tragic. What happened next is extraordinary.

In the midst of unimaginable pain and darkness, Azim forgave his son's killer. He even invited Tony's family into his home to talk about what had happened in an attempt to heal the wounds on all sides. As they sat together in Azim's living room, they created the safe space for an honest conversation in which both sides could be vulnerable. They openly shared their feelings and their experiences and grieved together in a spirit of forgiveness and empathy. "I didn't have this response that he should be hung from the highest pole, he killed my one and only son," said Azim. "I rather saw that he was a victim of society. The enemy was not the fourteen-year-old, rather the societal forces that cause many young men to fall through the cracks, especially young men of color."

After their initial meeting, Azim stayed in touch with Tony's guardian, his grandfather Ples Felix, and they struck up a friendship. Like many successful partnerships, Azim and Ples couldn't be more different. Azim is a Muslim and was an investment banker before his son was shot. Ples is a Baptist and was a Green Beret. They describe themselves as two opposites coming together for a common purpose, joking that they certainly can't be compared to Martin Luther King and Gandhi based on their early career paths.

Step-by-step, Azim and Ples deepened their relationship. As they learned more about the horrifying statistics of violence against young people in the United States, they knew they had to do something, and they agreed that the one thing they could do together was ensure young people don't end up dead like Tariq, or in prison like Tony. They found a shared purpose in tragedy.

When they first met, they felt an immediate sense of connection on a spiritual level. One was a Christian and one was a Muslim, so they were both committed to love, compassion, and empathy. This served as a foundation to build trust. Azim shared, "It takes time, it takes consistency, it takes behavior. I think that being able to rely on somebody is something we humans don't do overnight." He went on to talk about how their mission served as a compass for consistent behavior: "The purpose is really bigger than me individually or you individually. We're part of a story that's bigger than both of us."

Over the years of working together, they've built trust and proven that they would do anything for each other. They've created an environment where asking for help is a strength, not a weakness. And conflict is an opportunity to learn from each other. They've built an all-in relationship that is so deep that they refer to each other as brothers. "There's nothing that precludes us from being able to see each other and be together as brothers, as long as we understand that we are one," Ples said. Azim added, "Ples and I are different, but we respect and love each other as a human being, as one human race."

Azim founded the Tariq Khamisa Foundation, and reached out to ask Ples to join him in working to stop kids from killing each other and to spread the importance of forgiveness and empathy. They have multiplied the impact of their connection over a million times, traveling all over to share their story of forgiveness, compassion, and love across divides. Together, they have connected with hundreds of thousands of elementary, middle, and high school students, modeling the beauty of crossing racial, religious, political, and other divides to create a friendship united against violence, division, and fear.

A young girl who recognized Ples from a school presentation came and sat next to him on a trolley. She told him that the moment she'd heard him and Azim speak, she'd decided she would never be involved in gangs. She proudly shared that she'd finished school and had gotten a great job. Feedback like this gives Azim and Ples a sense of accomplishment that makes them want to spend the rest of their lives all-in for their mission.

Azim and Ples love to talk about the power in "opposing forces." No one would ever have imagined that the two of them would become friends, but their differences and story of forgiveness are exactly what make people listen.

At the end of our conversation, Azim summarized what it means to be part of an all-in partnership: "It is important in any partnership that it has to transcend cognitive and even emotional connection," he said. "It has to get to that deep spiritual connection for you to sustain, for you to be trusting, for you be respectful, for you to be able to look at conflict as an opportunity to be able to create love and unity."

Friends Before Partners

Like Azim and Ples, Ben Cohen and Jerry Greenfield could not appear more different: Ben is a visionary who has no limits or boundaries, while Jerry is an operational genius who makes stuff happen. Still, their partnership works. "Not only do we have different skills, but personality-wise, Ben is very entrepreneurial, doing things that he doesn't know how to do," Jerry said. "He tends to be very outspoken and spontaneous. Some people might say impulsive, but we say spontaneous. I'm much more measured, so I think, together, that's a really good combination."

Ben added, "Jerry has prevented me from doing a lot of really fucked-up *shit*."

They also have different approaches to leadership. "Jerry is a lot more diplomatic," Ben explained. "He's also much better at presenting and explaining things to people, in a way that they are able to hear it." Ben believes Jerry's approach is how they've kept their team inspired over the long term. "There was a stage during the growth of Ben and Jerry's," Ben said, "when I would walk around the company and say, 'Oh, this is wrong, that sucks, that's fucked up, don't do that,' and he would be walking behind me saying, 'Well, what Ben really meant to say was, you know, do this and do that.' He could say it in a way that people could hear it."

When I asked Ben and Jerry for the secret to their success, what was their immediate answer? Being all-in. "You gotta be all-in. All-in!" they exclaimed in unison, followed by joyous laughter. Ben continued, "How do you think we made Ben and Jerry's happen? We were both all-in. We were all-in!"

They became all-in thanks to their commitment to a common purpose. As they built their first store, which doubled as an outdoor movie theater, they both rolled up their sleeves and did any task that needed doing, including scooping ice cream and hosting movie nights (Ben was the projectionist and Jerry was the security guard). They grew their trust and respect for each other through the consistent hard work of building a business that would make a difference for their community. When they could get a break from twenty-four-hour workdays, they would crash on top of the ice cream freezers. In the process, they sacrificed basically everything to make the business work—everything except their friendship. "You would just be so exhausted at the end of the day, but there was nothing else you wanted to be doing," said Jerry. "Putting your all into something is very satisfying, knowing you are doing the absolute most you can do."

In working together, the two developed a mantra, "friends before partners." That mantra underscores one of the most extraordinary stories of deep friendship, with the side benefit of a hugely successful business.

In many of the interviews, the word *friendship* was often used to describe being all-in, no matter what type of relationship it was. There were many discussions about wanting to reclaim the concept of "best friend" from social media, where a "friend" can be had with the click of a button rather than through a meaningful relationship.

Ben shared, "I think loads of partnerships are partnerships of convenience. Somebody wants to do something, or both people want to do something, but they can't do it on their own. They didn't really know each other before, and they come together but they don't have the friendship basics to start with." For Ben and Jerry, though, authentic friendship and mutual hard work toward a common purpose are groundings for being all-in. Trust is also an important factor: "For us, I think a lot of it's just about trust. Being friends, you just trust each other," explained Jerry.

Love does not get talked about very often in the business world, so it was refreshing that Ben and Jerry discussed their love for each other freely. Everything they spoke about centered around love. When I asked them what they were most thankful for in their partnership, Jerry said, "Well, I'm really grateful for the love, the friendship, and the journeys that I am able to go on—places that I would never go. It's nice."

And Ben followed up with, "We have a tremendous amount of respect for the other person, and love for the other person."

Mutual Hard Work

This theme of mutual hard work to stay all-in was a consistent and important thread in all the partnerships I interviewed. All-in connections have to practice self-sacrifice, in which partners are willing to do what's right for the collective goals, even if that means stepping back from an individual goal. Many of the partnerships spoke about how this "sacrifice" for their partner actually ended up bringing them their greatest gifts.

When journalist and author Nicholas Kristof asked a gathering of people celebrating their golden anniversaries about the secret to a long marriage, he expected all kinds of fuzzy romantic stories. What struck him, however, was that every couple said, "It's hard work—hard work is what makes it last."

When I spoke with Nicholas and his wife, Sheryl WuDunn, a former journalist and author, he told me, "Sheryl and I have a wonderful relationship. We're so complementary in so many ways, and we love each other deeply, but it also does require compromise and hard work on both people's part. And that has to be grounded in mutual respect and a willingness to compromise, even when you are sure you're right."

Sheryl jokingly responded, "What? Hard work?"

With three children and high-pressure jobs that demand significant global travel, there is the inevitable hard work in simply coordinating everyday life. They acknowledged that having children adds another dimension of complexity, and at times it limits what you can do professionally. But it also "hugely enriches your entire life," shared Nicholas, "and at the end of the day, it's a legacy that you're going to be fundamentally most concerned with and value the most." Their close relationship with their children has helped them both stay all-in with each other.

Another important aspect of hard work is carving out the time to be present with each other. "You have to pay attention to the other person," Sheryl explained, "and not forget that they are a human being and they have desires and needs. It's not taking someone for granted." This understanding allows them to make sacrifices and trade-offs to ensure that there is a fair balance in the partnership. For Nicholas and Sheryl, this often meant holding back their individual fears when one of them traveled to a high-risk area. "We both weigh these trade-offs somewhat uncomfortably, and it sometimes leaves us both a little bit anxious," said Nicholas. "But I think it works because we have this grounding of deep mutual respect and love and understanding."

They shared a story about being in China during the Tiananmen Square crackdown. As the troops started to open fire on the crowds, Nicholas ran toward the square to ensure he could show the world what was happening. "I don't think any other spouse really could understand that," said Sheryl. "But that creates this enormous amount of empathy and sympathy and fear, all melded in one." Nicholas continued, "When you're being shot at—our compound was shot at as well—then you worry about each other, you feel a sense of outrage at seeing kids being killed. That was an incredibly traumatic thing to go through, but I think it really did unite us." They compared it to going to boot camp together, one that helped build an unbreakable bond of shared understanding.

The other critical dimension of hard work that keeps partnerships all-in is the hard work toward something bigger. Seeing someone commit and dedicate their life to a goal that matters increases one's respect, trust, and love for their partner. This is even more important when it is a shared goal. Working hard together ensures there is no resentment due to an imbalance in effort and builds a bond through their everyday experiences, as we saw with Ben and Jerry.

Sheryl and Nicholas know a lot about hard work toward their common purpose of ending fundamental injustices and inequities. During their careers, they've reported on the front lines of multiple natural disasters, and they have firsthand encounters with just about every war of the past several decades. Knowing all this about them made their words even more real for me.

The depth of their all-in connection was apparent in Nicholas's closing comments. "I just love Sheryl's company. If Sheryl is traveling . . . I feel like I'm missing an arm. . . . I feel complete only when Sheryl's around."

This mutual hard work cannot be underestimated, but hard work at the individual level is important, too. Being all-in demands that we work on ourselves in order to bring our authentic selves to a relationship. Hard work must start inside before we can ever be a great partner to someone else and achieve something bigger together. "There's an old saying that 95% of people try to change the world," said Jo Confino, former executive editor at *HuffPost* and now a partner at Leaders' Quest, "and only 5% try to change themselves."

A Consistent Long View

Robin Chase, the founder of Zipcar, flags a critical difference between many of the relationships in her life and the all-in connection she shares with her daughter, Cameron Russell, a storyteller, model, and activist: "She looks out for my long-term well-being when so many others are focused on short-term gain." In their interview, Robin spoke about how so many connections in our lives are transactional rather than long-term investments that help others thrive. For example, Cameron is completely honest with her mother when she feels a business partner or a decision will not serve her best long-term interest, while many others might have tried to push the partnership forward for short-term gain.

A partner also knows when to challenge us to live up to our something bigger. Robin shared examples of times when Cameron pushed her to step out of her comfort zone and express her views on sustainability and collegial leadership, knowing that doing so was important to Robin's life purpose. While Robin was used to doing what it takes to build and run a successful business, she was not used to going all-in and sharing her vulnerabilities and personal views on issues. Cameron kept encouraging her, helping her shape her stories, and slowly, Robin overcame her fear. Each time she spoke, she got more and more courageous. Now both are building long-term legacies of change by being outspoken advocates for the environment and a better way of doing business.

When asked what helped them to ensure they stayed all-in for the long term, when so many other parents and their children grow more distanced over the years, Robin emphasized a shared value system, one that would also help them navigate tricky times and "equalize the relationship."

A shared, all-in long view is not exclusive to families growing up together and partnerships you find in your early years. It can come in all shapes and sizes, and at all stages of life.

Ray Chambers and Peter Chernin's story is a perfect example of this.

They both had successful, decades-long careers in business and philanthropy. They could have spent the rest of their lives enjoying the benefits of their many successes, but instead, they joined forces to help end malaria.

Ray had built a successful career in private equity on Wall Street, where he oversaw such enormous deals as the 1985 purchase of Avis when he was chairman of Wesray Capital. But in the late eighties, he began to focus full-time on solving social issues. Ray has devoted countless hours and resources to a range of impact initiatives, from helping to revitalize his hometown of Newark, New Jersey, to volunteering as special envoy to the UN secretary-general. In 2006, Ray was working in Africa with the economist Jeffrey Sachs when he saw a photo of a roomful of sleeping children in a rural Malawi village. Then he learned they weren't actually sleeping. Every single one was in a malarial coma. Most of them would soon die. To this day, Ray still sees that image in his mind.

Ray learned all he could about malaria, a deadly disease that impacts millions. In 2019 alone, nearly a quarter billion people contracted the disease. Malaria kills more than four hundred thousand people a year, most of them children under the age of five. The tragedy is that malaria is both preventable and curable.

At a meeting in Sun Valley, Idaho, in 2006, Ray connected with Peter, then president and COO of News Corp and CEO of the Fox Networks Group. In his role, Peter oversaw global operations across five continents. Ray was looking for a partner, and Peter, though he may not have realized it that day, was ready to devote himself to something bigger that would become part of his life's work. Together, Ray and Peter founded Malaria No More, a nonprofit aimed at bringing a business mindset to the task of eradicating malaria. Between Ray and

Peter and the other Deep Connections they've built over the years, they've raised over $16 billion and prevented hundreds of millions of cases of malaria.

Peter and Ray came to their partnership with a lifetime-learning mindset and are both insatiably curious. Even after being at the helms of many companies and organizations, they approached this new chapter in their lives with deep humility and enthusiasm to learn from each other and their partners. They decided to be joint chairs of Malaria No More, and they got to work bringing in partners from all sectors: the World Bank, the Global Fund, the US government, *American Idol*, not-for-profits working to address malaria, and many more. They became master conveners and collaborators and built a network of partners that exponentially increased their impact.

Neither one of them was trying to be the hero and claim credit. They were both at a point in their careers where they were deeply grateful for their blessed lives and were laser focused on how they could end malaria. "We never ever try and get the limelight or the spotlight," shared Peter. "We show humility and modesty to one another and to everybody around us."

Ray and Peter, two fiercely competitive businesspeople, laughed when I asked if they were competitive with each other. The goal is too big, and the trust and respect between them is enormous, so there is no room for competition and other petty distractions. The only time they encourage healthy competition between themselves is around finding the best solutions to stop malaria.

It's much easier to jump all-in and stay all-in when there is no battle for recognition or first place. Because they met and partnered later in life, Ray and Peter had the experience, the humility, and the wisdom to understand the great value of joyful collaboration. "You can accomplish exponentially more in a partnership. It infinitely extends your reach," said Peter. "But it's also much more fun and so much more satisfying to know 'Hey, we did this together.' Ray is insanely willful and crazily patient. For him, being patient is critical to building larger collectives, as is staying out of the spotlight. I'd say it's humility and courage that have kept us going forward."

A core part of their secret is their "stick-to-itiveness," as Peter mentioned, and "not being a philanthropic dilettante." After sixteen years, countless hurdles, a successful global, cross-sector collaboration, and a Deep Connection founded on great love and respect for each other, Ray and Peter are clearly all-in for the long game when malaria is no longer one of the world's deadliest diseases.

And they were both clear that they will never give up.

Barriers to All-In

Opposing forces and the electric current of difference can wreak havoc on a relationship when they aren't channeled in the right direction. On the other hand, if people are too similar, they often end up competing with each other and not stretching themselves to be better.

The biggest barrier to being all-in is when one partner seems absent from the relationship. If one partner feels like they are putting in more time and energy than the other, distance will become the norm, and the relationship will suffer. An imbalance in commitment is one of the five key pitfalls in relationships, as defined by many of the scientists, therapists, and psychologists whose wisdom we tapped into for this book.

"There are two kinds of growing apart," the couples therapist Esther Perel says in a podcast for the *Knowledge Project*. "There's either bickering, chronic conflict, or high conflict; or there is disengagement and indifference and separateness. . . . That's really the choreography of growing apart. It's constant fighting, or it's so far apart that you don't even notice if the other one is there or not."

Acclaimed couples therapist John Gottman refers to what he calls "bids for attention"—the constant, nearly unrecognizable moments of reaching out from one individual to another within a relationship. Bids are actions. For example, one person in the relationship might complain to the other about a bad day at work. Does their partner ignore the complaints, or do they offer words of encouragement or empathy? In good, all-in relationships, Gottman says, those bids get acknowledged 86 percent of the time. In bad relationships, people acknowledge bids only 33 percent of the time.

Any relationship will ebb and flow as people go through their personal issues and their own evolution. Balance is important so people don't feel isolated and taken for granted over long periods of time. It might be that someone is going through a tough period like caring for an aging parent or a particularly challenging phase at work. Knowing that the other person has compassionate empathy and is giving you security is often all it takes to emerge stronger from these inevitable periods of difficulty and imbalance. It's also important to have the space for honest conversations so both partners can openly share how they are feeling in a way that creates solutions rather than increases any growing divide. Sometimes, a lack of interest links back to an inability to be vulnerable, in which someone is not willing to give 100 percent of themselves. When this happens, the other person eventually begins to disengage, too.

Letting Go of Fear

Embracing and sharing your own vulnerabilities is one of the quickest paths to becoming all-in. Often, this begins with letting go of your fears.

Keith Yamashita, founder of SYPartners, and Todd Holcomb, principal consultant at Becoming Human, met some twenty-five years ago on a retreat in the San Juan Islands, off the northern coast of Washington. They were attracted to each other through their shared passion for improving the world around them and their sense of optimism and possibility.

For a while, Keith and Todd had everything: a happy marriage, two beautiful children, and a thriving business. Then Todd became very ill with Lyme disease. It was the first time that Todd had not been able to function independently, as the disease was crippling. Keith stopped working during the worst of it to take care of Todd and their children.

It was in that vulnerable space that Todd realized the profound importance of their connection. The commitment Keith showed by sacrificing everything to be there for Todd opened up a safe space for Todd to let go of any fears he formerly held about the relationship and dive in completely, no longer attempting to hold a part of himself back in case things didn't work out with Keith. "You have to be willing to love before being loved," Keith told me, "and you have to be willing to trust before being trusted." Todd realized that one can be both intimately connected as a we, and be independent at the same time. In fact, it is perhaps that interplay between freedom and connection that allows partnerships to survive.

The two men went on to talk about how being all-in has allowed them to be the most loving versions of their original selves. "When you stop worrying about the perpetuation of the we—meaning we are going to go on until the very last breath as a we," Keith shared, "you can be more adventuresome and go out and be fully yourself and constantly return to the we." The security of their all-in commitment has allowed them to take risks because they know they will catch each other for the rest of their lives.

Fear of going all-in was also ever present in Chris Anderson and Jacqueline Novogratz's interview. When they were about to get married, Jacqueline was terrified to lose her independence and the freedom to follow her mission. To ease her fears, Chris surprised her at their wedding and added the vow, "I'll never hold you back."

Thirteen years after their wedding (and seventeen years after their relationship started), Jacqueline and Chris still feel safe and able to take risks, knowing that they are 100 percent there for each other and will always have each other's backs. Today, Jacqueline's advice to young people searching for Deep Connection in all types of relationships is "to realize that if you make the commitment in a real way, it'll set you free. It sounds so counterintuitive, but it allows you to fly."

Are You All-In?

When we think of being all-in, we might conjure up a picture of finding someone who is a mirror image of us so that everything will be familiar. In reality, complementary strengths and weaknesses can often make a relationship stronger. All-in partners give each other the safe space to be themselves, to celebrate rather than hide their differences.

In turn, an electric current of difference helps people stay all-in by minimizing competition, and by challenging each person to stretch beyond their comfort zone.

Alex Rappaport, cofounder of the education company Flocabulary, says the trick is waking people up to the importance of being all-in with someone. He asked: "How do we encourage people to look outside of themselves for support and additional skills and complementary skills, not be so proud to think that you can do everything? That's the ticket."

Here are some questions to ask yourself and your partner to determine whether you are all-in:

1. **Do you have each other's backs for the long run?** As we saw with Sherry and Mario, when you are doing something audacious, it is so critical to have someone by your side, especially when you are getting attacked from all directions. All-in connections are those in which you trust that someone will always have your back, and that same person or people will allow you to take risks while helping you minimize your fears. In safe, trusting environments, good relationships become like labs of possibility, spurring innovation and creating space to test new ideas and perfect Deep Connection skills. In these relationships, you can be confident that your partner truly has your best long-term interests in mind.

2. **Are you there when you need each other?** "When your partner speaks, the world stops," says Paul

Bennett, from IDEO. They are 100 percent there for you and you for them—a home to always come back to.

3. **Are you bearers of truth for each other, even when it is uncomfortable?** All-in relationships allow you to see things that you might not have previously seen in yourself, in others, or in the world. Your partner acts as a mirror, giving you a true picture of your strengths and a loving wake-up call when you are out on a limb and need to be pulled back (as we saw with Ben and Jerry). Ultimately, they give you the insight and freedom to be the best version of yourself.

4. **Do you support each other with a perpetual tailwind?** One plus one equals way more than two in an all-in connection, helping you achieve far more audacious goals than you ever could on your own. These partnerships are centers of learning, stoking the fires of curiosity, wonder, and enthusiasm. They are constantly helping partners lift each other.

5. **Do you provide a safe harbor for each other?** All-in partnerships allow individuals to fine-tune their interpersonal skills, such as opening space for honest conversations and managing conflict in a healthy way. This empowers individual growth and builds confidence to increase the depth and meaning of all the relationships in their lives.

6. **Are you loving enough?** Focus on giving love, not just getting love.

Being all-in does not mean losing yourself in a relationship. It means finding yourself through your Deep Connections. They give you the safe space and confidence to find your better self and the freedom to pursue something bigger. This doesn't mean that you have to be joined at the hip 24/7; rather, it means that no matter what happens, you will have each other's back. You will be there for each other through the best and worst of times.

CHAPTER FOUR

The Ecosystem

Third Degree of Connection

I think more than anything else, it's how
people construct their characters and how
they behave in the world.

—Uzodinma Iweala, author, doctor, film
producer, and CEO of the Africa Center

When geophysicist Joseph Farman and his team, Brian G. Gardiner and Jonathan Shanklin, at the British Antarctic Survey first saw the data, they thought that something must be wrong.

The data showed a worrying downward slope in the ozone level near the South Pole. Joe was known for his painstaking attention to detail and scientific rigor. So, they ran the same calculations again, over and over. They conducted systematic quality checks on years of data. They tested the equipment. The results remained the same. They were dreadful, as Joe said again and again.

They had just uncovered one of the most important scientific discoveries of the twentieth century.

When Jonathan first joined Joe's research team, he was skeptical about Mario and Sherry's research. "Well, that's a load of rubbish," he said. "How on Earth can aerosol cans possibly destroy the ozone layer?" He decided to plot a graph showing historic data from 1956 and current data that would prove that people did not need to worry about using spray cans. His skepticism rapidly diminished when he started to observe disturbing patterns in the data that helped lead to the discovery of the ozone hole and sparked the moral imperative to fix it. Years later he wrote about the damaging impact humankind is having on the environment: "Perhaps the most startling lesson from the ozone hole is just how quickly our planet can change."

In my interview with Jonathan, he spoke warmly of his decades-long friendship with Joe and Brian. They were a cast of unlikely characters: Joe the mathematical genius, Brian the physicist, a brilliant communicator and the glue that held them together, and Jonathan the enthusiastic, experimental scientist whose data analysis and visualization shined a light on the issue. Their different strengths interlocked to form an unbreakable bond. Their trust and unwavering respect for one another brought out the best in each other. Their combined breadth of scientific expertise demanded global credibility.

What Joe and his partners, Jonathan and Brian, discovered in 1984 was a hole in the ozone layer over the Antarctic. Working out the details, they concluded that indeed the combination of the bitter cold Antarctic temperatures and CFCs caused an accelerated ozone loss each spring. Fortunately, Britain had invested in gathering scientific data since 1956 and they were able to show that the damage was occurring fast. In 1985, Joe, Jonathan, and Brian published their findings in a paper in *Nature*, the same journal that had published Sherry and Mario's research eleven years earlier.

Not long after the British team published their findings, Susan Solomon, an atmospheric chemist with the National Oceanic and Atmospheric Administration (NOAA), led the National Ozone Expedition to Antarctica to gather additional data and understand how CFCs found in consumer products, appliances, and even battleships could cause damage to the ozone layer so far from where they were being used. Susan's findings validated what so many people had doubted. Her research was followed by many other scientific studies, all pointing in the same direction.

The data was irrefutable: Sherry Rowland and Mario Molina's research had been right all along.

"We had to be patient for more than a decade," Mario said.

These discoveries offered further support for Sherry and Mario's assertion that the crisis was a global one and revealed to the world the moral responsibility of global action. Soon the united belief that Sherry and Mario had in each other and in the urgent need to protect the ozone layer would ripple out into the world, preparing others to achieve the impossible.

Everyone I spoke with about the successful global collaboration to protect the ozone layer described Sherry and Mario as giants of moral character and integrity. Sherry, a tenured faculty member, could have legitimately taken most of the credit for discovering the impact of CFCs. Instead, he consistently shared the credit with Mario.

Sherry and Mario inspired the emergence of a core group of committed scientists, world leaders, policy makers, business leaders, and negotiators, each playing a different role yet all working toward the same audacious goal: to finalize a global agreement to stop the use of

CFCs and to ensure it was rapidly implemented. They built a network of friendships guided by a strong moral ecosystem. This ecosystem was instinctive to them, with respect, trust, and generosity, authentically alive in all they did, creating an environment of kindness, compassion, and grace.

At the center, building momentum and constantly keeping everyone on track, was a handful of very Deep Connections. Two of those Deep Connections were close friends of Sherry's and Mario's: Mostafa Tolba and Stephen O. Andersen.

Mostafa Tolba, a larger-than-life UN representative and a chief architect of the Montreal Protocol, was united with Mario and Sherry in the belief that if the right people came together to collaborate, the world could protect the ozone layer. Mostafa's respect and empathy for his partners and the needs and problems of less industrialized countries were critical to the world coming together. Stephen O. Andersen, an economist with the Environmental Protection Agency (EPA), was given the task of helping industries all over the world end the use of CFCs. Stephen would become one of Mostafa's trusted allies. The ultimate community builder, he was friendly, likable, and authentic. The two became extraordinary partners—Mostafa, a fiery but trusted leader from Egypt, and Stephen, an American from Logan, Utah, with a gift for getting people to feel part of something bigger, like a family focused on something that would impact many generations to come.

Mostafa fiercely protected the mission. He did not tolerate people who let their own interests get in the way, or who disrupted the virtues he held sacred to keep the wider community thriving. "This is a person who loved other people and the earth so much that he couldn't resist being stern and getting what was best for the environment and the people he loved," Stephen recalled. His unyielding focus on the higher purpose earned the trust of everyone and enabled him to build bridges. He could take two people with starkly different positions, figure out what their perspectives were, and find a solution.

Mostafa brought together a community of diverse professionals who helped forge an agreement, all using their complementary skills. Bit by bit, they respectfully discussed and debated their way to shared solutions. And on September 15, 1987, the Montreal Protocol was adopted, starting the process of banning CFCs and other chemicals to prevent further damage to the ozone layer. Eventually, 197 countries would sign. It was a monumental achievement.

But an agreement is nothing without a plan to implement it. Stephen was key to leading this implementation and continues to be committed to its success today, more than thirty years later. In 1989, Stephen, Mostafa, and other partners created groups of implementing bodies, including the Technology and Economic Assessment Panel (TEAP). This group was central to bringing together industry, science, and policy experts to eliminate CFCs and invent replacements.

Stephen had a strategy for building first a close team and then a movement: by paying careful attention to relationships and nurturing the ecosystem that promoted friendship, he identified best-in-class participants who wanted to work hard together. Then he set out to strengthen the connections between them. He built an environment of trust and appreciation. Stephen also realized the importance of empathy and compassion. He zeroed in on people's interests, sought to understand their cultures and their personal challenges, and then showed deep respect and empathy by paying attention to every detail, right down to what he would wear to make them most comfortable when they met.

Where Mostafa was the visionary, Stephen was the leader who rolled up his sleeves and made it happen. His path to get there was "suspending disbelief and cynicism, imagining success, watching the process and getting things to work." He evolved the ecosystem of virtues that Sherry and Mario embedded in the community from the start. Stephen centered his actions on respect and generosity, always praising people and celebrating their wins. He often sent letters of gratitude from the UN to the bosses of the TEAP members, giving them the opportunity to bask in well-earned praise for their work. Stephen went to extraordinary lengths to show authentic compassion to the community. When a member of the Solvents Committee, Jorge Corona, fell very ill from a parasite, Stephen mobilized the rest of the group, organized a worldwide search for the very expensive treatment, and arranged the financing, ultimately saving Jorge's life.

Sherry, Mario, Stephen, and Mostafa modeled the ecosystem of virtues for an expanding collective of scientists, economists, and industry representatives to hammer out the details and start implementation. "What they would implement, and how, has been based on . . . an ever-growing circle of friends [who have] worked tirelessly under conditions of personal trust," shared Mostafa. The bonds of trust and respect they inspired increased the speed, the level of innovation, and the effectiveness of the Montreal Protocol implementation process.

They were wise enough to know that as the community grew, they would need to create structures to keep a larger collaborative ecosystem thriving. The Montreal Protocol agreement was itself a huge success story, but the work of implementation was just beginning.

An Ecosystem for Collective Good

Talking about values and virtues is easy—we've all experienced them plastered on office walls and woven into political speeches. It is much harder to consistently live them. Sherry and Mario lived their values every moment, like a spiritual operating system that guided every word and every action.

This moral ecosystem appeared in some form in all the partnerships I interviewed, brought to life through the daily practice of essential virtues. Over time these virtues become reflexive responses, creating an environment of kindness, grace, and compassion among our Deep Connections and all our relationships. This ecosystem makes being all-in both possible and sustainable—and, just as important, it becomes the foundation for something bigger.

These virtues are not a pyramid or a ladder. They are interconnected—a living, changing ecosystem. The virtues can either feed and strengthen each other, or if any one of them is neglected, undermine the others. In a partnership, these virtues don't just magically appear. Building the ecosystem takes hard work, curiosity, and practice, until it becomes the center of everything you do, a way of being every day, even in the most mundane moments. I learned this when I met renowned anthropologists Wade Davis and Carroll Dunham, who have been friends for over forty years.

Standing in Wade Davis's home on Bowen Island in Canada, surrounded by artifacts he has gathered on his global travels as a photographer and anthropologist, I felt like I had been transported to another world, one in which cultural diversity is held sacred. Every bookshelf, table, wall, and even the floor felt like it held a little bit of magic. In the midst of all this, I sat and listened to Wade and Carroll Dunham talk for a full three hours. I was so enthralled I ended up missing not one, but three consecutive ferries back to the mainland.

As we discussed the idea of a moral ecosystem, they opened my eyes to how crucial but overlooked our collective virtues are. As Carroll said, "When we look at the glue that holds societies together, is the construct of who we are focused on us as an individual or are we part of a larger collective? If it's just me, me, me, I, I, I versus if it's we, we, we, the whole equation is profoundly different."

Wade and Carroll shared stories about biological ecosystems that work together to serve the collective good. The largest, oldest living organism in the world, called Pando, is a colony of aspen trees in Utah. Its connected root system is over eighty thousand years old. This community of trees stays alive by taking care of one another, protecting each other from disease and fire, and ensuring that any tree that needs water or nutrients receives them via an ancient root system. We can learn from the reciprocity that is alive and well in the ecosystems of this wondrous planet, as well as rethink our relationship with nature, moving from transactional extraction to regeneration and renewal.

Likewise, human cultures (and partnerships) survive because they look beyond the individual to the collective. Our culture clothes us in ethical and moral values, informing our capacity for great good . . . or great evil. We've lost this moral ecosystem, along with a respect for different cultures, which is one of the main reasons the world is being torn apart. In its place, we've gained a heightened sense of individualism.

Change is not a threat to cultural ecosystems, Carroll emphasizes: *power* is the real threat. The current power structures incentivize individual gain and ensure that control is held by a small handful of individuals. The focus is on power *over others* for short-term profit and fame, rather than a *shared, equal partnership* for long-term greater good for everyone. We need to figure out how we can reignite moral and ethical values in this new digital world that will bring us together. One place to start is through building ecosystems of virtues with our Deep Connections.

Carroll and Wade's rich insights, alongside those from the over sixty partnerships in this book, helped me see how **six key virtues** can help us transcend cultural divides, expand our aspirations, and build Deep Connections with a wider range of people:

- **Enduring Trust** is not just learning to trust each other. That's important, of course, but so is learning to trust in the unknown—trusting in life itself. Learning to live without fear, and trusting that the choices you make will work out, allows you to walk in grace. This then allows you to be fully present and bring your whole self to your partnership.

- **Unshakable Mutual Respect** for each person's unique contribution to a relationship must be maintained. Rather than trying to turn everyone into a version of yourself, celebrate differences. This starts with deep, respectful listening and opening yourself to ideas you might not agree with but are willing to try to understand.

- **United Belief** elevates partnerships, relationships, and communities, helping people believe in one another and in something bigger. "We've forgotten that belief and metaphor [are what have] always driven the human spirit," Wade says. "The measure of a culture is not just what they do but the quality of their aspirations, the metaphors that propel them forward."

- **Shared Humility** starts by recognizing that every person and every culture has something to contribute to society. In Wade's words, we need to "shatter the tyranny of cultural myopia." Being humble about what we don't know is critical to healthy relationships. As Wade says of his own field, "The whole message of anthropology is distilled in a simple idea: the other peoples of the world aren't failed attempts at you." Therefore, we must always begin relationships without assumptions, without judgment.

- **Nurturing Generosity** appears in all of Wade and Carroll's stories about Indigenous wisdom, focusing on the idea of competing in how much we can give instead of how much we can take. Wade pointed to the Penan nomadic people of Malaysia, who measure wealth in the strength of their social relations: "There is no word for thank you in their language because sharing is a reflex," mentioned Wade.

- **Compassionate Empathy** can be seen as the ability to step into someone else's shoes and not diminish them for their differences. This allows us to actively celebrate diverse dreams and alleviate suffering.

After my conversation with Carroll and Wade, Wade let me explore his office, a cultural treasure chest, for a bit longer. Every object on display has a human story behind it filled with Wade's deep sense of wonder and respect for other cultures—from the Aboriginal Elders in Australia, to the Inuit in the Arctic, to the Elder Brothers in Colombia, to the Gabra in Kenya, to the Penan in Sarawak. A symbolic ecosystem of the virtues that connect cultures and celebrate diversity.

Ultimately, Carroll and Wade always came back to universal compassion and love as the outcome of living the six virtues, bridging all human divides. As they describe it, an abundant love is a radiant generosity of spirit, not a limited commodity. We can build such love in our Deep Connections, by practicing these six virtues to help us be kinder and more loving toward everyone we connect with.

Exploring the Ecosystem

The ecosystem is alive with the daily practice of six essential virtues. Managing the balance and flow between the interconnected virtues is central to building depth in our relationships. For example, too much humility can undermine your united belief in something bigger, or a lack of generosity can crumble your foundations of trust and respect.

This is not an easy process. Living these virtues means doing the right thing, even when those decisions demand difficult trade-offs. We saw this when Leah Tutu trusted and respected Arch's decision to speak out against apartheid, even if it meant his being imprisoned or killed. This was certainly a painful decision for Leah, as she did not want to lose her husband, but she believed it was the right thing for Arch and the larger purpose.

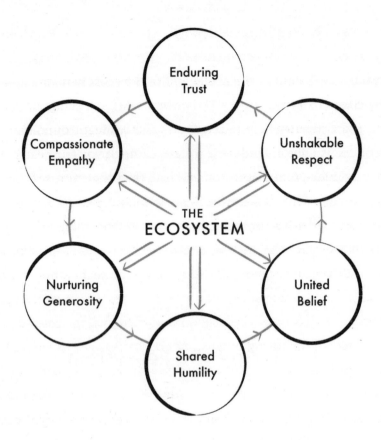

Over time, the virtues become reflexive responses, creating an environment of kindness, grace, and unconditional love.

These connected virtues help create psychological safety in partnerships and collectives. Google's Project Aristotle, led by Julia Rozovsky, found that this feeling of safety was one of the key factors in whether a team was successful.

As the moral ecosystem is at the heart of successful Deep Connections, the rest of this chapter explores each of the six virtues through the experience of the sixty-plus partnerships, including practical tips for each to help embed these virtues in your own relationships.

First Virtue: Enduring Trust—Faith in Each Other

Trust is by far the most critical element of the ecosystem of a partnership. "Trust is all-important. If you don't trust somebody, it doesn't work," shared Henry Arnhold, cofounder of Mulago Foundation. He went on to describe an enduring trust—in which you trust each other with your lives, grounded in something bigger than yourselves, with a consistent belief in each other's good intentions—as an essential component in cultivating meaningful lives and organizations.

Grounding our relationships in trust is fundamental to our well-being and to our businesses. The Edelman Trust Barometer study, which has polled thirty-four thousand people across twenty-eight countries every year for two decades, shows that "in the past 20 years, we have seen a fracturing of trust, but an increase in its value. Trust has emerged, like freedom and security, as itself a barometer of a successful society."

Whom we trust has shifted significantly over the past two decades of Edelman's research. In fact, the pyramid of trust has flipped upside down: in the early 2000s we put our trust in authorities, whereas today we reserve our trust for "people like me." Our peers, friends, and local communities are now our sources of truth in the sea of fake news that exploded with social media and the politicizing of the media. Our Deep Connections have become our most crucial centers for truth and trust.

Many of us think of ourselves as having a trusting nature, yet often our actions tell a different story. We want to have faith in others, but if our trust has been broken repeatedly, we may view life through a lens of suspicion and fear. We adopt patterns of behavior that, viewed objectively, reveal our distrust. We question others' intentions and fall back on the comfort of our own agendas. With commitment and the support of going all-in with Deep Connections, we can change, but it takes effort and intentional design.

Enduring trust is even more difficult, and often more rewarding, when you embrace connection with people outside your inner circle. And yet, it can be done, even among complete strangers. Consider the global success of Airbnb.

It seems obvious now, but when cofounders Joe Gebbia, Brian Chesky, and Nate Blecharczyk founded Airbnb in 2007, the idea of allowing strangers into your home seemed radical, even Pollyannaish. Investors, and basically everyone else, disbelieved their story—they were sure that strangers would never trust each other to that degree.

The team set out to counter this hesitation by designing a business model around trust and connection. They offered free professional photography to hosts, invited customer reviews, and designed a reputation system to bolster trust even further. Airbnb's leaders listened to find out what information guests needed to feel safe, and assured hosts that Airbnb had their back if something went wrong.

The three cofounders and friends instinctively knew that the measures that would matter the most would be those that encouraged Deep Connection—with each other, their team, their hosts, their guests, and local communities. They also realized that all these groups are interconnected and play a role in strengthening their business.

Most companies spend huge swaths of time creating and tracking all kinds of measures—profitability, retention of customers and staff, cost ratios, and more. Rarely do they focus on the depth of connection and level of trust—with customers, teams, and the communities they operate in. You can feel the absence of trust the second you walk into a company without it. An erosive current runs under the conversations by the watercooler, information doesn't flow, joy is missing, bureaucracy is high.

Joe, Nate, and Brian understood this and built a unique company based on connection and trust. This was made easier because their relationship had started with friendship. They had no agenda beyond wanting to enjoy one another's company. They were always thinking about what was best for each other and the company, anticipating each other's needs, and celebrating the combination of their differing perspectives to create better ideas. They wanted to create a culture inside the company that mirrored the fundamental trust they believed exists—and that they hold sacred in their own Deep Connection with one other.

To create trust, the Airbnb team realized they needed employees to understand there's no need to compete with one another; the only person to compete with is yourself. This was an important first step to developing respect for one another—and confidence that your coworkers will have your back. This then allows for a safe space of transparency and openness. Hard conversations are embraced and have productive outcomes because people trust in one another's good intentions.

This model of connection and communication appeared to be working well, as the company grew rapidly. By the end of 2019, its twelfth year in business, it was receiving more than a thousand résumés for every opening. Airbnb's rumored plans for a public stock offering became one of the most anticipated market debuts of 2020. Then COVID-19 emerged and travel skidded to a halt.

Faced with a barrage of communication from customers wanting to cancel their bookings and get their money back, Joe, Brian, and Nate made the decision to break with company policy and offer full refunds. They made the decision and implemented it without first consulting the network of hundreds of thousands of hosts whose livelihoods depend on bookings. The hosts felt blindsided. After twelve years of creating trust and goodwill all over the world, the founders realized that they had let their community down.

For another company, that breach of trust might have been the end of the business. For Joe, Brian, and Nate, it was an opportunity to show humility. To apologize. To reach out to their community and ask for another chance. They had the hard conversations that are possible only when you've created a culture of trust and openness. From these conversations came a decision to put in place a $250 million fund for their hosts, accompanied by a note of apology from Brian: "While I believe we did the right thing in prioritizing health and safety, I am sorry we communicated this decision to guests without consulting you—like partners should," Brian said. "We have heard from you and we know we could have been better partners."

Joe, Nate, and Brian's story is an important one, as it goes beyond their Deep Connection with each other—to their team, their hosts, their guests, and the wider communities they operate in. It is a shining example of connection and trust in a world that incentivizes the opposite.

Trust, of course, takes a different shape depending on the form of partnership, but in all circumstances, we are able to *design our partnerships to default to trust.*

Here are some guiding principles:

Assume good intentions. Don't jump to conclusions about the other person's actions, going immediately to a place of fear or distrust. Trust grows when you are confident the other person has your back, as well as the collective benefit of the relationship in mind. A strong purpose helps embed good intentions in every action. It deepens momentary trust into something enduring and profound.

Consistently defaulting to trust takes a leap of faith, which in turn encourages more trust.

Create a safe, honest space for trust to grow. This has a very literal meaning: create an environment where you and your partner can communicate safely. That requires time and regular moments that build stability, history, and joy. You'll see a whole host of great examples of these moments in the next chapter. When you make honesty and openness a central priority with your Deep Connections, people won't hide from difficult conversations.

Be transparent and clear. It's easier to be honest and open when you have a design principle of transparency. One software company, Buffer, took this to extremes. All their compensation packages and diversity data are available online, their open-source code is available to anyone, and they are transparent about their future product map. It has helped them build a much more connected, straightforward community, keeping team members focused on productivity rather than worried about fairness.

A clear operating framework, including clear roles and responsibilities, is fundamental in enabling trust to flourish. It allows people to be heard, make decisions, take risks, be efficient, and do something extraordinary.

Make hard conversations the norm. Don't be afraid to talk frequently about the tough stuff. At Airbnb, they talk about "elephants, dead fish and vomit." The idea was to open up dialogue throughout the entire company. "Elephants are the big things in the room that nobody is talking about, dead fish are the things that happened a few years ago that people can't get over, and vomit is that sometimes people just need to get something off their mind and you need someone to just sit there and listen." The idea is to communicate openly, always, so that people are free to express themselves even when what they have to say is hard to hear.

Trust can also get thrown off track by the demons of past experiences. When we take the time to learn and understand each other's hot buttons (as we also take responsibility for our own), we can help each other work through triggering situations when they arise, reinforcing the sense of the partnership as a safe space. The worst thing you can do is disengage, ignoring stressors on yourself and others until the tremors grow into an earthquake that could destroy the relationship.

Allow mistakes to build trust. No matter how carefully you craft a relationship, there are moments when trust can be broken, especially in the early stages, when you and your partner don't have a sense of shared history to help you understand why someone is doing something that might appear hurtful. Acknowledging and taking responsibility for mistakes can go a long way toward building trust.

Watch your body language. Rolling your eyes or turning your back when someone is talking to you could be all it takes to undermine trust. Trust was so deeply seeded in Ben and Jerry's partnership that you could feel it in every word they used, their body language, and even their laughter. In the fifteen years that I've known them, I've never seen even a moment when this trust was betrayed by an undermining glance, comment, or action.

Trust yourself. Ultimately, building enduring trust with someone else is impossible unless you already have that kind of trust in yourself. Many of the people I spoke with described fundamental questions you can ask yourself to better understand how to become a more trusting partner:

- Do you trust your intentions and your abilities?

- What do you need from your partner to help grow self-trust?

- Are you all-in and coming from a place of trust rather than fear?

- Is there a clear something bigger driving your life and your partnerships?

"The ability to give without feeling it's a sacrifice, that the winning is in the giving, is a kind of trust," says Will Marshall, cofounder of Planet, a satellite company. "A trust in the universe, but also in learning to trust that if you dedicate yourself to a big, audacious goal, you will be your best self, and you'll find a pathway to weave that into your daily work or life." As you better understand yourself, you will come to recognize that other people are simply trying to be their best selves, too. That understanding will enable you to collaborate with them more effectively.

Second Virtue: Unshakable Mutual Respect— Freedom to Live Your Truth

Trust will never flourish without respect. The two are deeply interconnected. I've seen them in all the successful relationships we've explored. In fact, the two were almost always mentioned in rapid succession when I asked interviewees about what kept their partnerships connected.

While trust is a belief that someone can be relied on, that their intentions are good, respect is the way we treat one another, how we accept and admire people for who they are. They are the twin virtues at the core of the ecosystem: trust will make sure you always have each other's back, and mutual respect will help you each become your very best authentic self.

Respect might seem like common sense. Of course we respect everyone we truly connect with. Yet a hard look at the graveyard of our past relationships reveals just how difficult it is to create the right environment for respect to flourish. When we get it right, we create *unshakable mutual respect*, able to weather mistakes, embarrassment, and times when our *self*-respect might be a bit wobbly. When we honor one another, that respect radiates to others.

Robert P. George and Cornel West spent their childhoods in wildly different environments three thousand miles apart. Robert was raised in the hills of West Virginia, the grandson of coal miners, and Cornel grew up amid the explosive racial activism of California in the 1960s. Today Robert is widely revered as one of the country's most influential conservative Christian thinkers. Cornel emerged as an inspired chair of the Democratic Socialists of America, an outspoken voice for left-wing politics who has been on the forefront of the racial justice movement.

Cornel and Robert have many polar opposite beliefs, but a Deep Connection has blossomed from their fourteen-year friendship. These two intellectuals, both Ivy League scholars (Robert went to Princeton and Cornel began at Harvard and left to go back to Union Theological Seminary), speak about each other with reverence and awe; they talk about their love for each other. When they sit together, their heads bend toward each other as if they're naturally drawn together—perhaps to make sure they hear every word.

While the world around them was being shattered by polarization and a degree of what they both call "spiritual decay," these two friends stayed connected and dedicated their lives to teaching, scholarship, standing up for things they believe in, and engaging and learning from fellow truth seekers with whom they have disagreements—including each other.

They do this through deeply listening to each other and creating a space for opposing views without losing respect for each other. "We have some profound points of agreement, despite our political differences," Robert said. "We're committed to truth-seeking. We're committed to ideas, to the kind of civil discourse that makes truth-seeking possible, and to freedom of speech, which is the condition of such discourse." As a result, he said, they've formed "a little evangelistic team for those principles and values."

To Cornel, respecting someone who holds profoundly different views is the path to growth. The point, he said, is to be "unsettled." But it works only if there is humility, an openness to self-scrutiny and respect for differing views. Robert feels similarly that reaching across to others with respect for different opinions is the path to greater understanding, but he admits it isn't easy. People need to force themselves to do it, and that takes humility and courage. "It doesn't mean you're pre-committed to change sides, but it means that you're acknowledging your own fallibility," he said.

It takes courage to get out of one's silo, Cornel said, "to get beyond whatever label and categories others have imposed." The important thing is to listen to each other, respect each other, "and hope that one is blessed enough to be able to have the deep sisterhood or brotherhood or friendship that we have been blessed with, so that it could be transformative in one's own life to make one a much more loving, courageous, critically minded, humble, tenacious human being."

Their last words of advice were to go out and find a friend who *unsettles you*. To have deep respect even across divides to allow for differing views to challenge and shape your thinking.

Respect helps reverse the poisonous lack of basic human civility in the world, as Robert and Cornel are demonstrating by bridging very large divides. It's not about respecting what someone may become, it's respecting who they are now. "Love is respecting your partner in the place they are in," says Jo Confino, whom you met in chapter three.

Any kind of partnership can be designed to default to respect. Through the interviews, I identified **six common principles** that build unshakable mutual respect:

Legos, Not Jigsaw Puzzles. We mistakenly look for partners who we believe are mirror images of ourselves and will fit us like the perfect jigsaw puzzle piece. Richard Reed, one of the founders of Innocent Drinks, adamantly rejected that approach. Focus instead on whether someone's skills complement yours, whether their upsides balance your downsides. He likened it to respecting each other's differences and creating a Lego structure, with all kinds of different shapes and sizes building upward and outward toward something bigger and wondrous. At times the structure will feel unsettled by the multitude of different pieces that make up the whole, but the right moral ecosystem will lead to building the most extraordinary things. Our virtues must match, but our perspectives or skills can (and often should) differ. Honoring and respecting differences strengthens relationships over time, pushing us toward greatness.

The World Stops. "The world stops" when you are listening to your partner. Paul Bennett, partner at IDEO and photographer Jim Cooper's spouse, went back to this phrase again and again during their beautiful, creatively charged interview. They discussed how respect is as much about deep listening and being present as it is about praise and affirmation.

Cornel and Robert joked that someone eavesdropping on their conversations might be perplexed by long periods of silence—moments when they have deeply listened to each other's opposing views and are reflecting and testing their own thinking.

We've all had the experience of trying to communicate something important to someone who is mentally somewhere else, not listening at all. We've also all been guilty of doing the same ourselves. Not only is this disrespectful, it also undermines connection, sapping both people's willingness to share and damaging their confidence. Author, film director, and entrepreneur Uzodinma Iweala said, "First and foremost, you need to listen. Not listening to someone is as good as saying to that person: *you don't exist.*" It's the ultimate signal of disrespect.

Disagree, Never Disrespect. Differences of opinion are the heart of a good relationship. To have these differences without discord, we must learn how to discuss and respect opinions without launching into an emotionally charged war of words.

Part of this process comes from letting go of any sense of competition. "We always had an in-built sense of respect for the other two's opinions," Richard Reed told me. "[At Innocent Drinks,] we would always make decisions as a threesome by listening to each other's arguments, by getting to the logic and the facts and the reasons rather than [getting] caught up in ego and competition."

Grow Respect. Like trust, respect has a mutually beneficial connection with the first degree, Something Bigger. Respect grows by supporting each other's efforts to accomplish something of meaning. Knowing when someone is focused on making a difference to others and not just themselves, and being there for them in that process, is central to the growth of mutual respect.

A Web of Respect. Community plays an important role in creating a welcome embrace of respect. Daily life has a way of fraying respect in a partnership as you see each other at your best and at your worst. Someone in your wider community can often play an objective role in reminding you why your partner is so uniquely special—reigniting that spark of respect for each other.

Just as you must trust yourself in order to trust others, this web of respect must start with self-respect—an understanding and appreciation of your own unique skills. Mark Twain is purported to have said, "The worst loneliness is not to be comfortable with yourself." Respecting yourself, and being comfortable with who you are, gives you the strength and openness to give unshakable respect to others.

An Imperfect Pedestal. One of the biggest impediments to mutual respect is putting our partners on a pedestal. When they make a human mistake and tumble off, we go into a negative spiral of disappointment and criticism. We must ground our awe of each other in reality. No one is perfect, and if we try to hold people to unrealistic standards, respect will be eaten away, and the fabric of our partnerships will fray beyond repair.

Respect and trust open the door for belief in each other and a belief that together you can achieve something far bigger.

Third Virtue: United Belief—Make the Impossible Possible

United belief, built on the bedrock of trust and respect, is like having your own personal fan club cheering you on and lifting you up. It is a shared confidence in each other, as well as a faith that together you can make the impossible possible. This belief pushes you to be the best version of yourself and propels even the most difficult, audacious ideas into reality. United belief is a bit like the fuel that helps you get to something bigger, believing in each other and believing in your ideas, even when others might think you are crazy.

United belief does not always mean that you share exactly the same dreams, as we saw with Cornel and Robert. It means that there is an underlying confidence in each other, a respect for differing approaches, and a mutual awareness of common ground.

In September 2003, during my first week with Virgin Unite, Richard Branson handed me a letter from Nelson Mandela and his wife, Graça Machel. The letter was a positive response to an earlier letter from Richard and his dear friend Peter Gabriel, about their shared idea of The Elders, a vision for a group of morally courageous leaders to work on peace and human rights. As he handed me the letter, Richard said, "Mandela and Graça are in. Can you please help us make The Elders happen?" My first thought was, *Oh my gosh, I've just quit a great job in Australia to come to work for a crazy man with outrageous ideas.* Then I pulled my jaw up off the floor, suspended my disbelief, and got to work.

In May 2006, we hosted a series of gatherings on Necker Island in the British Virgin Islands to co-create the idea of The Elders. On the first day, jittery with nerves and squinting in the morning sunlight, I stood barefoot in the Balinese-style great room in front of a group of philanthropists, tech founders, social activists, heads of foundations, religious leaders, and government leaders from all over the world. I could never have imagined myself in the same room with such an illustrious collection of people, let alone presenting to them with a flip chart. (Peter and Richard had banned the PowerPoint deck we had spent months creating, as they felt it was not human enough—which was a wise decision.)

As nerves made it difficult to hold my pen steady, I caught the piercing blue eyes of President Jimmy Carter, who was sitting next to Archbishop Tutu in the front row. I thought, *Wow, he's listening so intently. He must love this idea.*

He did not.

Moments later, President Carter stood up. "I don't think this idea makes sense," he announced. "I don't believe in it."

I wanted to melt into the cement tiles under my feet and disappear forever. Quickly, I glanced at the back of the room and saw Peter and Richard, mouths agape, frozen in shock.

During the break, the three of us went into Richard's office with heavy hearts. What we and so many others had put so much love and hard work into shaping had just been smashed in front of a room of people who were critical to getting it off the ground. Not a good start. After a few moments of muddled discussion (I've never before or since seen Richard or Peter at a loss for words), we took a deep breath, united in our belief in the idea and one another, and stepped back into the room. We were shaken and humbled, but not beaten.

What happened next was extraordinary. Everyone in the room rolled up their sleeves to co-create a better, stronger idea. Peter, Richard, and I, alongside key partners Scilla Elworthy and Andrea Brenninkmeijer, took turns hosting small groups to fill in some of the holes in the idea, always staying true to the concept that we so deeply believed in: a group of global Elders courageously and independently working on peace and human rights, but never assuming we had all the answers. Instead, we narrowed in on the idea of The Elders collectively encouraging nuclear disarmament, working behind the scenes to end conflicts, and fighting for human rights, such as ending child marriage and encouraging climate justice.

President Carter's initial disbelief stemmed from his worry that the effort would be just a "talking shop," leading to more words and no action. To ensure that was not the case, he and Archbishop Tutu huddled together for five days to shape the purpose and values of The Elders. They would often laugh at each other's different ways of working, with President Carter wanting to start at the crack of dawn and work through to evening, and Archbishop Tutu wanting breaks throughout the day to reflect and pray. The collective perspective of the group made the final concept far better (of course) than our banned PowerPoint deck.

This wisdom we achieved through united belief was captured in Mandela's speech at the launch of The Elders on July 18, 2007, almost a year to the day after that melting-into-the-cement moment on Necker Island. All The Elders watched with respect as Mandela took the stage and spoke about how governments around the world are struggling to respond to our interconnected global problems. His face lit up when he shared his belief that this group of Elders, who had no other agendas or vested interests, could help tackle what often seem like intractable issues. He set a North Star for The Elders that still holds true today: "Gathered here today we have the makings of such a group. Using their experience, their moral courage, and their ability to rise above the parochial concerns of nation, race, and creed, they can help make our planet a more peaceful, healthy, and equitable place to live."

President Carter and Archbishop Tutu, alongside many others in that initial group, became the most steadfast supporters of The Elders over the years. When President Carter retired from The Elders after his ninety-second birthday, in May 2016, he held up a glass and toasted his colleagues, telling them, "The Elders has been one of the most significant things I've done in my life."

United belief will help you and your organizations step into your highest potential, as it did for The Elders.

Here are **four ways** successful partnerships are able to sustain a united belief over time.

No Boundaries, No Limits. United belief gives you the freedom to live a life of exponential possibilities together, breaking through boundaries and limitations that might hold you back if you were on your own.

Alex Rappaport and Blake Harrison are the founders of Flocabulary, a company delivering educational hip-hop music videos to help millions of young people master vocabulary, math, science, and more. Think *Sesame Street* meets Jay-Z. Alex told me, "It's easier to leap if you are holding someone's hand. . . . Knowing that someone else is just as crazy as I am is a really good feeling."

That doesn't mean that united belief encourages reckless, ridiculous risks. "I feel like you are the second half of my brain. You're the skeptical to my impulsive a lot of the time, which is great," Alex told Blake. "[I ask myself,] am I chasing a shiny object that actually doesn't mean anything to our business? And often you pull my balloon down to Earth." They figured out ways to challenge each other, to become devil's advocates to ensure that their united belief gave oxygen to their best ideas without shattering each other's dreams.

Jerry Greenfield describes Ben Cohen's approach to life as one of "no boundaries, no limits." This led them both on adventures of a lifetime that expand rather than limit their united belief in a better way of doing business.

Anchor of Confidence. When President Carter moved into the White House in 1977, Rosalynn Carter declared that she had no intention of being a typical First Lady. She did not want to be confined to the traditional role of hostess. Instead, she used her platform to advocate for important issues that were unpopular at the time, such as mental health.

Rosalynn was not always that confident. "I was very insecure about what I was capable of, and Jimmy believed I could do anything," she said.

As mentioned in chapter three, President Carter credits Rosalynn as the most important person in the White House during his presidency. "Rosa was deeply involved in domestic and international affairs, and when I couldn't go on an important mission, Rosa would go for me—not my secretary of state, but Rosa," he said. "She visited seven countries in Latin America to strengthen international relations and heal the wounds. She had to deal with very troubling issues such as nuclear proliferation and the drug trade. She assumed enormous responsibilities that related to all aspects of governing America."

Confidence is both an output and an input of united belief. Not self-interested confidence, but a confidence that grows through honest feedback from your all-in partners.

Competing with Yourself. Self-belief and the constant bettering of yourself are the grounding forces for a wider united belief with others. Often, what knocks this off track is our culture's emphasis on competition over collaboration. How many times have we sat at awkward dinner parties watching couples try to outsmart each other? Or sat in a business meeting where everyone is trying to be the most important person in the room?

As Bertrand Piccard said of his solar flight efforts with his partner, André Borschberg, "The goal is not to be better than the other and make it a competition; the goal is to be better than what we were before. I have to be better than what I was before. André had to be better than what he was before. Competing with ourselves."

Lift. Pat Mitchell has achieved a lot in her life: she's the former CEO and president of PBS, the president of CNN Productions, founder of TEDWomen, and much more besides. Still, it was clear during my interview with her and her husband, Scott Seydel, a successful business leader, that the most important thing they've ever done is nurture their Deep Connection.

"I value so many things about this partnership, and every single day I think to myself I'm the luckiest woman in the world," Pat shared. In unison, they continued, "We lift each other up."

What if, in every interaction with our Deep Connections, we asked how we could lift them up in this moment? How can I choose to focus on the positive rather than the negative? How can I celebrate their strengths? How can I pause to show them how much I value and believe in them? How can I use this approach to lift others?

Fourth Virtue: Shared Humility—Tame Your Ego

Shared humility is all about remembering how little we know and coming to everything with a curious, learning mindset. This virtue relies on the presence of united belief; one without the other will wreak havoc in a partnership. If united belief is not tempered with humility, outsize egos can make you overestimate your own abilities and underestimate your partner's abilities, leading to an unhealthy imbalance in the relationship. If you have humility without belief, it will be hard to do something bigger.

Shared humility is informed confidence—an understanding of our own limitations and the healthy ego that will emerge from that.

When I arrived at the offices of Draper Richards Kaplan (DRK), a global venture philanthropy fund, I expected to meet and interview the three cofounders, Bill Draper, Robin Richards Donohoe, and Rob Kaplan (who was phoning in from Dallas). Instead, the tiny office was crammed with five voices: Bill, Robin, Rob, Jim Bildner, the managing partner, and Christy Chin, a partner at the time. Bill, Robin, and Rob had decided that they didn't want to be interviewed on their own or take the credit for the work of the team, since DRK's culture is all about others.

In 1994, Robin was still an MBA student at Stanford and Bill was impressed by her leadership at a university meeting. They had a long breakfast and by the end of the four hours, they decided to start a private equity company together—a twenty-six-year-old student with four years of experience alongside one of America's first venture capitalists, who had also held the second-highest position in the UN as administrator of the United Nations Development Programme. Bill described their partnership in his typical self-deprecating manner: "Opposites attract. You've got youth and you've got brainpower on one side—her side—and you've got age and experience on the other."

Robin was stunned when Bill asked her to partner, and pleasantly surprised by his humility. He insisted that this was an equal partnership and that her name had equal billing. When Robin tried to convince him otherwise because she felt she was too young and he might want a more senior partner later on, Bill's reply to her was, "Why are you doubting yourself? You are my partner and I want your name on the door." This same ethos led to Rob joining the partnership later on.

For seventeen years, Bill and Robin had lunch together every day, a ritual that deepened their relationship. Robin was immediately struck by Bill's ability to listen authentically to a twenty-six-year-old. She also remembers learning an important lesson from him early on when he got in a taxi and asked the driver, "Where are you from? What do you enjoy doing?" Bill tries to learn from everyone he meets.

The genesis of DRK began in 2001, when, after many years of successfully running their private equity business, Draper Richards, Bill and Robin decided to start what would become DRK, a fund focused on supporting early-stage social and environmental impact entrepreneurs—founded way ahead of its time, before impact investing became popular. They were joined in 2010 by Robert Kaplan, who was a professor of leadership at Harvard and who later was the president and CEO of the Federal Reserve Bank of Dallas. The partnership is now on their third fund, this one $65 million, dedicated to entrepreneurs with the potential to change the world for the better.

The members of the team at DRK come from all kinds of backgrounds. They've put structures in place to benefit from their differences and tame egos, leading to an extraordinary example of a highly collaborative workplace. "When we play, we're playing like a symphony," the partners said, "because in our DNA we've taken out a variety of components so that they are not competing [with each other]; they are competing on *how I can make my life material to others*." From the start, they've put at their core a sense of always being in it together, sharing both failure and success. They've also created the right incentive structures, replacing rewards based on short-term profit with those linked to long-term, shared impact. Removing the focus on warped individual incentives that promote the ego encourages team members to do all they can to support their social entrepreneurs from a place of shared humility.

Their impact is measured on the lives served by their portfolio, what they refer to as their "family." Over the years, DRK has helped get organizations like Room to Read, Kiva, Education SuperHighway, and One Acre Fund off the ground, all now multimillion-dollar social enterprises driving significant change in the world.

Robin, Bill, and Rob sent a clear message of humility in all they do by bringing their colleagues into the interview. Consistent shared humility in how we approach each other, how we approach different cultures, and how we approach the environment and different belief systems is fundamental to nurturing Deep Connections.

Here are **five principles** to help embed humility in your relationships and life.

Make no assumptions. DRK is about service to others, not about the résumés of the team. They have a shared commitment to good that is free of constraining assumptions about who can add value and who cannot.

Shared humility in a partnership begins with letting go of any assumptions you might have about your partner and coming at every conversation open-minded and ready to learn. It's also an important skill to learn to ensure you don't miss a partnership that just might change your life.

Understand your limitations. Andy Kuper and Jim Roth, founder and cofounder of LeapFrog Investments, which invests in companies that provide lower-income families with financial services and healthcare, believe that when you have an audacious idea, it is impossible to do it on your own. It has to be done by "the flotilla of co-captains."

If you need an easy reminder, there is no better way to understand your limitations than to step outside and look at the stars, or head into the high mountains, or go scuba diving in the vast ocean. Nature is the true great equalizer, keeping us humble and grounded, making us realize how insignificant some of our outbursts of ego truly are. Nature can also teach us about the power of the collective and stretch us toward something bigger. As Amory Lovins, the cofounder of RMI (Rocky Mountain Institute), put it, "I'd say we learn everything from nature. Where else would you learn anything?"

Value diversity. Celebrating rather than fearing diversity is fundamental to shared humility. This applies not just to different cultures but also to all kinds of diversity, from race to gender to sexual orientation to political views. Interestingly, many of the successful partnerships we spoke with bridged divides across vast differences. This electric current of difference made them even stronger together.

Be in service—not in control. The sense of humility in all the partnerships was aided by their focus on something bigger and the realization that we are in service to our partners and our mission—not in control of them. As Paul Bennett mentioned about his marriage to Jim, "I think one of the best by-products of our relationship is that my ego has gone in a very healthy way. I feel like I'm in service in this relationship. I feel like I'm in service in my work."

Letting go of total ownership, of having to be the one in charge, allows you to focus more on impact and on the well-being of your partner. A bold something bigger checks any egos that might get in the way of the larger vision. As Andy from LeapFrog Investments shared, "What about the next hundred million people? What about the next billion people that we could reach, and whose lives we could impact?"

Lord Hastings, a member of the House of Lords in the UK, and his friend Gloria Abramoff, whom he met and worked with at the BBC for many years, spent much of the time I interviewed them generously praising each other. "We've gone beyond a world of controls, dictation, and ordering," proposed Lord Hastings. "We're in a world of conversation, collaboration, and partnership—how we can do this better together. Bringing the best of all the skills and talents we can possibly find into the room, rather than I'm the one who knows the only way to do this."

No one does it alone. In 2018, I visited the Apartheid Museum in Johannesburg, South Africa, for a celebration of what would have been Nelson Mandela's hundredth birthday. Much of the discussion and celebration took place in a room named after George Bizos. George was one of the renowned lawyers who defended Mandela and other anti-apartheid heroes in the famous Rivonia Trial in 1963–64. He went on to become a critical legal figure who fought for many of the African National Congress leaders. Bizos was a dear friend and partner to Mandela, Archbishop Tutu, and many others.

We were fortunate that George, then ninety years old, was with us that night in the museum. After a moving concert from the Soweto Gospel Choir, I nervously went up to him to say thank you for all he'd done to end apartheid.

He turned to me with a sparkle in his eye and said, simply, "No one does it alone."

Fifth Virtue: Nurturing Generosity—Give Freely

In his book *Give and Take*, Wharton professor Adam Grant showed that takers, who focus on self-interest, might win in the short term, but people tire of constantly giving to them. It is the givers, as long as they protect themselves from being exploited, who have better prospects for success and happiness in the long run.

Generosity was a critical virtue in the ecosystem of the over sixty successful partnerships I spoke with. Not one of the partnerships was based on the lopsided relationship of a taker. Instead, enormous generosity created a mutually beneficial ecosystem of balanced giving. The individuals in these partnerships found a rhythm of generosity that nurtured everyone, grounded in the wisdom that you always receive more than you give.

At seven forty-five p.m. on March 3, 2017, celebrated conservationists Dereck Joubert and his wife, Beverly, were walking through their camp in Botswana's Okavango Delta, getting ready to celebrate Dereck's birthday, which happens to coincide with World Wildlife Day. After a full day filming in the African bush, they were looking forward to a relaxing evening together.

They turned their heads as a snorting sound from the darkness caught their attention. In mere seconds, before they could even comprehend what they had just heard, Dereck and Beverly were charged by a Cape buffalo. After ramming into Dereck, breaking a number of his ribs, the buffalo slammed one of its horns into Beverly, impaling her underneath her arm, penetrating her lung, and continuing up through her throat.

Suddenly, Beverly was being swept away by the buffalo and out of the camp. Dereck struggled to stand up and chase after them. He managed to kick the buffalo under the right leg, and when it flicked its head in response, Beverly was thrown to the ground. Dereck rushed to Beverly, but before he got to her, the buffalo charged again. Instinctively, Dereck ran toward the buffalo, placing himself between the animal and Beverly in an effort to protect her. He was run over, adding a broken pelvic bone to his fractured ribs.

After that second blow, however, the buffalo retreated into the darkness. Once they had struggled back to the camp, Dereck sent out a distress message, got painkillers for Beverly (and himself), and started first aid to stabilize Beverly while waiting for the arrival of emergency services. Several hours later, as Beverly began to realize the full extent of her injuries, she gently asked Dereck to stop the medication—she wanted to be fully conscious if she had to say goodbye to him.

She had lost five pints of blood by the time medical assistance got to them at dawn. Eleven hours after the incident, they reached the nearest hospital safely after the flight to South Africa. It was a harrowing, unbelievable experience, and they were lucky to have survived.

Two years before the accident, Dereck had told me that selfless generosity played a big role in their relationship: "If anything happened to Beverly, I would save her first." Little did he know that a Cape buffalo would give him the chance to do just that.

Thankfully, most of us will never have to go to the extreme of throwing our bodies between our partners and the horns of death to show generosity. All that is required is an ongoing effort to find ways to be helpful to others. All we have to do is get joy from giving.

Here are **five ways** you can put generosity into action.

Gratitude Scorecards. Gratitude is a beautiful expression of generosity. It is integral to an enduring relationship and a healthy life.

Jacki and Greg Zehner, former Goldman Sachs executives who left to start a foundation for social justice, have gratitude scorecards—not literal scorecards, but a competition for who can be more generous and grateful to the other. When we practice exploring the world from

a place of gratitude, thanking and inspiring each other instead of crit-
icizing, we infuse generosity into all our actions.

Most of the partnerships I interviewed have rituals to ensure they
never take each other for granted and that they express gratitude for
the world around them. Brothers and cofounders of Life is Good, Bert
and John Jacobs, told me how, when they were children, their mother
made a request at their family dinner table every night to remind
them to be grateful: "Tell me something good that happened today."
Many of the other partners shared with each other something they
were grateful for every single day. It is a wonderful way to start the
day and shift your lens to one of gratitude for everything around you.

Shared Good Fortune. Many of the business partnerships I explored have thoughtfully built structures based on generosity to share
prosperity with everyone in the company. "Every single person in the
business has a stake," Sangu Delle (whom you met in chapter two)
told me. "Everyone is part of a profit-sharing agreement that we do at
the end of the year. Everyone from the receptionist to the security
guard to the guy who cleans the windows, because fundamentally
our goal is that we want to be able to create a situation where there's
shared prosperity and it doesn't just accrue to people at the top."

Shared fortune does not have to be measured simply as financial
gain. It can also be expressed by sharing an opportunity or welcoming someone into your wider circle of friends.

Shared Glory. Shared glory multiplies the feeling of generosity and
allows you to celebrate your Deep Connections. Remember how
Sherry always shared recognition for discovering the impact of CFCs
on the ozone layer with Mario, leading to both of them winning the
Nobel Prize? Likewise, you would be hard-pressed to find any media
articles about Detroit Vegan Soul that don't feature both of the

company's founders, Erika and Kirsten. They are very thoughtful about making sure that both of them get the chance to be the public face for their successful business. But shared glory does not always have to come in the form of a grand prize or a front-page article. Small, frequent affirmations help build respect and belief in each other. Conversely, a refusal to share glory can cause a partnership to blow up, as you will see in chapter six.

Extreme Altruism. Research by the John Templeton Foundation found that generosity has its roots in our biology and evolutionary history. Dereck and Beverly shared a beautiful perspective on generosity with me that they'd gleaned by watching a herd of elephants. Whenever there was a perceived threat of danger, females in the herd quickly and deliberately stepped out in front of the other elephants to protect them. "It was the most basic form of altruism," explains Beverly. "The females in the herd were sending a very blunt, generous, and protective message: 'Take me first and save the others.' This kind of extreme altruism should shame us as humans and embarrass us as a self-involved culture."

Not Me, Us. Many of us are so focused on a belief in separation and individualism that we have largely forgotten to take care of one another in the spirit of generosity. As Jo Confino said beautifully, "We've created a society of grasping." He went on to share that we need to shift this to "not about me, but about us." We will look back on these times of individualism, of shareholder capitalism, of systemic racism and vast inequality as one of the largest collective acts of selfishness the world has known.

Being all-in and giving of yourself 100 percent is the most important act of generosity. Being generous with your time, with yourself, and with each other can be an act of compassion that gives you the opportunity to build a depth of understanding and empathy that you could never realize on your own.

Sixth Virtue: Compassionate Empathy— Loving Action

Imagine being taken from your home while you were mowing the lawn and forced into a police car. Imagine being told by a police officer that it didn't matter if you didn't commit the crime. You were guilty because you were Black.

Imagine being put in a prison cell and thinking that this nightmare would all be over soon because surely someone would right this very bad misunderstanding.

Imagine then being thrown into a five-by-seven-foot cell on death row, with no evidence against you.

Then imagine remaining in that cell for twenty-eight years.

This is Anthony Ray Hinton's story. He was wrongly convicted of the 1985 murders of two fast-food restaurant managers in Birmingham, Alabama.

At nine thirty a.m. on April 3, 2015, Ray was released from prison, his conviction completely overturned and all charges against him dropped. After almost three decades, he left prison an innocent man.

Ray survived this horrific ordeal in large part thanks to two Deep Connections. Lester Bailey, his best friend from childhood, drove 257 miles each way every single week for twenty-eight years to visit Ray in prison. The other was his lawyer and friend, Bryan Stevenson, founder of Equal Justice Initiative, who for more than sixteen years worked tirelessly to prove Ray's innocence and finally get him released.

Theirs is a story of compassionate empathy at its very finest.

When we think of empathy, we think it's the ability to stand in someone else's shoes, an attempt to understand someone's emotional reality and how they are feeling. This can be exploitive, like being a voyeur of someone else's suffering.

Compassionate empathy goes beyond that. It is not just standing in their shoes, it is walking alongside them in a respectful, equitable way and helping to alleviate their suffering. Compassionate empathy means taking loving action, providing support that is guided by the person who owns the shoes and knows what's needed. Stanford psychologist Jamil Zaki refers to this as empathic concern. "Empathy is an umbrella term that captures at least three ways that we connect with one another's emotions," he explains. He goes on to outline three different types of empathy: "Emotional empathy, which is vicariously catching somebody else's feelings. Cognitive empathy is your attempt to understand what someone else is feeling and why. And then empathic concern or compassion is your motivation to improve others' well-being."

Lester and Ray had been friends since they could walk. They did everything together. After Ray was arrested, Lester could have called Ray a couple of times a week and told him how sorry he was and then got on with his life. Instead he drove ten hours every single week to ensure he was there for Ray, standing by him with love and grace.

For fourteen years after his unjust arrest, Ray could not obtain the legal help he needed to prove his innocence. Bryan went to meet him in prison after getting a call from Ray in 1999. "He made quite an impression," shared Bryan. "Thoughtful, sincere, genuine, compassionate, funny, it was easy to want to help Anthony Ray Hinton." Bryan could have simply felt Ray's pain and walked away, leaving Ray to die on death row. He didn't. Bryan took loving action every day for six-teen years to prove Ray's innocence.

Ray in turn had consistent compassionate empathy for what Bryan and Lester were going through. He refers to it as "thirty years inside and thirty years outside," to highlight their shared pain. Ray was con-stantly worried about the death threats and attacks both of them en-dured for standing by him, worried that Bryan was working too hard, concerned that Lester would be upset if he heard another appeal was turned down. He did all he could to help minimize their suffering, comforting Bryan and Lester when they got bad news about his case. He even used humor to lift their spirits when his own heart was breaking.

Even in his unimaginable pain from being unjustly incarcerated on death row, Ray lived with compassionate empathy permeating all his relationships, from the guards who held him captive to his fellow inmates. He even found a way to empathize with Henry Francis Hays, a notorious Ku Klux Klan member who had brutally lynched an inno-cent nineteen-year-old Black man in 1981.

Ray and Henry first met through a book club that Ray had started in the law library at Holman Correctional Facility. Ray didn't know who Henry was when he first joined the intimate group, but he soon found out about Henry's background. Ray and the others in the book club decided not to continue the chain of hate, and to instead prac-tice compassionate empathy. "Everybody knew Henry had shame, and here we were, five Black men in the South trying to comfort the white man who would forever be known for doing the last lynching of a Black boy."

Ray learned from Henry that his mother, his father, everyone in his family had taught him to hate Black people from the day he was born. Henry had also endured vicious beatings at the hands of his father his entire life. "All his life he was taught hate, and I felt bad for him that this mother and father didn't love him enough to show him love," Ray said. "I thought, I have enough love given to me by my mom that I really believe I could give to the whole world. I just started talking to him and started trying to deprogram him to show him that I'm no different than you are."

The two men deepened their relationship through their honest conversations during the book club meetings. Ray took loving action by never judging Henry, by authentically listening and understanding *why* he had become a person so filled with hatred and violence. Henry was transformed by Ray's compassionate love. Right before his execution, he shared that the very people he was taught to hate were the ones who taught him how to love.

Compassionate empathy starts with deep listening, understanding, and loving action. As Jo Confino said, "Understanding is love." Yet in today's always-on world, we often don't have the time to really listen to and understand one another, let alone to take action to help alleviate suffering. Cracks in a relationship emerge when people feel not listened to, misunderstood, ignored, or abandoned in their pain. Building compassionate empathy into all your relationships takes work.

Here are **five ways** successful partnerships in this book strengthened this virtue in their lives.

Letting Go of Judgment. Azim (whom you met in chapter three) could have easily fallen into a spiral of hatred, revenge, and bitterness after his only son, Tariq, was shot by Ples's grandson Tony that night in January 1995. Yet he didn't. He had such a great depth of compassionate empathy that he forgave Tony and did not judge him. He understood that it was not this fourteen-year-old's fault; it was the fault of the society that put Tony in that position.

When Tony got out of prison some twenty-four years later, Azim and his daughter, Tasreen, embraced him without judgment and brought him into the fold to work at the Tariq Khamisa Foundation. "The biggest impediment to empathy, compassion, and forgiveness is judgment," shared Azim. Letting go of judgment frees you to truly listen and understand your partner—and then act in service with compassionate empathy, as he has with Tony.

Proximate Experiences. Bryan Stevenson often speaks about the importance of proximity: getting close to each other in a meaningful way to truly understand each other and the issues we need to solve together. This is important for our Deep Connections for a couple of reasons. First, proximity helps us better understand the history of our partner, where they grew up, what their struggles were, what injustices they faced, when they were most joyful, and more. Second, proximity helps us better understand the difference we are trying to make through our something bigger. When we walk alongside the people who are on the front lines of any issues we are trying to solve, we are close enough to hear their answers and solutions.

Permission to Be Vulnerable. Compassionate empathy can be deepened only if the right safe space is created for people to be vulnerable. It's not just understanding someone else's pain; it's having the courage to share and know your own. Your vulnerability allows your partner to be vulnerable. "It's people who have the courage to touch their pain and to do it in a way that opens everyone else's heart and it's literally like a tuning fork," shared Jo Confino. "If you're prepared to show your own vulnerability, what you do is you give permission to other people to be vulnerable."

I'm acutely aware of how difficult it is to be vulnerable in the workplace. My father, who wanted to protect his daughter in the war zone that can be corporate America, constantly said to me, "As a female, you can't cry, you can't show any vulnerability, as you will not be taken seriously." I became a master at biting my tongue, remaining calm, tucking my feelings safely away . . . until one day when I was balancing on one of the upper steps of the corporate ladder. I burst into tears in a board meeting in front of the chairman of the company.

In a meeting with the chairman the next day, I was so mortified about my emotional outburst that I had my resignation letter ready to hand to him. But he did something unexpected. He opened his heart and shared with me a story about a time when he was CEO of a company that was in a serious legal dispute. He had been grilled all day by an imposing panel of lawyers. The pressure was so intense that at one point in the middle of difficult questions being thrown at him from all sides, he burst into tears in front of the entire panel.

This honest, vulnerable story he shared was a huge gift for me. It gave me permission to be vulnerable and see it as a strength that opens doors to deeper connections. Relieved of my shame, I tore up my resignation letter.

Urgent Patience. None of the partners I interviewed had mastered all the virtues with a snap of their fingers. It takes hard work, patience, and an openness to allow each other to make mistakes. It also takes compassionate empathy to understand that change is not easy. Alongside a sense of urgency about wanting to help lift each other into the best possible version of yourselves, hold space for patience as each person evolves at their own pace.

Urgent patience linked to your something bigger might mean taking immediate action to change a broken system while also having the patience to see it through. Bryan has had this in spades during his lifelong fight to change the criminal justice system in the United States and throughout his sixteen-year fight for Ray. Other times, that urgency takes on an immediate need to ease someone's suffering and then the patience to sit with them as they emerge from their pain.

Freedom Through Shared Understanding. In 2018, I traveled with Ray, Lester, and The Elders to South Africa to celebrate what would have been Mandela's one hundredth birthday. We took a bumpy boat ride from Cape Town to Robben Island to visit the prison where Mandela and many other political prisoners were incarcerated for decades.

Our tour guide, Thulani Mabaso, met us on the dock when we came off the boat and walked through what was now a welcoming gateway into Robben Island. Thulani had experienced a different entrance in 1985 when he was brought to the island as a political prisoner, where he remained and was brutally tortured for the next six years.

When we got to the small seven-by-eight-foot cell where Mandela was held captive with only a thin mat to protect him from the cold cement floor, Ray could not bear to enter it (understandably). Thulani felt Ray's pain and grabbed his arm, and the two walked off into the courtyard together. As I watched them hug beside the small garden that Mandela and others had planted many years ago, I could feel the compassionate empathy between these two great men. A meaningful connection that helped set them both free from an unthinkable shared experience.

&

CHAPTER FIVE

Magnetic Moments

Fourth Degree of Connection

Our partnership is fluid. It's not rocky. It's
not difficult. It flows. And sometimes, it
flows down, but we manage to rise back up.

—Tony Hawk, president of Tony Hawk Inc.
and founder of the Skatepark Project

S tephen O. Andersen had been waiting for just the right moment.
It was the end of a long day of ozone negotiations in Paris when
Stephen pulled aside the Russian delegation. Dr. Ya. T. Shatrov, the
chief scientist in the Russian delegation, had played a central role in
the Soviet space program, as had many others present that day. The
space program was a source of tremendous pride for the country.

Stephen proceeded to recount the many scientific contributions of
Russia not only to the Montreal Protocol but to advancing the world's
understanding of space. He then presented the group with a memento:

a collection of Soviet postage stamps commemorating early Soviet space exploration, which Stephen had stumbled upon years earlier when he was browsing a flea market. The Russians were deeply moved by his generosity; many of the scientists had tears in their eyes. The stamps, it turned out, while not particularly valuable, would have been impossible for the Russians to obtain on their own. The scientists then burst into descriptions of how they had contributed to the space program. They beamed with pride—and gratitude. They stayed connected, and years later, the Russian scientists worked with Stephen on documenting how alarmed they were when Soviet research confirmed Sherry and Mario's hypothesis.

Stephen loved to give thoughtful gifts of deep significance to members of the community. He knew instinctively the importance of connection in effective negotiations, and how to foster thoughtfully created moments of meaning and warmth, which often turned into laughter. After a long day, negotiators from all over the world would sometimes gather in the hotel lounge after dinner to unwind from the busy day and to forget how far they were from home. On the occasion of someone's birthday one night, Stephen went around the table and asked each person to sing happy birthday in their own language.

He routinely recognized individuals publicly for their good work, identifying and celebrating "Ozone Champions" for doing something extraordinary. Over the years, on behalf of the EPA, he gave out hundreds of stratospheric ozone and climate protection awards, describing what someone's accomplishment meant to him personally and relishing the joyful impact it would have on the group. He joked that he was really in the "awards business." "It's contagious actually," he said. "Once people view themselves as a hero of the stratospheric ozone, it's more likely that they would work on some other problem in their company because it would also be the right thing to do, and they would know it wasn't impossible. And if you help people do good, they'll do more good."

Another practice of Stephen's was to invite spouses and other family members to the conferences and receptions to bring them into the shared history of the community. The impact, he said, surprised even him. "I tried to humanize the process," he said. "I realized that these spouses were often clueless about what their spouse had done. But they were suffering because of my demands on their spouse's time." So Stephen spent time talking with spouses, making them allies in the cause, and building family pride in what was accomplished. Thus, one magnetic moment led to another.

Mostafa, Stephen, and the other people who followed in Mario and Sherry's slipstream began to build a community of Deep Connections and world-changing friendships, putting aside their individual interests to build an epic global collaboration on behalf of humanity and the planet. While Mostafa was the grand master, Stephen was often working behind the scenes, with characteristic energy and resolve, keeping participants on track and encouraging collaboration.

Mostafa and Stephen also had their own rituals, carving out time together to debate the best solutions and approaches. This could get heated at times, as they were often coming from two very different perspectives, yet they always came out the other side with a better solution than they ever could have created on their own.

Much like Stephen, Mostafa deeply understood the importance of creating a culture of friendship, and he was also a master at creating magnetic moments for deepening connection, especially linked to creating relaxed spaces for honest communication. Mostafa believed that "informal social relations formed the basis of the successful treaty negotiations." He was constantly looking for opportunities to get the right people into the room and to create a space where they could understand each other's perspectives. Lengthy negotiations would be sprinkled with moments of awe and wonder as the community started to better understand the evolving scientific data and the enormity of what they were working on. These rituals of curiosity and innovation were the backbone of the implementation as industry, scientists, governments, and not-for-profits worked in concert to create new solutions to replace CFCs.

Decades after the Montreal Protocol was signed and its implementation well underway, thoughtfully crafted magnetic moments still created wonder in the ozone community. "There was a pulse in the room, some type of vibration," said Professor Kevin Noone, a chemical meteorologist at Stockholm University, looking back on a meeting of the ozone community years later. "It had to do with relationships. It was a bit like when you watch snowboard competitions and they are all high-fiving each other . . . moving forward by helping each other out rather than competing."

As innovation after innovation emerged, these moments of success became fuel for moving toward the negotiators' shared goal and allowed them to weather many a bump along the way.

Traditions, Rituals, and Practices

On July 18, 2007, Nelson Mandela marked his eighty-ninth birthday by launching The Elders, a collective with the shared goal of tackling tough global issues. He was joined by leaders whom he and his wife, Graça, had selected back on that morning in October 2006 at their home, including Archbishop Tutu, former US president Jimmy Carter, former UN secretary-general Kofi Annan, and former president of Ireland Mary Robinson. The founding ceremony took place at Constitution Hill in Johannesburg, South Africa, where many anti-apartheid heroes had been imprisoned at the height of South Africa's apartheid government. Musician Peter Gabriel brought the crowd to tears by closing the ceremony with his song "Biko," written about the anti-apartheid hero Steve Biko, who was assassinated by the brutal apartheid regime in 1977.

I remember standing by the stage, basking in the moment, and thinking, *We did it! We've launched this amazing collective into the world. The hard work is done.*

It wasn't.

Much of my life, I've mistakenly believed that relationships should form spontaneously, without the need for effort and planning. As you may have realized by this point, this isn't the case. Deep Connection is not a gift bestowed by the universe. It requires what I now call *magnetic moments*. These are intentional experiences that allow for people to be present together. Magnetic moments give space for spontaneity and wonder to flourish. Creating them takes thought, planning, and effort, but they are worth it because of the way they increase the depth and meaning of the connections you form.

Mostafa and Stephen thoughtfully planned magnetic moments that occurred on a consistent basis, including an annual gathering where everyone in the ozone community came together in person and built a family atmosphere that has since prevailed for decades. Magnetic moments take the form of rituals, traditions, and daily practices. They deepen wonder and love in relationships. From the Carters meeting every afternoon on the Truman Balcony of the White House to debrief on their day, to Anthony Ray Hinton and Lester Bailey going to the barber together every Saturday, to Richard Branson and Peter Gabriel pouring water on each other whenever they are taking themselves too seriously, to Azim and Ples planting a tree with students at every school where they share their story, we see magnetic moments in the stories of every great partnership.

As we'll see, magnetic moments fall into four key categories: joy and play, curiosity and wonder, space for honest communication, and time with a supportive community. They are "magnetic" because they ultimately bring us closer, deepen our connections, and help us stay connected without binding us together.

Before I came to Virgin Unite, I had worked in start-ups, and the frenetic pace of that life had pushed joy way down on my list of priorities. Initially, I created an agenda for The Elders' gatherings that had everyone working from eight a.m. right through to dinner at six p.m., a schedule I considered an efficient use of everyone's time. Richard Branson quickly tore up my proposed schedule, stopping the work sessions at lunch so that people could play together in the afternoons, a ritual we've maintained over the past fifteen years. He was right. The lifelong, world-changing Deep Connections, the true purpose of these gatherings, emerge not from the morning sessions but from those relaxed afternoons of play, those magnetic moments. There is an old saying, "You learn more about a person in an hour of play than in a year of conversation."

These moments become the storybook of your shared history, the pages you turn to again and again to remind yourself why you love someone. They're bookmarks on those moments of joy that make you laugh out loud, the times when a moment together profoundly shifted your lives forever, the pages that are alive with something bigger that rippled out to many other people's stories. Often they also have some type of physical manifestation that serves as a reminder of those moments and your connection to one another. No matter what form they take, these magnetic moments deepen connection and increase shared understanding. Ultimately, they create the energy that strengthens your ecosystem of virtues, lifts people above the drama, creates continuity, and constantly stokes the fire to keep a Deep Connection alive.

It was in my interview with Richard Reed, cofounder of Innocent Drinks, that this idea crystallized. That company is all about rituals of joy-filled connection.

A Twitch of an Eyebrow

As students at the University of Cambridge in the early 1990s, Richard Reed, Adam Balon, and Jon Wright bonded over a shared love of nightlife. After graduating, they began separate careers, but they held on to a dream to start a business together. On a snowboarding trip in 1998, they dreamt up a natural fruit smoothie business.

Richard, Adam, and Jon spent six months and £500 creating an array of fruity concoctions that they could sell at a music festival in London. To get feedback on their smoothies, they set up two trash bins at their stand: one with a sign that read "yes" and one with a "no." Customers were asked to chuck their empty cups in the "yes" bin if they liked the smoothie so much that they thought the three friends should quit their jobs and start a fruit smoothie business. If the smoothies did not stand the taste test, they were asked to chuck the cups into the "no" bin. At the end of the festival, the "yes" bin was overflowing and the "no" contained only three cups. Innocent Drinks was born.

The three cofounders started their company based on a commitment to both goodness—pure, wholesome, and natural ingredients—and social purpose. At one point, they were donating nearly half their profits to charity. When they realized this would lead to bankruptcy, they changed that to 10 percent. They created a very successful business that has also donated over £10 million to good causes.

Richard, Adam, and Jon each volunteer that they would never have created Innocent Drinks without the others, especially at the start, when they struggled to find investors and met with one closed door after another. It was a brutal time, but when one of the three friends was having a bad day, the other two could pick him up. Jon was the "operations guru," Adam "Mr. Commercial," and Richard "brand, brand, brand."

From the beginning, Richard, Adam, and Jon were obsessed with making sure that the success of the company was a team sport. They put all kinds of rituals, traditions, and practices in place to continually renew their friendship and build a strong community among their staff and customers.

One such practice is Innocent's Home Juicing Guarantee. If a customer decides an Innocent orange juice isn't sufficiently fresh, someone from the company will travel to their home and squeeze fresh orange juice on the spot.

Another important ritual for the company is its quarterly off-site meeting. At first, these meetings were held in the pub at the end of the road. As the company became more successful, they moved the meeting to Nature Weekends across Europe, from Salzburg to Ibiza. These relaxing team-building weekends featured themes like Desert

Island Disco. They also hosted AGM (A Grown-Up Meeting) at their Fruity Towers headquarters for their customers to drink smoothies, eat cake, and ask questions. On a grander scale, they held Fruitstocks that eventually became Innocent Unplugged, an off-grid festival for people to connect with each other through activities like yoga, morning dance raves, and Fergus the Forager forest tours.

Innocent's rituals have built lasting, meaningful connections among its employees and with their customers. In 2003, they started an annual tradition called the Big Knit. People all over the UK are encouraged to knit small caps for the tops of the Innocent Drinks bottles and then mail them to the company. Innocent then places them on bottles before distributing them across the UK. When someone buys a bottle with a hat, Innocent donates 25 pence to Age UK, a charity that supports the elderly. Since the tradition's inception, thousands of volunteers have knitted over 7.5 million mini hats, raising over £2.5 million for Age UK, and, just as important, building an incredible, connected community.

Innocent's magnetic moments weren't all fun and games. Richard, Jon, and Adam believed in creating space for more serious moments of honest conversations. One enduring ritual, a meeting that the founders called the CEO Show, took place every Monday afternoon. They spent the first thirty minutes catching up with one another. For the remaining ninety, anyone in the company who needed input on a decision could come in and meet with them directly. Richard, Adam, and Jon also initiated monthly all-team gatherings to share transparently about what was happening across the company.

The three founders had a collective communication practice that required them to have a conversation with one another and agree on a shared approach for any material decision in the company. One of

their investors mentioned that they were the slowest to make decisions out of all the companies he had invested in. But they also had
the highest rate of making the right decisions, because there were
three brains coming up with solutions, rather than just one. When
Richard, Jon, and Adam needed to make material decisions, they
would get together, leave their egos at the door, have deeply honest
discussions, and take turns playing devil's advocate so they could
look at the options from all vantage points. Their goal was to ensure
what was right for the business before coming to an agreement. This
shared decision-making practice and the bond of trust between them
made for a highly efficient business, with less time wasted both on
wrong turns and by destructive arguments.

Eventually in 2013, the three founders decided that Innocent Drinks
had a great team in place and could continue to fly without them.
On their last day, the trio boarded a little motorboat in the canal next
to their office, and slowly putt-putted to the pub. That day, as they
drank their beers, they decided to start an investment firm. Shaped
by their principles of partnership, JamJar rarely invests in individuals.
Instead, the firm focuses wherever possible on partners who come together around an idea. They look for businesses that function like
gatherings around a campfire, where each partner feeds the fire with
their own unique contribution.

After close to thirty years of mutual collaboration, multiple successful businesses, and many moments of joy, Adam, Richard, and Jon
remain best friends, "first-phone-call people," who, after countless
magnetic moments, know one another so well that, as Richard said,
"you can tell just by the twitch of an eyebrow what they're really
thinking."

At this point, you're probably saying to yourself, "I'd love to have such moments, but how do I create them, let alone on a regular schedule?" Mostly, it requires thoughtful planning and the discipline to create that space amid all life's demands. Beyond that, I've found that **four categories** are helpful when crafting your own magnetic moments.

Joy and Play: An Unlimited Resource

Despite their many professional successes, I never found that any of the people in this book take themselves all that seriously. But I did find that many take joy and play seriously, weaving it into all their daily practices. In most of these partnerships, frequent moments of joy are the norm. They relieve tension, nurture vulnerability, and foster a way of being that builds trust, respect, and love.

There is inherent joy simply in forging Deep Connections. As mindfulness expert Susan Piver writes, "The joy of connection, whether to a person, animal, flower, idea, or sensation, is the most profound of all the joys." Joy can't be manufactured, but it can be welcomed into your relationship through the magnetic moments you shape, and in turn, it can create memories that warm our hearts continually.

Jo Confino, whom you met in chapter four, believes joyful play is central to all we do: "You get so much more done when you're playful, when you're joyous, when you're light," he said. "That's where the creativity comes from, that's where the grace comes from, that's where the community comes from. That's where the connections come from, that's where the collaboration comes from." Jo also talked about how important it is to stay joyous even when you're in a place of pain, or when someone makes a mistake. This gives others an opportunity to step back into a place of joy from wherever they've landed. I've witnessed Jo do this many times. Joy is a daily practice for him. He will crack a joke to relieve a specific moment of tension, or lift someone up with kind words after they've made a terrible mistake. Jo uses joy to encourage others to move forward rather than judging, punishing, and pushing them backward. He did exactly this during our interview, when the director spent twenty minutes dealing with a battery problem. Instead of getting annoyed, Jo teased the video team when they came back with the clapper board. "Paz and Jo, take three," the director said.

"Why isn't that Jo and Paz?" Jo said. "I'm furious." Then he burst out laughing.

When Richard Branson and Peter Gabriel were building The Elders, they took their mission seriously, but never themselves. "It was a lot more fun doing it with somebody," Richard said. "I don't think either of us could have done it on our own. We had an end purpose that was so wonderful that if we could make it become a reality, we were going to give it everything."

Peter and Richard's Deep Connection is based on many years of friendship infused with laughter—and frequent pranks. Peter is an extraordinary musician and a visionary full of big ideas. Richard is a successful entrepreneur who focuses on making stuff happen—or, as they often say, "Richard is the *screw it let's do it* guy, and Peter is the dreamer." Over the years, they've respected each other's differences and have brought great joy into each other's lives.

This was clear during The Elders' Necker Island gatherings, when the two friends were competing to teach Archbishop Tutu how to swim. "Richard's approach was just to throw him in," Peter joked with me, "whereas mine was to sort of get him into a meditative space, floating with a snorkel." They still argue about who played a more important role in the feat, but there is no doubt that there was plenty of laughter and joy as the Archbishop learned to swim.

Mick and Caskey Ebeling met thirty years ago, when they were twenty. They were complete opposites: he was in the military, and she was a "hippie anarchist." They fell in love, got married, and, in 2009, cofounded Not Impossible Labs, a company designed to change the world through a potent mix of technology and story. They joke that if they had not met each other, she would be somewhere on the mountain alone doing meditation while he would be in an office, wearing a suit and tie. Instead, they are creating a life of joy and "living their truth" together.

Mick and Caskey have created a host of magnetic moments to ensure that "play is like breathing air" in their partnership and family. Some of these moments are spontaneous: "We're goofy and silly and dance in the kitchen in front of the kids. We scare each other and play pranks on each other," explained Mick. "If you can't goof off and laugh, then you're not in the right relationship."

They have also created their own ritual vocabulary. One phrase they use when someone is taking themselves far too seriously is "dotysofus." When I first heard this word, I visualized some special sofa in their house that you were banished to when your ego was out of control, but they explained that it stood for "Don't take yourself so f****** seriously." Another phrase they use to remind themselves to live in the adventure and pause to remember their good fortune is BLE, which stands for "best life ever." To ensure they are living their BLE, they go on a date night every Thursday, a "touchdown" ritual that keeps them connected amid the chaos of work and raising three children.

For those who shy away from silliness, joy may come from rituals centered on shared experiences and purpose. President and Rosalynn Carter's rituals were shaped from the hobbies that brought them each joy. They took the time to learn each other's passions, including skiing, fly-fishing, and hiking. I saw this last ritual in action at every Elders gathering. If I got up around six a.m. and went for a run, I would often see the two ninety-plus-year-olds striding easily up the hills, side by side, with exhausted security guards desperately trying to keep up.

The poet Ross Gay reminds us that joy is not simply about play and happiness. In his essay "Joy Is Such a Human Madness," Gay poses a question in verse: "What if we joined our sorrows, I'm saying. / I'm saying: What if that is joy?" Perhaps sharing moments of profound sorrow with one another helps make us human and is its own form of joy.

Curiosity and Wonder

"It would be an empty universe indeed," Stephen Hawking wrote, "if it were not for the people I love, and who love me. Without them, the wonder of it all would be lost on me."

Magnetic moments that spark curiosity and inspire wonder make life a giant classroom. Curiosity keeps partnerships alive, in a constant state of excitement and flow. These moments keep us in awe of our partners as well as of the wider world.

One common theme found in many rituals of curiosity is an emphasis on asking and listening over talking and being "right." For example, Caskey and Mick value naivete because it leads them to find the answer to their problems together instead of coming up with inferior, precooked solutions. They make a practice of starting every discussion with a question.

Caskey and Mick extended this thinking to their company, Not Impossible Labs, by introducing a ritual to foster innovation and curiosity. Every time they begin a new project, they gather together unlikely partners to tackle problems others say can't be solved. Naive questions and ideas are encouraged and celebrated. For example, no one thought that deaf people could truly experience live music beyond just feeling low-end bass, that is until Music Not Impossible was born. They brought deaf people together with scientists, musicians, and designers to create a wearable solution that translates the individual instruments of a song into vibrations that the deaf music lover feels on specific points on their body. So now a deaf person can actually precisely feel the music. In other words, they figured out how to use the skin as an eardrum!

It's also important to have rituals that spark curiosity when something goes wrong. Andrew Maxwell Mangino and Kanya Balakrishna, cofounders of the Future Project, hold a forty-eight-hour intensive Dream Summit weekend, from Friday night to Sunday night, designed to create a new sense of possibility—and reimagine the path when there is a breakdown on the way to their vision. They create an experience, full of magic and surprise, so it's something they can look forward to. During the weekend, they always frame the questions with an authentic sense of positive curiosity rather than blame—and use the chance to re-center on the ultimate vision and commitment that gave rise to the project in the first place. Other companies, like Innocent Drinks and Planet, have annual traditions to come together and review what worked and what didn't from the previous year—and to hold space for dreaming and wonder about the year ahead.

Ingrid Rowland shared with me that her dad, Sherry, was always driven by his curiosity: "He just wanted to go out into the darkness and cast light on the complicated things." This curiosity kept him humble and connected to his partner, Mario, when they were trying to figure out what would convince people about the dangers of ozone depletion, and to his students as they explored different scientific interests—and to his wife, Joan, as they explored opera, the best dance moves to Frank Sinatra's music, and the wonder of each other for close to sixty years.

Many of the other partnerships we explored also have rituals of wonder linked to nature. Sisters Severn and Sarika Cullis-Suzuki like to say that they grew up with three parents: their father, David Suzuki, their mother, Tara Elizabeth Cullis, and Mother Nature. For over thirty years, the sisters have been connected in their mission to use science and advocacy to protect the natural world.

For the Cullis-Suzuki family, nature is central to their wider family rituals. They believe that there is no place better to spark curiosity and wonder. Almost every story Severn and Sarika shared with me linked back to a tradition that the family had nurtured over generations, particularly when it came to harvesting food together from the generosity of nature (something most people living in urban areas no longer even think to be curious about). Their summers were spent together swimming, collecting clams, fishing, and sharing meals from their catch cooked over the campfire. These summer rituals created moments of curiosity and flow. They taught them the importance of slowing down to pause and wonder at nature—and each other. Severn and Sarika remind us that rituals of play, curiosity, and wonder have an important role in shaping memories for generations to come.

These joyful magnetic moments hold the family together, building a shared history and keeping it grounded.

Nature has also been central to the life of environmental activist Stewart Brand. In 1966, he led a campaign to get NASA to release its satellite photo of Earth as seen from space. That image changed the way we understand our shared destiny with each other and the planet. For forty years, Stewart, now president of the Long Now Foundation, has partnered with his wife, Ryan Phelan, executive director of Revive & Restore. Their connection revolves around curiosity, wonder, and questions that spark long-term thinking on how we live in harmony with the natural world. The two are also co-skippers, making their home in a working 1912 wooden tugboat called *Mirene*, moored in Sausalito, California.

We've been told most of our lives that being able to "finish each other's sentences" is the sign of a good relationship. Stewart sees it differently: "I can't finish her sentences, and I hope she can't finish mine, at least not most of them."

Stewart and Ryan keep their life uncluttered. This is made easier by living on a sixty-four-foot boat. They also reduce the time spent on mundane activities as much as possible; for example, by hiring a cleaner as soon as they could afford it, and by keeping separate bank accounts to reduce administrative effort and conflict. This minimalistic approach gives them the freedom to explore moments of curiosity and wonder. "I always say to people it's the secret to our marriage," Ryan explains. "The boat keeps our lives simple and uncluttered."

The two have breakfast together whenever possible, "reinventing the world" over a cup of coffee. Often these breakfasts are spent discussing their joint project, Revive & Restore, which seeks to revive extinct species using state-of-the-art technology—no small subject with which to start the day. Stewart and Ryan's reinvention rituals continue throughout their day as they challenge each other to be their best selves, "poking the fire and saying this is not as good as it could be." Every night, they bathe together in a deep Japanese tub.

Honest Communication

Creating space for people to communicate in an honest, open way is critical for building Deep Connections. We see that in the range of rituals and traditions at Innocent Drinks. All the partnerships we've studied carve out time to be present together, talk through issues, share dreams and sorrows, celebrate each other, and give each other honest feedback. "Communication is at the core of it," Peter Gabriel said. "If you hold back, you're screwed."

Jo Confino and his wife, artist Paz Perlman, are a living example of honest communication. Both have incredibly busy lives, but they understand that love is not enough—a partnership needs nurturing and maintenance to stay strong. They've shaped a host of rituals and daily practices to keep themselves grounded and connected. The primary imperative of their relationship is to be there for each other.

To help them be present, to be vulnerable with each other, they've set up a ritual called Friday Talk, which they have been practicing from the time they met more than fourteen years ago. Its roots are in a practice created by Zen master Thich Nhat Hanh called Beginning Anew, which the monastics use regularly. Every Friday, Jo and Paz go to a café and each person has time to talk about the positive things that happened that week, to voice any regrets, and then to raise anything that upset or worried them, all with an open heart and no accusations. The other person practices deep listening, without defensive interruptions, and then they swap places. This helps the couple on a number of fronts. Often in relationships, small grievances or annoyances are swept under the carpet but build up over time and harden into bitterness and resentment, just like stalactites and stalagmites in a cave, where the drip, drip of water eventually creates a calcified monolith. Friday Talk also prevents eruptions during the week when they hit a bump, as they both know they have a formal space to express themselves on Friday and often the time in between allows issues to be put in perspective.

To help each other reach their aspirations, Jo and Paz created a dream book, in which they annually record their individual and shared dreams, and then work together to make them reality. This gives them the space to create a shared life of possibility and deepens their understanding of what's important in their lives. Out of that ongoing collaboration, they realized the depth of their shared love for art—Paz in mixed media, sculpture, and monotype printing and Jo with his photography—and took the opportunity to hold joint exhibitions in New York. One exhibition was called *Call & Response*, in which they chose pairs of works that spoke to each other.

While in New York, they also helped found and moderate a Zen community that met weekly; it included walking and sitting meditation as well as deep sharing. The Zen Buddhist practice has been integral to their life and approach to their partnership, and it has led to an annual tradition of going on retreat to Plum Village, Thich Nhat Hahn's monastery in southwest France. In fact, in 2020 they bought a house just a few minutes' walk from the monastery, and during the worst of the COVID-19 pandemic, they supported the monastics in leading online retreats and workshops to help relieve people's suffering.

Almost all of Jo and Paz's rituals, as they explained to me, are about everyday living. Together, they focus on being there for each other. "We are not a perfect couple," Jo says. "We are not trying to be an inspiration to the world. We're trying to inspire each other."

Entrepreneur and activist Sangu Delle calls continuous, open, and transparent communication "food for the partnership." He started Golden Palm Investments in order to create tangible economic growth on the African continent by investing in technology businesses. His brothers, Banguu and Edmund, work in partnership with him. Their partnership has worked over the years because it is based on trust and a shared understanding that they have their collective best interests at heart, as well as a clear vision of socioeconomic transformation in Africa.

The three brothers have thought deeply about practices and rituals for opening up lines of communication, minimizing conflict, and creating magnetic moments. For example, they established an independent investment committee in order to take the egos out of their decision-making. When one of the brothers feels passionately about an investment, the committee steps in to make the final call, reducing friction among them.

Some of their communication rituals began with their mother, who, Sangu jokes, is the "CEO of us." When they were children, she told them to look in the mirror every night and ask themselves, "What have you accomplished today? How have you helped someone?" This ritual continues to influence the siblings today. Their mother always had a collective celebration for their individual successes, but she also believed in shared punishment. If one sibling did something wrong, all were punished, teaching them to look out for one another and always have one another's backs.

The brothers talk every day on the phone, but they also ensure they are there for each other and the company at the most critical moments, a phone ritual they call Code 10. When you receive a text with "Code 10" in it, Sangu explains, "unless you're in the middle of a meeting with Obama," you drop everything and call each other immediately.

One of these Code 10 incidents happened two weeks before our interview. A driver with the trucking company they had contracted with was in a bad accident and in need of immediate surgery. Even though it was the trucking company's responsibility, it refused to pay for the thirteen-thousand-dollar surgery. After one brother sent a Code 10 to the other two, they hopped on a conference call and made a unanimous decision to cover the costs to ensure the man could walk again.

The Delle brothers make good use of the phone to foster connection. Most people are comfortable with texting and email to stay in touch. However, where video calls are concerned, this hasn't always been the case. That changed almost overnight in early 2020, when the COVID-19 pandemic made Zoom calls the new norm. Video is a terrific way for people to stay connected when they can't be together in the same place. All kinds of rituals, such as birthday parties, weddings, funerals, and even romantic dates have moved to video. Online connections can help us begin new relationships, bond more closely with one another, and make us feel loved when someone we care about checks in. The danger, of course, is when virtual connection replaces other forms of connection entirely, separating you from others and leading to inauthentic self-expression. Relying too heavily on these tools can make it difficult to build depth and meaning in your relationships and distract you from nurturing the relationships that mean the most.

Nothing can fully replace in-person touch points. For most of their more than four decades of friendship, the three scientists who discovered the ozone hole, Jonathan, Joe, and Brian (whom you met in chapter four), had a wonderful ritual called a "smoko," borrowed from a term used in the Second World War to describe a smoking break. In the early years, the name was taken literally with Joe furiously puffing on his pipe, leaving Brian and Jonathan coughing and spluttering, yet happily willing to risk smoke pollution for their invaluable time together. As the years went on, even after they retired, they continued to get together with other scientists from the department at half past ten every Friday, now for a slightly healthier version with biscuits and coffee rather than pipe smoke.

Community

Magnetic moments with your wider community help build stronger connections with your partner. Each community tapestry has different designs and textures based on the individual relationships and the role the community plays in them. Friends, spouses, children, neighbors, coworkers, and the wider community all play an important role in the tapestry, just as we saw with Stephen's welcoming of families into the ozone community.

All partnerships need help, in good times and bad. Many of the people I spoke with referred to the old African saying, "It takes a village"—not about raising a child, but about ensuring that a partnership thrives. Jane Tewson, founder of Igniting Change, shared some words of wisdom from the vicar who married Jane and Charles Lane, her wonderful partner: "It's going to be bloody hard for this couple. Don't think it's going to be easy, and each and every one of you needs to be there in support on this journey with them."

In his Blue Zone research, the National Geographic explorer and author Dan Buettner found that one of the communities with many centenarians was Okinawa, in Japan. One of the secrets to the Okinawans' long, healthy lives was what they called "moais," groups of five friends who committed to come together and support one another for the rest of their lives.

Moais do not happen by accident. In Japanese, the word means "meeting for a common purpose." People are assigned a group in childhood, and members of each group support one another in their social, financial, health, and spiritual interests. Moais meet on a weekly, even daily basis. They are a beautiful example of how a lifelong community ritual can help encourage and catalyze long-lasting, healthy partnerships.

There are many other community rituals that can strengthen your Deep Connections, from cultural gatherings, book clubs, family traditions, and special interest meetings all the way to formal rituals like the YPO forum meetings. YPO is a community of successful CEOs structured around ritual meetings of tight-knit local forums that allow members to forge deep, trusting relationships. YPO members support each other around the most difficult personal and business issues. I've heard again and again from YPO members that forum meetings give them a chance to work through hard challenges and gain perspective in a safe space, sometimes saving their businesses and even their personal relationships.

To thrive, Deep Connections need rituals and traditions that connect to wider communities. Community members can act as sounding boards, advisers, and witnesses to hold us accountable and remind us of the importance of our partnerships. Magnetic moments with our wider community can also simply bring more joy and love into our lives, deepening our connections with one another.

The Willis family has realized the importance of community rituals for generations. Artists Deborah Willis and her son, Hank Willis Thomas, are united through both love and art. The magnetic moments that keep them close began when Hank was a young boy. Deborah would gather her extended family on the phone to talk for an hour first thing every morning and catch up on the news. Hank loved the stories that flowed from that daily ritual so much that Deborah had to force him out the door to go to school.

Hank is the first to acknowledge that the virtues that shape his partnership with his mother and his relationship with their wider family and community have also shaped who he is. "I don't really have much choice but to maintain those values," he said, "which are hopefully dignity, honesty, trust, respect, self-love, and love for one another. Sometimes, it is a heavy burden. But it makes life easy."

Community is central to Deborah's and Hank's lives and their work. They also believe it has been central to the survival of African Americans. In their opinion, one way love manifested in twentieth-century Black families was through the ritual of photography. Taking pictures became a form of loving preservation of shared history, critical in a community that has been treated unfairly and whose cultural narrative has not been properly shared and celebrated.

The Willis family has one ritual that has been passed down from generation to generation: an open-door policy. Everyone in the community is welcome, as long as they come with love. They don't have to hold the same views or look like them—an open heart and love are the determining factors. This ritual strengthens their community, and it even had unexpected lifesaving benefits. When Deborah was sixteen, she had an allergic reaction to a medicine. To survive, she needed infusions of fresh type O blood every two days. The city did not have enough blood, so the community created their own blood bank, giving Deborah the lifesaving blood she needed.

This sense of community and moments of connection were omnipresent in the childhood home of world-renowned skateboarder Tony Hawk. His mother also had an open-door ritual, one that encouraged skateboarders from all walks of life to join family dinners. That spirit of openness and those moments over dinner encouraged Tony to become the extraordinary athlete and entrepreneur he is today. Following in his mother's footsteps, he has created an extended family with his fans that he is deeply and personally invested in. He creates magnetic moments by responding to social media requests, posting frequently himself, and donating millions to build skate parks in underserved communities.

Most of us will spend over a third of our lives in the workplace, so it is critical that we extend this sense of community and family to embrace the people we work with and those we serve. We saw some examples of community-building moments with Innocent Drinks. Global design company IDEO offers other examples.

In 1978, David Kelley and a group of friends started a company to collaborate on meaningful projects. That company eventually turned into IDEO. They've stayed true to the intitial philosophy by minimizing hierarchy and creating a social contract that emphasizes collaboration and mutual support. Tim Brown, the former CEO and now the company's chair, talks about the value of rituals in constantly nudging and strengthening the culture of a company. Here are a few IDEO rituals that build deeper connection and community:

- **The end-of-project celebration.** Every participant gets celebrated, inspiring a sense of connection and completion.

- **The humble-brag ritual.** When someone new starts at the company, the team invites them to share their accomplishments: "We know you're humble, but go ahead and brag."

- **The three-minute workout.** The whole team in one department puts on ceremonial headbands and does a quick workout together.

- **Unlocking hopes and fears.** At the start of every project, they share both their hopes and their worries.

Tim's work community also includes his family. Since Tim started working for IDEO more than thirty-four years ago, he and his wife, Gaynor, have completely blurred the lines between work and personal life, with IDEO becoming a central part of the success of their partnership. Gaynor does not work at IDEO, but she is still a central part of the IDEO family. The couple even refers to having two shared thirty-year partnerships: one with each other and the other with IDEO.

An Unimaginable Magnetic Moment

Magnetic moments don't just deepen existing connections. They have the power to bring together people with deeply opposing views, creating a bridge of respect and care despite genuine differences. The most extraordinary example I've seen of this was the relationship between Bob Vander Plaats and Donna Red Wing. Unfortunately, I never got to meet Donna before she passed away, but I spent time learning about their friendship from Bob.

In July 2014, Bob's organization, the Family Leader, invited conservative political and religious leaders from all over the country to Ames, Iowa, for its annual Family Leadership Summit. Donald Trump was there and, much to Bob's surprise, so was Donna Red Wing. Though he had never met her, he knew that Donna was Iowa's most visible advocate for LGBTQ rights. The Family Leader organization had spent countless hours trying to persuade national leaders to oppose same-sex marriage. The Christian Coalition of America had even branded Donna "the most dangerous woman in America."

On the day of the summit, during a break between speakers, Donna introduced herself to Bob and asked him if he'd be willing to meet her for coffee sometime. He cordially agreed, though he never expected her to follow up. Then she called his office the following week to schedule the meeting. His staff was incredulous. Bob and his team prayed for the meeting to go well. The plan was to meet in a coffee shop in Des Moines, Smokey Row. Little did they know then that this magnetic moment would be the start of a ritual that would change both of their lives.

Over coffee, Donna explained that she hoped the two could have a civil dialogue despite their many differences. Though they differed in their opinions, beliefs, and worldview, they shared a hope that they could learn from and come to understand each other—not convince the other one that he or she was wrong. To achieve such a level of civil discourse and honesty, they both agreed, would take trust. In the end, Bob jokingly called it "a good first date."

"We didn't start by talking about the issues that divide us," he said. "We started by talking about her family, how she grew up, how she went to a Lutheran church, had been married, had a son, and then a painful divorce," he said. She told Bob about her longtime partner, Sumitra, and about her activism. Bob spoke about his wife, Darla, and their four sons, and he gave Donna a copy of the book he had written about raising their son Lucas, who was born with a severe brain disorder.

"We got to know each other as people before we started talking about issues or an agenda or things that divide," Bob said.

Bob and Donna continued to meet for coffee at Smokey Row every month. Whenever their honest discussions started to get too emotionally charged, they learned to take a breath and pivot the conversation. Their moments together were filled with well-intentioned curiosity to better understand each other's perspectives. As their connection deepened, their coffee ritual turned into a place of great joy and learning for both of them. They joked about their "coming out party" when a journalist found out about their meetings and wrote a front-page article about their friendship, encouraging people to realize that you can disagree, but you don't have to hate.

The emotional connection between the two deepened after Donna's son fathered a child with developmental challenges. "Right away there was a closer bond," he said. "It was at a human-to-human level and not about what defines me and what defines you." They discovered they had important things in common, such as a determination to help end human trafficking. At the time, Bob had no idea that LGBTQ individuals were particular targets. "It opened up my eyes when she was able to give me real stories of real LGBTQ individuals who were trafficked, how they preyed on that community," he said. "I was able to see at a deeper level." Through many hours of honest conversation, they learned how to see through each other's eyes and have each other's backs. They did not change their own core beliefs, but they learned to connect rather than repel each other. They both welcomed each other into their wider communities—and together they weathered the brunt of anger that sometimes followed these introductions. Bob joked that one time when Donna was in the hospital, he and his wife went to visit her and immediately cleared the room.

The day the Supreme Court declared that same-sex couples could marry anywhere in the country, Donna was being interviewed by a local TV station. When she got up to leave her chair and walked backstage, she ran into Bob on his way to be interviewed for the same show. Their eyes locked and then they hugged. Bob joked, "You're buying coffee next time." The reporter marveled, "I just saw something I never thought I'd see."

After four years and many magnetic moments, Donna very sadly passed away on April 16, 2018. Bob was invited by her community to attend her funeral and gave a moving eulogy celebrating their extraordinary friendship—sharing how much he truly loved and respected Donna and how he would never be the same because of her.

Renew You

Magnetic moments create a path to improving your ability to grow through your relationships, but it's equally important to be able to understand and take care of yourself. As I mentioned previously, the adage goes that 95 percent of people try to change the world and only 5 percent try to change themselves. If you choose to become part of that 5 percent, look for renewing rituals and practices that work for you. They will help you approach your relationships with an open heart and give you the strength to do the hard work needed to build Deep Connections with others.

Magnetic moments to connect with yourself might show up in daily practices like taking a walk in nature, writing in your journal, getting enough sleep, meditating, and eating healthfully. Other moments might occur during a trip or taking lessons in something new or embracing a physical challenge like hiking. Making the time for moments when you can go inward to renew yourself will lead to much stronger partnerships with others. Give yourself space to practice self-reflection and do things that bring you joy. Spend more time with friends and family. Many of the partnerships I spoke with told me about times of burnout in their lives, when they were so focused on impact, on work, on trying to be a good partner that they lost sight of themselves. They stressed the importance of building rituals and practices to course correct and ensure you can give yourself and your relationships the love, care, and time they deserve.

Daily practices of gratitude help reframe how you live in the world. Shift your focus to "what's good," as Bert and John Jacobs's mother did. Take time to appreciate the wonders of the world around you. In my own life, my husband and I each write down five things we are grateful for each day and share it with each other. Choosing five, rather than one or two, really forces you to think. Over time, a gratitude list helps you appreciate everything and everyone around you. It has been amazing to see how a practice so simple has so effectively deepened our own connection.

Of course, one of the most wonderful ways to take care of yourself is being of service to others, focusing on something bigger than yourself. Taking the time to work in your local community or fight for an issue that you are passionate about can reenergize you. As Mahatma Gandhi once said, "The best way to find yourself is to lose yourself in service of others."

Magnetic Moments Architecture

Magnetic moments, repeated over time, helped make Innocent Drinks an enduring success. They have strengthened all the partnerships shared in this book. Such moments coalesce to create a "story of us" and bring all the people in a partnership closer. This includes small moments, like the daily practice of making someone a cup of tea or sharing something you are grateful for at the end of each day. Here are a few things to consider as you shape your own practices, rituals, and traditions to keep everyone connected:

- **Always evolve.** Magnetic moments are never fixed.
  They evolve as the connection deepens. The conscious
  effort that creates successful results at the start of your
  partnership may evolve into "the way things are done."
  You will need to spark new life into your rituals or

practices by introducing an innovative twist, as
Innocent did by going from the pub to off-site Nature
Weekends.

- **Respect individuality.** Give everyone an equal chance
  for expression and leave room for healthy
  disagreement. Compromise even on where you meet to
  help everyone feel safe and open.

- **Share ownership.** Let everyone work together to create
  magnetic moments rather than force it on them. Every
  partner should feel a sense of ownership and belonging.

- **Consistency is key.** When magnetic moments happen
  regularly, they help deepen connection and identify
  potential conflicts in the relationship before they've
  had a chance to grow to an unmanageable size.

- **Ensure breadth.** To get the most from magnetic
  moments, incorporate all four elements: joy and play,
  curiosity and wonder, honest communication, and
  community.

Magnetic moments offer the space to nourish your Deep Connections. They allow you to laugh, shout, cry, and simply be together. These moments also give you an opportunity to practice gratitude for the world around you and better appreciate how interconnected we all are.

&

CHAPTER SIX

Celebrate Friction

Fifth Degree of Connection

We are happy each time we disagree, because
we know we're going to learn something
new; it's going to make some sparkles.

—Bertrand Piccard, cofounder, Solar Impulse

Lee Thomas, the head of the Environmental Protection Agency and chief negotiator for the United States in Montreal, was discouraged after a long day negotiating with the representatives from Europe. It felt like they were getting bogged down in conflicts, and discussions were not moving forward. Around midnight, he caught word that the negotiator for the European Commission, Laurens Jan Brinkhorst, had left for a bar with colleagues.

Lee walked down to the bar himself, joined the European group, and asked Laurens if they could chat over a beer. That night, in the joviality of a local watering hole, Lee and Laurens reached a critical compromise between the United States and Europe that was ratified the next morning at eight o'clock. They were left with little sleep but a deepened friendship.

The participants in the Montreal Protocol learned time and again that friendships were essential to keeping talks on track and defusing conflicts. They invested significant time in creating the right culture for friendships to flourish and the best structures for friction to help create better solutions rather than blowing up progress.

Stephen O. Andersen had a way of avoiding conflict before it happened by paying attention to who would be in the room so that he could structure meetings to harmonize interests. First, he never issued a broad invitation but instead started by recruiting the most talented, knowledgeable, and influential experts in a given subject. He identified these people based on careful investigation, drilling down through professional networks until he found the right set of skills, the right personality fit, and people who were open to fresh thinking. He would avoid anyone who was not a team player. That reduced the number of detractors and pessimists in a meeting and avoided people who might slow things down or poison the atmosphere with negativity. Instead, the meetings reflected a sense of optimism and a profound desire to get things done, while still holding space and respect for very differing views.

Second, before any major meeting, Stephen spent time thinking through how it might unfold and mapping out the reasons someone might have a contrary view. Then he structured the meeting to make sure everyone was heard and that their views were taken into consideration. He also ensured that everyone had specific roles and responsibilities in the meetings and on the committees to avoid conflict.

This was an intentional approach, based on a foundation of environmental, technical, and economic science.

Third, he set up some rules for meetings (for both his own colleagues at the EPA and others)—guardrails to keep them on track and out of the spiral of negativity. "You are welcome to come to this meeting," he told his colleagues, "but if you come you have to follow these rules: no reference to past things the company has done, no [negative] motives, no name calling, no anger."

Lastly, he always had a path to harmonizing interest and an agreement in his sights. On some nights before a big meeting he would even dream of people agreeing.

Mostafa Tolba had his own approaches for preventing friction from derailing negotiations, but like Stephen he started with connection and honest discussion. To mobilize a wider collective behind a goal, Mostafa courageously put aside his diplomatic hat and became a philosopher, a convincing visionary who swept people up, almost like hypnotizing them, with the larger purpose of the mission. He brought key parties into a safe space and asked them to put aside their "cloak of authority" and move into what Stephen described as "jury instruction," removing all biases linked to national identity. This helped them to frame their decisions from the perspective of global citizens deciding what is right for humanity. The group would then come up with a shared vision and set of solutions.

Mostafa often asked respectful questions like, "What is stopping the United States from agreeing to this vision and set of solutions? What would need to change to make this work?" Country after country would then work together through their issues and possible paths to solutions. When they left the private meeting, they put their cloaks of authority back on, and went back to the negotiating table, this time with a map of the paths to a solution rather than roadblocks.

There was a genuineness to Mostafa. He knew that seeing another perspective might not change his opinion, but it helped him understand how to solve the problem. He always searched for a "third way" solution, bringing together the best ideas from all parties to navigate a path through differing perspectives. Sometimes Mostafa assembled informal groups of ten to fifteen people of opposing positions and then announced that the meeting was private—no one was to take notes or distribute papers, and the identity of participants was confidential. They would just talk. In doing so, people behaved as if they were freed from their obligations, and they were reminded of the humanity of everyone else in the room. "They gradually become friends working for a common cause even if it is from different angles," Mostafa said.

Collaborating with someone radically different from you can lead to amazing things, and the negotiations proved this time and again.

Stephen O. Andersen and Steve Lee-Bapty, a scholarly British negotiator, were about as different as two people can be, one an outlandish and optimistic American and the other a Winston Churchill–type of character. "No one could figure out whether we were friends or foes," Stephen said with a chuckle. It was impossible for people to imagine how these two radically different men could successfully work together. They, of course, used this to their advantage in the negotiations. Steve Lee-Bapty had infiltrated the diplomats and Stephen was integrated into the technical community. "He'd give something a try and when it wasn't working, I would try something," Stephen said. "We each had something to give and we each had something to gain from the other person." And in the end, they harnessed their differences and achieved things together that neither one could have alone, building an unlikely friendship in the process.

Protecting the ozone layer has not been an easy process. Countries' delegates often disagreed and representatives from different sectors dug their heels in. Mostafa, Stephen, and a much wider community jumped over every hurdle by consistently being open to diverse perspectives and putting in place productive approaches to manage conflict.

Now was the time to act. They had no time to waste on debilitating drama.

Harnessing Friction

Even with a perfectly architected set of magnetic moments, friction is inevitable. The trick is not taking on the impossible task of trying to eliminate it. It's harnessing it to deepen your connection.

When I first started interviewing the partners you've met in this book, people told me, "You have to find the drama, and dig into the fights, the breakups, and the dark side of the relationships." In interview after interview, I looked for the plate-throwing, screaming arguments to no avail. We've been so programmed by the media and the entertainment industry to think that high drama and raging conflict are the norm that we no longer question whether it really has to be that way.

This isn't to say these relationship stories are devoid of conflict. These people don't live Disneyland lives—none of us do. But by focusing on something bigger, by embracing an ecosystem of virtues that transcends the partnership, by shaping magnetic moments to keep them in flow, they've learned how to harness conflict gracefully, which allows them to channel it into supporting each other and work toward goals that matter. It's a beautiful rebuttal to the world's obsession with drama and negative conflict.

When they do have friction (which is inevitable), they see it as a moment to step back, to listen, and to use it as a learning moment, not a finger-pointing opportunity. They approach friction as the "sparkles" of learning something new, as defined by Bertrand and André—the outcome of the electric current of difference that will help each partner become their best self.

When I was researching relationships that failed, I found that drama is normally fueled by people's inability to approach friction as a learning moment. Instead they turn it into a personal attack worthy of a dramatic response. Forgiveness also plays a crucial role, as people often get stuck in past offenses, opening up wounds again and again and creating a cycle of conflict.

Let me be clear: It's not about agreeing with your partner all the time. It's about the way in which you disagree.

Rebecca Zucker, a leadership consultant and founding partner at Next Step Partners, connects our approach to disagreement to our ability to grow. "Friction can offer opportunities to learn, to step back and say what went badly," she said in an interview. "Having a growth mindset means putting your ego aside and asking yourself, how did I contribute to that problem? Constructive conflict means you don't personalize it. Rather, you hold contrary ideas as compatible." The key to being able to embrace conflict is complete trust that your partner always has your best interests at heart. "In a good partnership, you assume good intentions," she said. "And you avoid drama."

John Gottman uses the metaphor of the Four Horsemen of the Apocalypse to describe the four factors—criticism, defensiveness, contempt, and stonewalling—that can point to difficulties in a relationship. Gottman and his team have observed and tracked couples over time, and they've identified what the successful, happy ones all have in common: they skew toward the positive even in times of conflict. "We examined couples across the whole life course," he said. "We videotaped them talking about how their day was, or about an era of conflict, and even when they disagreed, we saw they had five times as much positive than negative emotion when they talked."

How we approach and manage conflict is also impacted by our "always on" lifestyles—cutting into the time and space we give to resolving differences and adding a layer of complexity when communication happens on a device rather than in person. When we aren't able to see someone's facial expressions or body language, when we can't hear the tone of their voice, it leads to potential miscommunication, which can add fuel to a conflict. More frequent unhealthy disagreements might also be sparked by the rise in perfectionism, causing a heightened fear of failure.

Knowing how to use our partnerships as safe spaces to grow from failures and turn friction into learning moments has never been more important to help us navigate a society that is increasingly divided and fearful. We need to cultivate the humility to realize that we don't have all the answers and that our partners are some of our best teachers and our support system.

The Sparkles

On July 26, 2016, after spending 558 hours flying 26,000 miles, André and Bertrand successfully completed the first solar-powered flight around the world. They credit their success to their Deep Connection with each other—a friendship built through years of twists and turns as they made their dream a reality.

They are also the first to admit that their partnership was not devoid of friction.

One of the early tests of their relationship was sparked by unequal public recognition, when the media began calling Bertrand the founder of Solar Impulse, without even a mention of André. Naturally, this caused some early tension in their relationship. At one point it got so bad that Bertrand's wife, Michèle Piccard, lovingly nudged him to do something about it before it tore the relationship apart.

This was the moment when Bertrand and André learned how to celebrate friction and take the heat out of conflict. They sat down together for private, uninterrupted time—as they have many times since, at the earliest sign of tension—creating a safe space where they could honestly share their feelings without feeling accused. They eventually realized that the tension between them was an unintentional by-product of Bertrand's past speaking experiences and his enthusiastic love of communicating the vision. He was comfortable being in the limelight, having given more than two thousand speeches on his family tradition of exploration and his nonstop balloon flight around the world, before Solar Impulse had even started, and therefore he became the de facto spokesman of the effort. His intention was never not to share credit with André or to eclipse him.

Together they came up with a shared solution that would lift both of them and give them equal public recognition. André trained Bertrand how to be a pilot and Bertrand trained André how to be a speaker. "On the same day André had his first standing ovation as a speaker," Bertrand recalled with a huge smile, "I was making my first high-altitude flight on Solar Impulse." Now they are very conscious that it is the responsibility of each of them to bring the other partner into the limelight to ensure fair share of the credit. André joked, "I'm a bit more like a psychiatrist now and he's a bit more like an engineer."

Celebrate friction is purposely the fifth degree of connection, as the other four lay the groundwork for moving from shared drama to shared learning during a conflict. André and Bertrand mastered this by leaving their egos behind—in large part because their shared vision of shifting the world to clean technology was much larger than any petty conflict that might emerge between them.

André and Bertrand raised themselves above competition and conflict in part by becoming mirrors for each other, constantly checking each other's egos. Bertrand elaborated on how André gives him honest, straight feedback: "André will say to me, 'Bertrand, I don't understand, you give such good advice in your speeches and your books, and now, in this practical situation, you do exactly the opposite and it's so bad, what happened?' And I say, 'Okay, thank you, you are absolutely right.'" No defensiveness, no anger, simply trust stemming from the realization that André has Bertrand's best interests at heart and would only ever criticize him from a place of love.

The next step, what they call "the sparkles," is the chance to use conflict to spark innovation. Grounding the conversation in curiosity and humility, they shift to brainstorming solutions—neither of them trying to win, both intent on finding a third way that transcends their original positions. This helps them nip conflict in the bud and build a deeper connection with each other. "Combining our experiences makes a new vision of the world where we can move ahead,"

Bertrand explained. "We should never be the same after a discussion; otherwise it means we learned nothing."

Now competition is healthy, not hurtful. It is an opportunity to improve themselves. "I've worked a lot with other people," Bertrand said, "but never anyone who was as brilliant as André. Each time I'm good at something, he becomes good also, so I had to push myself to be better. . . . The goal is not to be better than the other and have a competition, the goal is to be better than who we were before."

Twelve Approaches to Celebrate Friction

Celebrating friction is not about a blissful moment when everyone holds hands in a circle and suddenly everything is all right. It's about hard work and discovering the tools that are best for you and your partners. One thing is certain: all partnerships have bumps and disagreements. But we have a choice in how we address them. Here are twelve approaches that emerged from listening to great partnerships.

Understand the Why

The best way to defuse a conflict starts with compassionate, empathetic listening. As André and Bertrand demonstrated, this means prioritizing time for each other through intentional magnetic moments, hearing each other out without judgment or interruption, and focusing on questions to understand someone's perspective, rather than just trying to prove yours. Jo and Paz did this with their ritual of Friday Talk.

You need to take the spotlight away from your own personal feelings if you really want to understand what someone else is feeling and why. Understanding what past experiences are informing those feelings helps you stop making defensive assumptions that turn small rumblings into major earthquakes. This does not justify or make someone's actions and reactions right; it simply allows you to start from a place of understanding so you can work toward a solution and help someone see the patterns that might be causing them pain.

Andy and Jim, from LeapFrog Investments (whom you met in chapter two), constantly make difficult decisions as they navigate the rapid growth in the nascent field of impact investing. They have developed a way of working where they are always challenging each other to get to the best outcomes, but they've learned to "disagree without being disagreeable." "When you're younger, you have a sense that you need to absolutely find the solution in conversation," Andy said. What Jim and studying philosophy helped teach Andy is that rather than having all the answers, you need to come to a conversation with a frame of thinking, an understanding of where someone is coming from, a perspective on what is material and worthy of discussion, and then open yourself up to a spirit of discourse rather than proving your way is the right way.

Part of understanding the why is building a rich history together so you can see how past life experiences influence people's decisions or hot buttons. Ben and Jerry referred to this as the practice of separating the deep history of "us" from the issue so it will never blow up your friendship.

What If the Other Person Is Right?

In any disagreement, André and Bertrand always start by asking themselves, "What if the other person is right?" Even if they don't shift their perspective fully, this allows them to embrace other ideas and not just stubbornly hold fast to their own.

When we recognize our own fallibility and acknowledge the need to learn from others—especially from those who challenge some of our most cherished convictions—it creates space for deep listening, understanding, and learning.

Cornel West and Robert P. George have mastered the art of self-scrutiny. "The first thing I want to know is whether I might be wrong. If Cornel thinks something and I think the opposite, then the first thing I want to know is, if somebody as brilliant, gifted, and intellectually and morally serious as Cornel thinks such and so, then it's possible I'm wrong about this and he's right," Robert told me.

When a controversial idea came up for discussion, rather than blocking it or fighting about it, the Delle brothers would take turns playing the "hard question game," each thinking through why it might be a bad idea. Alex and Blake, who cofounded Flocabulary, did something similar, flipping positions to test their thought process and understand differing perspectives. Doing so allowed them to understand the idea from all sides, taking the heat out of it and often leading them to a better plan.

Joe, Brian, and Nathan, the cofounders of Airbnb, whom you met in chapter four, also used hard questions to review all their actions. They promoted this process in the company as the AAR, the "after-action review." People would come together to openly discuss what worked and what didn't, giving room for friction to be aired in a safe space and then pointed in a positive direction.

A Third Way

Like Mostafa, Bertrand and André celebrated friction by "constructing a third idea" based on both of their experiences and insights. This is an idea that takes the best of both of their individual ideas and creates a third idea that is a better way, a combination of their thinking. They did this by living with a constant learning mentality, which also demands a heavy dose of humility, acknowledging how much you have to learn from your partner. Respect plays a significant role in this co-creation process; you don't crush your partner's dreams—you find ways to cooperate and create shared dreams, just as we learned with the creation of The Elders in chapter four.

Cindy Mercer and Addison Fischer co-created the Planet Heritage Foundation to protect the natural world. As two successful, determined personalities, they had to take time to structure a productive way to approach conflict. Cindy told me there are two ways people normally approach conflict: domination, where the person with the most power wins, and compromise, where both people give up something that is important to them. Cindy and Addison wanted to find a third way, focused on integration. "It was a way that we could come up with answers that worked for both of us, that made the outcome bigger," Cindy explained.

A Courageous Space

Space took on two meanings throughout our research process. There's the space and time in which to have brave, difficult conversations (as we saw in chapter three), and there's also the need for partners to give each other the space to take a break, to give things time to settle down. Both are important.

Azim (whom you met in chapter three) created one of the most courageous spaces one could ever imagine when he invited Ples, the grandfather of the teenager who shot Azim's son, into his living room. This was not easy for either of them, but by having the hard conversations and opening the door for forgiveness, they freed each other from bitterness and hatred. They've now taken that safe space from Azim's living room into grade schools and high schools, where they help students have open, honest conversations about vulnerability, forgiveness, and love.

Jo and Paz have Friday Talk, as we saw in chapter five. Committing to this ritual ensures they have a time to share the good and the bad in their relationship. This brave space has had a couple of benefits: it has enabled them to deepen their understanding and love for each other, and it has offered an opportunity to minimize disagreements that emerge earlier in the week—by the time Friday comes around, they've taken some space away from the heat of the conflict.

Sarah Kay and Phil Kaye, two accomplished spoken-word poets, described how hard it was in the beginning for them to have difficult conversations, as they were both conflict avoidant. "I had to learn how to say, 'This actually didn't make me feel very good,'" Phil said, "'and I trust that you didn't intend to do that, but I still feel kind of crappy about it.'" Sarah talked about three promises she made to Phil to create a safe space for hard discussions: "I will always be honest with you to the absolute best of my ability. I would never do anything to intentionally hurt you. If I do something that hurts you, trust that it is because I didn't realize it was hurtful. Please tell me so I can do everything to adjust my behavior, so I no longer hurt you. That's what I promise and what I expect back."

Nature can play an important role in shaping a courageous space. Many of the partners I spoke with talked about going for a walk or getting outside to create a space that grounds you and gives you perspective, either by yourself or when you need to have a difficult conversation.

Veto Power

No matter who you are, there are moments when celebrating friction feels like an impossible dream. Thoughtfully thinking through how to design "correction mechanisms" can help protect your relationship from blowing up in moments of exhaustion, or when you're so passionate about something that you can't see straight, much less listen deeply to someone. For example, early on in their relationship, Ben and Jerry decided that either of them could veto any decision they felt they absolutely couldn't live with. This happened very infrequently, but it was key to making sure their friendship always came first.

Putting structures in place to defuse conflict early is also critical (as Mostafa and Stephen did so well). As mentioned in the previous chapter, the three Delle brothers would decide jointly which investments their company would back, and this was a recipe for conflict, as they each had different approaches to risk and differing ideas on which business opportunities were the right fit. The solution was to create a structure that would depersonalize such decisions. The first step was to ensure they each had very clear roles and responsibilities. They then set up an independent investment committee with final decision-making authority. This allowed them to have rich debates and discussions about investment opportunities without having to disappoint one another and rip the family apart.

In any organization, a failure to delineate clear roles and responsibilities can lead to confusion and bruised egos, and in turn conflict and a lack of trust. The cofounders of LeapFrog Investments often refer to it as a flotilla of speedboats rather than one large central command boat. Every team in the company and each of the partners are like individual speedboats, with unique roles, yet still part of a shared flotilla headed toward the same purpose. This allows them to move at speed with a clear vision rather than having one dominant, lumbering boat that has a captain shouting orders to everyone.

Humor

As Peter Gabriel said, humor can be "the best oil for any problems." A moment of laughter, a self-deprecating joke, or a silly prank can bring lightness and joy to difficult situations. As I mentioned, Richard Branson and Peter have a consistent magnetic moment linked to water throwing, as they demonstrated in their interview. When the conversation got too serious, Richard threw a glass of water on Peter, who in turn threw a pitcher of water at Richard, and before we knew it, everyone in the room—including the film crew and the waiters—was in a water fight, soaked and laughing hysterically.

Humor is so important for defusing conflict and for keeping people connected—so I've included it as a category of magnetic moments, and a way to manage conflict. There can never be too much joy and humor in your partnerships!

The Other 99 Things

Don't sweat the small stuff. Remember the ninety-nine things you love about someone when that one irritating thing happens. To check themselves on level of importance, Beverly and Dereck ask themselves, "Will this be in the memoir we write when we are in our nineties?" If not, talk it out and let it go.

A sound perspective can keep you from being drawn into unnecessary, debilitating drama. Your something bigger will always lift you above the petty rivalries and disagreements and allow you to turn friction into positive energy toward your mission.

Language is also important. Stay away from blood pressure–raising words like *always* and *never*—these all-or-nothing phrases are usually exaggerations showing that you've forgotten the other ninety-nine times your partner actually didn't (or did) do something.

Positive Amnesia

I remember spending an hour trying to get Peter and Richard to talk about their disagreements, but they simply could not remember any, even though, after working with them for seventeen years on The Elders project, I know there have been a few!

As this pattern continued in subsequent interviews, I came to realize that *positive amnesia* is a sign of deep respect between partners—and it highlights a healthy practice of forgiveness. Successful partnerships can work through bad experiences and then release them, forgiving and literally forgetting so they don't undermine their collaboration by hanging on to any negative reflections. The ecosystem of virtues plays a critical role, as having the foundations of trust and respect in a relationship reminds you that your partner would never intentionally hurt you (as Sarah and Phil shared in the fourth approach, "A Courageous Space").

Sometimes forgiveness is not so easy—whether that is forgiving your partner or forgiving someone outside the partnership. It is worth the effort because it frees you from bitterness and anger and allows you to move on with your life from a place of love rather than resentment.

Azim demonstrated the ultimate act of forgiveness after his son was killed. He clarifies that forgiveness does not mean condoning the killing, but rather separating himself from bitterness toward the killer. Unless you forgive, you remain a victim. Staying in anger and resentment only hurts you. It becomes a form of self-abuse. Forgiveness is a healthy approach that gives you freedom and control of your own life. He frequently quotes Mandela: "Resentment is like drinking poison and then hoping it will kill your enemies."

Peace with Yourself

It's super hard to have a positive approach to friction if you don't have peace with yourself. Jo and Paz stressed the need to "take responsibility for your own buttons." Focus on understanding the things from your own history that will trigger a negative reaction so that you can be aware of them, accept responsibility for them, be honest about them, and really work on them.

Part of working on your own hot buttons is giving yourself the space and time for self-reflection. Deepening your own understanding of yourself will allow you to step back and observe your behavior, to separate out the emotions and understand where you need to change.

Healthy partnerships also allow us to see ourselves mirrored through the eyes of someone we love and trust. These relationships help us understand both our strengths and the areas in which we might be letting ourselves down. Opening up space for honest reflection with our partners is one of the fastest paths to achieving peace with ourselves.

Greg Zehner (whom you met in chapter four) was trained as a pastor and has seen many couples whose marriages are in trouble. One of the most common issues is that each spouse is trying to change the other, thinking that will save the relationship. We have to accept the other person unconditionally, he says, "and it's the love and that unconditional acceptance that actually causes change, versus the criticism and staying on top of somebody." Freed from the burden of trying to change someone else, we also become free to be at peace with ourselves.

You Can't Read the Label from Inside the Jar

This one is simple to say, but not always so easy to do: be courageous and get help when you need it. We often think we've failed if we need to reach out to someone for help, when in truth we've failed if we don't realize that we might need some external perspective to help us get

through a particularly rocky patch. Most of the successful partnerships needed a little bit of extra support at some point—some reached
out to friends (like the Carters in chapter three), others reached out to
family members, and still others found the right expert help.

Gro and Arne Brundtland have been together for sixty years. They
met over a beer at a student gathering and, as Gro recalled, "Light-
ning struck the moment our eyes met." Everyone was stunned that
a Social Democrat and a Conservative could fall in love so deeply
and so quickly. No one thought it could last. Yet instead of allowing their differences to dominate, they embraced their curiosity and
had discussions about everything under the sun. They supported, inspired, and learned from each other as both pursued their political
careers, with Gro eventually becoming the prime minister of Norway
and Arne holding a range of political analyst roles as well as becoming a well-respected journalist and author.

Their shared values—trust, respect, openness, and self-sacrifice—
and continual communication built a partnership in which they
respected each other's independence while always cooperating as a
pair. As with every partnership, it was not always smooth sailing.

When they had been married for ten years, they found they were
having more and more disagreements. Rather than simply letting
themselves drift apart, they decided to seek advice from an experienced psychologist, someone "outside the jar" who could help them
navigate their situation. "During five hours of sharing concerns, and
telling each other how we felt about each other and ourselves, things
improved greatly," Gro recounted. "Our harmony and genuine respect for each other resurfaced. It was a great experience, for which
we are forever grateful."

Finding Common Ground

Lawrence (Lawry) Chickering and James (Jim) Turner, both trained as lawyers, have spent the past twenty-five years seeking to reduce political conflict. They do this in large part by focusing on areas of common ground instead of on political differences. Coming from different political backgrounds—Lawry from the right and Jim from the left—they shared from the beginning an intuition that each side contains important but incomplete truths. The whole truth, they believe, will best be realized by interactively integrating views from all sides, which often leads to a new insight not discovered previously.

They met at a publication party for Lawry's first book, *Beyond Left and Right: Breaking the Political Stalemate,* and quickly recognized they share a fundamental belief that people are more similar to each other than they are different. Lawry's conservative background came from his long friendship with the late conservative writer William F. Buckley Jr., and Jim traces his progressive activist roots to taking on the FDA with consumer activist Ralph Nader in the late 1960s.

They call their political vision "transpartisan." Lawry and Jim's vision goes beyond a binary, two-dimensional spectrum of left and right. Citizen empowerment and engagement provide the glue. They argue that this is the most important ingredient in shaping all social change programs that succeed, working with the most marginalized populations as well as the most privileged.

Their partnership rests on the strong and enduring bonds of friendship built up over years of exploring each and every issue from very different beginning points. Seeing the same things from different angles enriches both their views. "Lawry makes me look at things at a hundred and eighty degrees," Jim said. "When people see things from a different angle, they get a better picture than if they looked at it from just their own angle. If you look at something from an angle, all you see is that side."

The Long Game

Part of building an enduring relationship is the ability to embrace self-sacrifice. As Gro and Arne learned, that's not always easy. Gro was successfully moving up in the Norwegian government as a parliamentarian and deputy leader of the Labour Party when Arne, who was also becoming recognized as a leader with great potential, was approached with an opportunity to become a candidate for parliament— through the opposing Conservative Party.

Either their marriage was going to have to end or one of them would have to step down, as it would have been untenable for both to sit in parliament together on opposing political sides. After many heartfelt, difficult conversations, Arne decided to step back and, as Gro said, "support the sum of the two of us." His sacrifice saved their marriage.

Later, it was Gro's turn to give back when she trusted Arne to write a book about their life together and promised to let him write it freely, without having to get her approval or have her standing over his shoulder. When Gro stepped down from her role as prime minister, Arne published *Married to Gro*, which rapidly became a bestseller.

To celebrate friction and practice the approaches shared in this chapter, you need partners who are in it for the long run. Building a shared history together is like clearing a path in the forest so you can walk calmly with "sparkles," rather than stumbling around bushes and trees as you navigate a difficult situation.

Most interactions and relationships in our lives are short term and can't provide continual love and support across our lifetime. Similarly, most people focus primarily on short-term gain for themselves, rather than protecting each other's long-term well-being. It is our Deep Connections, the people who are with us for the long game, that really make us who we are in this world. It is also far easier to celebrate friction and look at it as a learning moment if you have a shared history with someone and you know that they will always have your back.

If you are able to celebrate friction with your Deep Connections, it will permeate through all your relationships and alleviate much of the stress and anxiety that comes with being in fight mode, rather than partnership and cooperation mode.

CHAPTER SEVEN

Collective Connections

Sixth Degree of Connection

What they would implement, and how, has
been based on a circle of friends, an ever-
growing circle of friends, that has worked
tirelessly under conditions of personal trust.

—Mostafa Tolba, executive director
of UNEP, co-architect of the Montreal
Protocol to protect the ozone layer

British prime minister Margaret Thatcher was skeptical about reports of damage to the ozone layer, until she spent a weekend poring through a briefing that was assembled by her staff and British technical experts, including the scientists Joe, Jonathan, and Brian (whom you met in chapter four), the partners who discovered the ozone hole.

As a trained chemist, by Sunday evening she had joined these

British scientists, Mostafa, Stephen, Mario, and Sherry as a converted leader in the movement to protect the ozone.

She and her team sprang into action, helping to rally countries to deliver results. "We need to go further and act faster, to accept higher targets and shorter deadlines," Thatcher told the delegates at a conference she was hosting in London in March 1989. "Please do not set your sights too low." Her voice was a beacon for global cooperation, for sharing information and experiences, for working together across borders to fully understand the extent of the damage and then take concerted action to fix it.

Throughout the 1989 and 1990 negotiations to strengthen the Montreal Protocol, Thatcher expressed compassionate empathy for the countries who did not cause the problem. "Clearly it would be intolerable for the countries which have already industrialized, and have caused the greater part of the problems we face, to expect others to pay the price in terms of their people's hopes and well-being," she said. She was steadfast in her view that no country should be left behind. Humanity needed to come together in our collective interest, rather than be divided by selfish nationalism.

She effectively used the media to pressure other industrialized countries, and even inadvertently to pressure her own country. When asked by reporters how much Britain was going to pay into the multilateral fund to support countries who had not caused the ozone damage, she told them £1.5 million. Nicholas Ridley, the British environment minister, whispered to her, "Actually, Prime Minister, it's one and a quarter million," to which Thatcher replied, "Well then, you'd better make it one and a half million immediately. That will teach these people to give me the wrong briefing, won't it?"

In her speech in London that day, Thatcher warned representatives of industrialized nations, including Britain and the United States, that destruction of the earth's ozone layer was proceeding even faster than scientists had first thought and that efforts to reduce ozone-destroying chemicals must be hastened. It was an impassioned plea that didn't fall on deaf ears. President Ronald Reagan, who had already been convinced of the urgency by his secretary of state, George Shultz, was also scaling up the US response to the crisis. Thatcher and Reagan became a formidable pair of unlikely environmental activists.

This was a new era, an unprecedented moment in the history of diplomacy. "Politicians from every bloc and region of the world are setting aside politics to reach agreement on protecting the global environment," Ambassador Richard Benedick, the lead of the US delegation, said in an interview in 1990. "The Governments are backing off hardened positions to get an agreement, and even the customary disagreements between North and South—the developed nations versus the developing nations—lack their usual edge."

There were many unlikely collaborators across sectors at the center of the negotiations and the ongoing implementation of the Montreal Protocol, and we are indebted to them all. They were not trying to be individual heroes; they were trying to collectively save the world. From awareness through implementation, it was an inclusive process that brought everyone into the tent to collaborate on an unheard-of scale.

They were friends, global citizens all working together for a common cause. Here was human achievement at its very best, this vast collective of people who delivered what everyone thought was impossible.

Why was this collaboration a success when so many other global efforts have failed?

When I started this exploration of partnerships, I knew that Deep Connections were important to our individual lives and our ability to do something bigger in the world. What I did not grasp in the early stages was how fundamental they are to most significant human achievements. As I studied extraordinary collective accomplishments, such as protecting the ozone layer, ending smallpox in India, and ending apartheid, it was clear that the success of those endeavors was not linked to one individual, or to money or fame or social media likes. The keys to success were the strong Deep Connections at the center, friendships that weathered many challenges, coupled with a unique approach to collaborative architecture.

As we face complex global issues such as pandemics, climate change, nuclear threat, and many others, we need to architect effective collaborative solutions that know no borders.

The sixth degree, collective connections, is a framework of design principles to scale collaborations, with Deep Connections at the center as role models, as hubs of momentum, as connective tissue, as collaboration architects.

I was reminded of the importance of collective connections on a damp London day when I sat in a tightly packed conference room with a group of academics, business leaders, scientists, and politicians, all distinguished in their fields and all concerned about climate change and the growing loss of biodiversity. Over the next eight hours, with the hiss of the barely functioning heater as background noise, people mentioned the word *collaboration* close to fifty times. Yet the meeting felt more like a battleground. People were talking over each other, not listening, with everyone trying to be the smartest person in the room. Talk of collaboration was simply that: words that were trampled on as everyone climbed on top of each other. People were all-in for the cause, but not all-in for each other.

We mistakenly expect groups and individuals to be able to collaborate spontaneously. Yet this is like expecting a group of amateur gymnasts to come together and instantly perform a gravity-defying double backflip in unison before they've even mastered how to spot each other in a simple cartwheel.

Often, we aim for immediate "moon shots" rather than starting with more accessible steps with a handful of Deep Connections, the hub from which to build and forge a path forward—dependent not on one single leader, but on a group of committed friends who become the "critical mass from which I spread," as Mostafa has said.

If two or three people in that London meeting already had Deep Connections with each other, they could have modeled the five degrees of connection we've explored in this book and changed the whole dynamic and impact of the group. Yet, when designing collaborations, we don't often consider depth of connection as an important factor for selecting the group. Instead, we focus on technical skills, levels of experience, and name recognition to give the group credibility. Those things may be important, but a group is far more likely to achieve something extraordinary if there are a few people with all-in Deep Connections at the center, along with a clear purpose, an ecosystem of virtues, and a thoughtful framework to keep people connected. In that scenario we have a collaboration that can last for the long run, where trust, respect, and generosity rule, rather than egos and individual interests.

The importance of the right collective composition and dynamics for scaled collaboration is even more vital when we realize how interconnected and dependent we are on each other for our very survival. Architect and scientist Buckminster Fuller articulates this beautifully in his short book *Operating Manual for Spaceship Earth*. He uses the analogy of Earth as a spaceship, a shared home where all our actions have flow-on impacts to other global citizens and to nature's systems. His perspective is that we are all passengers together on this spaceship, flying through space with limited resources and a need for innovation and cooperation "to keep the machine in good order or it's going to be in trouble and fail to function." His visionary book is a callout to the world for planetary scale, cooperative strategies so that everyone on Earth can thrive and live with dignity and freedom, on a "spaceship" that is healthy and regenerative. Although Buckminster's book was written in 1969 during the Cold War, when the world was deeply divided, it is just as relevant and useful today.

"The most important thing about Spaceship Earth—an instruction book didn't come with it," Buckminster said. Fortunately, we have many examples of copilots who have led our spaceship to much better outcomes through collective cooperation. These are people who created frameworks for collaboration to flourish and who used their Deep Connections as a springboard to exponentially increase the number of collective connections working toward a specific outcome.

A Human Story

The effort to protect the ozone was successful because it grew far beyond a handful of copilots. It relied upon global collaboration across sectors and borders, grounded in science, at a scale that stunned even the most hardened critics. In her closing speech at the March 1989 London conference, Thatcher's words were chilling and still very relevant today. "For centuries mankind has worked on the assumption that we could pursue the goal of steady progress without disturbing the fundamental equilibrium of the world's atmosphere and its living systems," she said. "In a very short space of time that comfortable assumption has been shattered."

Thatcher, Reagan, and other global leaders were the unlikely megaphones and partners that the movement needed. The monumental achievement of the Montreal Protocol was delivered by thousands of people and has since saved millions of lives. It shaped the first successful international treaty to address a common global environmental challenge, with all sectors—business, government, scientists, multilateral institutions, and not-for-profit organizations—playing a critical role. And it came about as a result of Deep Connections between citizens from diverse backgrounds who humbly dedicated their lives to the global good.

This is one of the most important examples of scaled collaboration in the world, yet it is oddly absent from many of our textbooks, and from case studies on how we should approach our growing interconnected global issues. The true heroes at the center of this achievement are largely uncelebrated.

Much of the historic writing about this unrivaled global accomplishment focuses on the negotiation tactics, the scientific process, and the technological innovation. The story that unfolded during my research and interviews with people like Mario, Jonathan, Stephen, Penelope, Nancy, Ingrid, and Jeffrey was something different.

A human story.

A story of Deep Connections who together built and nurtured a massive global network of friends and allies. This relational approach was especially critical as nations began the challenging process of phasing out CFCs, which started when the ink was not yet dry on the Montreal Protocol and continues today.

Nancy Reichman and Penelope Canan, the authors of *Ozone*

Connections, spent years documenting the importance of this relational approach. They also have their own story of Deep Connection, which they shared with me during a Zoom interview that was buzzing with laughter, respect, and love.

When they met some thirty-seven years ago, they were sociology professors at the University of Denver. They bonded in their fight for equal pay and became fast friends. Together, they attended their first ozone community meeting and became deeply curious about the camaraderie, joy, and trust in the group. It operated like a family, yet with a group of people from a wide diversity of backgrounds. They had never seen anything quite like it. Here were scientists, business leaders, environmentalists, and government policy makers all rolling up their sleeves with a sense of urgency that would be sustained over decades.

After years of research, they found that the secret to this massive "family" was explained by a core group of tight relationships at the center, combined with an innovative organizational structure that encouraged bonds of friendship across a global network—or in my language, Deep Connections that inspire and mobilize a vast network of collective connections.

They concluded that people like Stephen and Mostafa, masters of collaborative leadership, propelled the entire group forward. "They inspire others, create the institutional space for co-operation among equals, determine membership and create norms of reciprocity, action, consensus and camaraderie," they wrote. "They literally create the conditions for shared excellence."

Stephen woke up every day motivated by a singular mission: protect the ozone layer. Like Mostafa, he understood the profound power of something bigger. "A shared experience of this kind can transform a collection of individuals into a group and unify them around a set of values and a common purpose," Nancy and Penelope wrote. Never before had a global environmental agreement assembled such a combination of technical expertise and political savvy.

The independence of the TEAP committees allowed them to create their own achievable targets for phasing out CFCs, and to invent replacements. This opened up the tent for unlikely partners, including competitors, to experiment together and then fast-track the best ideas to go to scale. Stephen and the TEAP committee leaders clustered collectives by industry to allow them to reinvent their own futures. By connecting a cross-fertilization of experts who trusted each other—from scientists to economists to people working in manufacturing to activists—they created multiple innovation hubs, where all ideas mattered and relationships flourished.

As a "super motivator," shared Nancy about Stephen, "he made people feel good about themselves." Nancy and Penelope's connection data analysis showed a clear mapping of what some people jokingly referred to as "the Steve Andersen effect," a central hub in tightening the overall network that helped everyone stay connected and be effective over long periods of time.

Through an expanding collective of world-changing friendships, participants put aside individual interests and built an epic global collaboration on behalf of humanity and the planet. That does not mean it was always an easy process; there were moments of conflict and misaligned priorities that threatened the outcomes. Ultimately it came down to a set of innovative design principles and several Deep Connections at the center becoming hubs that took care of people, paid attention to the small things, and made people feel part of something bigger.

The result was bonds of trust and friendship that were unbreakable.

Collaborative Design Principles

As we watched the pandemic race around the world in 2020, it became ever clearer that our interconnected world demands a new order of global cooperation.

Fortunately, we can learn from the collective connections built by copilots like Mario, Sherry, Mostafa, Stephen, and so many others. Their stories inspire confidence that well-designed collectives of willing partners can literally change the course of history. As we also saw, building collective connections of people from diverse backgrounds and keeping up the momentum as they drive toward shared goals is not an easy process.

Over the past fifteen years, as part of my work with Virgin Unite, we've worked with partners to incubate or support the incubation of more than a dozen different collectives. Every one of them had at least one Deep Connection at the center that helped it weather the chaotic start-up years, created an achievable path, and ensured it blossomed into a sustainable movement with long-lasting, systemic impact.

Deep Connections at the center of larger-scale collaborations model the first five degrees and keep the wider collective together. But there are also a number of other lessons that were omnipresent in the collectives we've built and studied. The lessons were similar whether it was a local community effort of hundreds of people; The

Elders, with a group of twelve leaders and hundreds of partners; or the ozone community, made up of thousands of people from all over the world. All of them had several Deep Connections at the center that then served as hubs to mobilize many more people, who formed their own Deep Connections in the wider community, leading to unstoppable distributed networks.

Here are **six collaborative design principles** that combine with the Six Degrees of Connection to create the conditions for shared excellence in larger collaborations.

An Intoxicating "Something Bigger"

Mostafa, Stephen, Sherry, and Mario all had something in common that lifted them from a singular, personal purpose to a collective, world-changing purpose: a sincere belief in saving humanity by closing the ozone hole, and the humility to know that they could not go it alone. They needed thousands of people who were also "hypnotized" by this critical mission.

They did not just talk about their mission and write long reports, they dedicated their lives to action, building one of the most successful global partnerships in the history of humanity. To this day, people still call Stephen "the ozone guy," reflecting the centrality of this work in his life. This sincere, clear commitment to something bigger gave the partners authentic trust and respect that rippled out to create the wider movement. Their belief and persistence were intoxicating. People wanted to be part of it. They wanted to be on the right side of history to make a difference for generations to come.

As you expand your Deep Connections and start to create much larger collectives of connections, it is even more important to have a clear purpose to serve as inspiration and as a compass as the group grows ever more diverse. Without the first degree, a compelling something bigger, it is impossible to achieve liftoff.

The something bigger does not have to be perfectly articulated from day one; in fact, co-creation bonds the collective. Where The Elders are concerned, it took several years, many workshops, and a moving speech from Nelson Mandela to arrive at the moral compass for the collective of twelve Elders. That speech (shared in part in chapter four) still stands today, some fifteen years later, as a North Star for The Elders and their ever-widening circle of partners.

Even with clear North Stars, such as the imperatives to protect the ozone layer and to end apartheid, there needs to be flexibility for them to evolve as the science advances, policies are tested, and approaches are fine-tuned. They also need to be inspiring enough to hold people's attention. For the ozone community, this was the chance to change history for the better, as shared by Richard Benedick, chief US negotiator: "The 'spirit of the protocol,' often invoked by participants in this process, reflected genuine feelings of solidarity and partnership to protect the ozone layer, in what was regarded as a noble and historic global movement." It also helped tremendously that the science was respected, the term the "ozone hole" was simple to grasp, and there was an immediate threat to human health.

Within that framework, people's individual purposes were lifted to ensure they had fulfilling experiences. "Inspiring a shared vision does not mean that others must share the exact purpose of the leader," Stephen told me. "A leader honors others' goals and dreams and enables them to see that there can be a mutually rewarding outcome."

Start and Strengthen

Sometimes the issues we face, whether in our community or in the world, seem way too daunting to imagine we personally can do anything to help solve them.

Yet the road to the Montreal Protocol started in a lab in California with Sherry and Mario. They were morally courageous, wise scientists who took those first steps and kept going, leading to movements that changed the course of history.

Rather than being daunted by the challenge of engaging the entire world, Mostafa focused on getting started with those countries who were already willing, rather than waiting to bring everyone into the tent. He built core circles of friends and then widened them, using these circles to strengthen and scale. His straightforward demeanor neutralized any feelings of bias, leading him to joke that he was equally attacked by all sides, which he took as a sign of success.

Stephen mirrored that in his approach to phasing out CFCs and other ozone-depleting chemicals with companies by creating manageable working groups by sector. Incrementalism was celebrated, not dismissed. The process of experimentation, failing quickly, learning, and then moving on was encouraged. This was supported by small, nimble clusters working together on manageable steps. For Jay Baker, the Ford Motor Company TEAP lead, this meant "moving early on easier targets" and then building on success.

Rather than one big moon shot, there were hundreds of new challenges and success stories every step of the way. The TEAP committees and company representatives focused on setting achievable targets, suspending any disbelief, co-creating solutions—and moving to the next challenge. This kept people engaged over the years and gave them a tremendous sense of shared accomplishment. Decades later, their Deep Connection of friendship lives on.

When I asked Stephen why other global treaties and collaborations have failed, he said that most of them set unachievable goals, were inflexible, and focused on deficiencies rather than successes. Who would want to be part of failing at every turn?

Yet that's how we approach many of our global collaborative efforts.

Open Tent

If we linked The Elders to one individual or organization, with a closed tent exclusive to our community, I'm 100 percent certain the initiative never would have gotten off the ground. Completely independent initiatives allow for diverse partners to enter the tent and feel a sense of belonging, united by something bigger.

I frequently see organizations wanting to "own" a collaborative effort, to mark it with their brand or their name. But if one brand, one individual, or one set of interests tries to steer the ship, it will crash. The people in the collective must have the freedom to follow their path within the wider purpose and live the collective's ecosystem of virtues, or the impact will be biased and only as big as the organization or individual trying to steer it.

This is not just about opening up the tent, it is also knocking down some of the barriers to entry. Growing up in Egypt, Mostafa personally understood that to open the tent for the Montreal Protocol beyond the industrialized countries, they would need to level the playing field, giving tailored support to the less industrialized countries who did not create the ozone problem. (Industrialized nations used 88 percent of CFCs with only 25 percent of the world's population.) The answer was a multilateral fund, including technology and knowledge transfer, support resources, and grace periods for less industrialized nations, which allowed everyone to be part of the ongoing solution.

An open tent also encourages thoughtful recruitment of people from diverse backgrounds, who will in turn encourage others to join. Stephen spent hours finding names, cold-calling people to find more names, and then doing his homework to make sure that the experts in the network were the best in the world. This helped the network bond quickly, as there was an immediate sense of trust and respect based on strong reputations. But he selected people based not just on technical skills but also on their "social capital"—their personal networks, their willingness to share knowledge openly, and their understanding about the importance of building strong relationships with others in the tent.

In addition, Stephen had no tolerance for those who would come into the tent and try to undermine the wider collective and not show equal respect to everyone involved. He was quick to show them the exit so they did not poison the wider group. This was an important lesson for me because in my quest to bring together unlikely partners, I've at times kept people for too long who were undermining the wider mission. I thought that I was allowing for differing views to have a voice, when in reality I was just creating space for ego-led individuals who were not all-in for the shared mission.

Unlikely Connections

Sherwood and Mario, Mostafa and Stephen are very different people with diverse backgrounds, yet they built collectives around their partnerships. Their electric current of difference and their equality within their partnerships fueled the wider collectives. I've seen similar collaborative success among unlikely individuals in The B Team, a group of leaders working toward a better way of business. The B Team is a diverse group of business, union, government, and not-for-profit leaders whose success lies in the ability to work across different sectors, such as when Sharan Burrow, the head of the International Trade Union Confederation, shared the stage with Paul Polman, CEO of Unilever at the time. Though Sharan and Paul had some different opinions, it was precisely the contrast and honesty between them that fostered a richness of debate, better outcomes, and immediate credibility.

Stephen and Mostafa were masters of this kind of cross-pollination. They understood from the beginning that industry, government, scientists, environmentalists, global institutions, and others would need to come together if the Montreal Protocol was to be a success. As I shared in the previous chapter, much thought went into how to harness friction for better outcomes. Stephen and Mostafa used what they called "reverse jeopardy" by determining who they needed to answer the questions to solve the problem, and then going out and finding those people. This diversity of thinking led to fewer mistakes and far better outcomes, as everyone was looking at the issues and solutions from different angles.

Some of the leaders they brought in were known as "super experts," well-respected chairpersons of the different TEAP committees who fostered a spirit of community and never focused on gaining the spotlight—only on getting the work done. "Many were network spanners," shared Penelope and Nancy, "connective leaders who advocated, facilitated, and fostered sectorial network action and created bridging networks that connected sectoral innovation to policy decisions."

The scientists, diplomats, and business leaders were an uncommon, courageous mix of people who normally did not work together. They also forged unlikely partnerships across sectors with the media, the public, and NGOs to further the mission. This consistently helped to speed up the collaboration process as people and organizations then put pressure on their governments and industries to act. NGOs and the media helped get companies to act via public pressure, like when Greenpeace hung a huge "#1 Ozone Destruction" banner on DuPont's water tower. This also happened through public celebration, like when Stephen got the US Environmental Protection Agency to publish newspaper ads celebrating companies who were doing the right thing.

There were also unlikely partnerships across generations. At the event in London in June 1990, the negotiations were not going well at one point—there was a deadlock and they were running out of time. A group of young Australian leaders, organized by the Australian Conservation Foundation, presented an eloquent declaration of frustration to help speed up the process. They said they had been watching the negotiations, sometimes with fascination and in other moments horror, fearful that the inaction of the negotiators was going to condemn them to a devastating future filled with skin cancer, cataracts, and depleted natural resources. "At the moment we are afraid," they pleaded. "Do not leave our generation without hope. Our fate lies in your square brackets. You are making history. Have the courage to save the ozone layer."

Their plea crossed the generational divide and helped to break the deadlock.

Relational Scaffolding

Mostafa and Stephen did not want to be a command-and-control center. They knew that success lay in distributed leadership across thousands of people all over the world. Architecting the scaffolding to encourage and support this level of distributed leadership across networks takes significant thought at the outset. Relational scaffolding provides the framework to encourage people to build strong relationships, to take on leadership roles, and to minimize disruptive conflict.

To Mostafa and Stephen, protecting the ozone layer was not simply a task to be completed, it was a purpose for living, woven into the fabric of their very beings. They built relationships, rather than merely conducting a transaction. They built incentive structures that cleared the runway for traction and gave everyone the best possible chance for success. For example, they worked with governments to establish specific phase-out dates for CFCs, which gave companies the clarity they needed to set targets for inventing alternatives to aerosol products. They also used trade restrictions to encourage countries to become a part of the Montreal Protocol. Both of these approaches were tremendously successful.

The Montreal Protocol was wisely created with a flexible, distributed relational scaffolding that allowed for periodic reevaluation and localized, relevant targets. Relational scaffolding can also create a successful company. Natura, a Brazilian cosmetics company, is built on its relationships with over six million consultants in one hundred countries as well as a thoughtful partnership with Mother Nature. Since 1969, the three cofounders, Luiz Seabra, Pedro Passos, and

Guilherme Leal, have partnered to grow Natura into an $11 billion global company.

Natura's distributed collective of consultants is not only incentivized by profit potential. They are also rewarded for encouraging sustainable consumption and recognized as key partners in the company's success. Their relational scaffolding includes policies geared toward transparency and co-creation. As a result of all this, each year consultants generate hundreds of new ecologically sound product ideas.

The wider Natura network includes partnerships with over thirty indigenous communities in the Amazon supporting more than forty-three hundred small farmers who supply the unique ingredients in their products, like Brazil nuts and ucuuba berries. These independent communities use their traditional farming know-how, helping to conserve almost 1.8 million hectares of Amazonian forest. This is an incredible virtuous circle created by thoughtful relational structures that make partners want to be part of Natura's wider mission.

Natura was an early pioneer in changing business for good by setting clear local targets, allowing their diverse network of partners to help them become carbon neutral in 2007. "I believe that one plus one makes way more than two, when you're willing to live with difference," Guilherme offered as a response to why diversity is so critical. "Disagree cheerfully, unite agendas, and build commitment around them—that's when real change happens."

Natura's mission from the start has been "to create and sell products and services that promote the harmonious relationship of the individual with oneself, with others and with nature." They credit their success to their belief that life is a chain of relationships and that valuing relationships is the foundation of "the great human revolution."

Here are twelve tips for creating the right relational scaffolding, for an organization, a company—or a movement:

1. **Agree on the destination, have clear roles and responsibilities, and then let people choose their own route**—with as little interference as possible.

2. Allow space for **localized, accountable ownership**— including the setting of relevant, achievable targets and deadlines.

3. Build in **as much independence as possible** from any type of biased influences.

4. Be **adaptive and flexible** at every turn—establish periods for honest feedback and evolution.

5. **Create positive incentives and support structures** that encourage collaboration and level the playing field so everyone has a "fair go."

6. **Transparently and openly share information.** Share stories. Build a shared history together and a foundation of trust.

7. Create informal spaces for small clusters so people can have **safe opportunities to disagree**, debate, and work toward pragmatic, fast consensus without the glare of a large-group spotlight.

8. Encourage an atmosphere of **cooperation, not confrontation**. Look for ways to create a harmony of interests and don't reinforce the negative skeptics—never burn bridges; create soft landings.

9. Create **ongoing points for connection**—standing meetings and committees that allow people to continue to collaborate and build relationships.

10. Put effort into **orchestrating meetings** to ensure the right people are in the room, the nurturing of relationships, an efficient use of time, and speed of outcomes.

11. **Make people conspicuous, not anonymous**, so they feel ownership and pride at being part of the collective.

12. **Celebrate success and people** every chance you get—create contagious shared glory. Bring audacity, equality, and joy to the table at every point of connection—inspire everyone to be part of something bigger.

Culture of Service and Friendship

The March 26, 1988, issue of *The New York Times* carried a story about what led to DuPont's abrupt reversal on the subject of CFCs. The company, which as the world's largest producer of CFCs had the most to lose, had steadfastly refused to acknowledge publicly that these chemicals might be dangerous. Representatives had harshly attacked Sherry and Mario's findings. But everything had changed ten days earlier, when new, irrefutable scientific evidence emerged. "Du Pont's policy has always been to be responsive to the best scientific information available," said DuPont's chief scientist, Mack McFarland, "and this is the best scientific information as of March 15." McFarland saw that it was time to turn the ship around. He and another leader at DuPont, Joseph Glas, set out to convince DuPont leadership that they had to shift course immediately.

This was no easy process. Yet based on Mack's courageous stance, the company made the decision to start phasing out CFCs. Mack called Mario, as he wanted to tell him the news personally. Mario and Sherry were stunned that DuPont decided to phase out CFCs before a government mandate. Sherry told the *Baltimore Sun*, "Their decision is welcome now and would have been welcome anytime in the past fourteen years." That night Joseph went home and told his wife and six children what the company had decided to do. "They said, 'Dad, that's fantastic,'" he recalled. "I know I'm doing something that's important, and it felt good."

Mack was DuPont's representative in the TEAP community for many years before and after that pivotal moment in 1988. Stephen shared that when Mack eventually retired from DuPont, his Montreal Protocol family held a party for him in Paris, packed with people from across all sectors, including many environmentalists. This would normally have been completely unheard of, as industry and change makers didn't mix socially—except in the ozone community, where adversarial divides were bridged through deep friendships.

Through living and promoting the six virtues in the ecosystem (the third degree of connection in chapter four) and the creation of many magnetic moments as shared earlier in the book, a unique culture of "fast friends" was nurtured for all those who were lucky enough to be part of this special community. The fast-tracking of friendships came down to the enormity of their shared something bigger, careful selection of partners who garnered immediate respect, authenticity of their commitment to service that sped-up trust, and the relational scaffolding that kept people connected and moving forward together.

Successful collectives need to have individuals who are working in service to others, not trying to control others or to push their individual agendas. My dear friend Andrea Brenninkmeijer loved to call this ingredient "working for the universe on behalf of humanity and the planet." This demands a "quiet power" that is not ego directed but focused on building outcomes for others, allowing collectives to flourish.

The community working on closing the ozone hole had a golden rule that everyone had to leave their own agendas at the door; the only agenda in the room was in service to protecting the ozone layer.

Impossible Is Not a Fact

Using these six collaborative design principles and standing on the scientific groundwork laid by Sherry, Mario, and others, Mostafa and Stephen worked with many others to create and implement the most successful global treaty of our time. Without the Montreal Protocol in place to halt the depletion of the ozone layer, someone living in 2050 would get a fierce sunburn in five minutes. The EPA estimates that in the United States alone, there might have been an additional 280 million cases of skin cancer and 1.5 million cancer deaths if the world had not acted to halt the use of CFCs. Just imagine how many deaths were avoided worldwide by protecting human health and agriculture.

And it did not stop there. In 2016, over 150 countries signed the Kigali Amendment to the Montreal Protocol, to phase down the use of hydrofluorocarbons (HFCs), an ozone-safe chemical and potent green-house gas that significantly contributes to global warming. HFCs were one of the solutions that replaced CFCs. As soon as scientific data showed that they were contributing to global warming, the Montreal Protocol community sprang into action. More than thirty years after his initial engagement with the Montreal Protocol, Stephen was also involved in Kigali. He recalls a collective of people working twenty-four hours straight through the night to complete the Kigali Amendment. The next morning at the signing, they were all still awake, their faces filled with enthusiasm and shared success, and no sign of their sleepless night.

Eight years after the 1987 agreement, Sherry and Mario—along with Dutch scientist Paul Crutzen—accepted the Nobel Prize in Chemistry for their discoveries. And on the twentieth anniversary of the Montreal Protocol, in September 2007, Sherry's wife, Joan, and his children, Jeffrey and Ingrid, stood by proudly as Sherry and Mario received a standing ovation from their peers in academia, governments, and public interest groups.

When I asked Jeffrey whether his father realized how important his discovery was, without hesitating he smiled and said, "He would never claim that kind of credit—he didn't have an ego that needed to be fed."

The legacies of scientists like Mario, Sherry, and Paul are not limited to their collaborative efforts to protect the ozone. They also inspired a generation of scientists who followed in their footsteps to collaborate across divides not just to publish reports but also to co-create solutions. You'll meet some of these visionary scientists in the next chapter.

The ozone partners also inspired a different approach to collaborative negotiations. Nearly thirty years after the Montreal Protocol, Christiana Figueres used the same sense of humility and collaboration to work with her Deep Connections, including Tom Rivett-Carnac, a former Buddhist monk and activist, and many others, to secure the unanimous (195 countries) adoption of the Paris Agreement, an ambitious plan to reduce global warming. The importance of this agreement for the survival of humanity cannot be underestimated. Today, when her brother and lifelong Deep Connection José María Figueres introduces himself at a public event, he says, "I used to be known as the president of Costa Rica. Now I am known as Christiana's brother."

During the years leading up to the negotiations, we worked closely with Christiana to mobilize business leaders through The B Team and global leaders through The Elders. I'm in awe of her relentless determination and commitment to ensure that countries live up to their Paris Agreement commitments.

"Impossible is not a fact," Christiana told me. "It's an attitude. Only an attitude. We have got to change the tone of this conversation. Because there is no way you can achieve victory without optimism."

This collective spirit of optimism toward something bigger can be unstoppable, as demonstrated by the unlikely circle of friends who successfully implemented the Montreal Protocol. Now we need to do the same thing with the Paris Agreement to ensure that the commitments of nations to reduce their greenhouse gas emissions are achieved in time to avoid global climate catastrophe.

180,000 Collective Connections

The environment isn't the only issue requiring collaboration at scale. Such scale is needed to address all the interconnected issues we face, from pandemics to conflict to inequality. Fortunately, across all these areas there are successful collaborations that shine a light on the way forward.

One worth sharing that brings to life the collaborative design principles to tackle a deadly health issue is the global eradication of smallpox, a scourge that crisscrossed the world for nearly three thousand years. In the twentieth century alone, it killed at least 300 million people, many of them children. In India, the last place where the disease was killing people in the millions, its arrival with the end of the monsoon season was considered as inevitable as the heat itself.

The beginning of the end of smallpox in India came one night in 1974, when a brash young American doctor banged on the door of Russi Mody, a corporate executive in Tatanagar, an industrial city in southern India.

Although it was almost midnight, Russi was just sitting down to dinner. A butler answered the door and promptly shut it, telling Larry to call in the morning. When the butler opened the door a second time, Larry pushed past him until Russi's Tibetan mastiff clamped his jaws around Larry's wrist.

Such was Larry Brilliant's determination to help rid India of smallpox, a feat considered nearly impossible.

Larry could barely contain himself. Russi was the local head of Tata Group, at the time India's largest corporation, famous for its steel exports, and Tatanagar was a company town. That year, the city's major export was disease, spread from an outbreak in Tatanagar to the rest of India and beyond through the company's vast distribution system. The source of the outbreak was right there in Tata's steel factories.

"Do you know what your company is doing to the world?" he blurted out. "You are exporting smallpox to every country. You are exporting nothing but death."

At hearing this, Russi was incredulous. He had been unaware of the swath of misery smallpox was cutting across India and other parts of the world. He wanted the facts. Russi offered Larry dinner and they spoke until almost dawn.

Then Russi phoned the company's CEO, J. R. D. Tata, waking him up at his home in Bombay. The news of Tatanagar's role in the spread of smallpox came as a surprise to Tata as well. Together with Larry they launched a complex plan for containment of the disease in the region—and built an unlikely Deep Connection that became the center of a much wider collective of connections. So began a partnership that would reverse Tatanagar's staggering rate of smallpox infection and death and halt the spread to the rest of India. Tata Group committed $50 million, 500 jeeps, and 500 of the best Tata managers to help take on India's smallpox epidemic.

Larry worked for Dr. Nicole Grasset, the Swiss-French medical virologist and microbiologist-epidemiologist who led the WHO's smallpox eradication program in India. Larry described Nicole as building a team with no *I* in it. Everyone was equal, and everyone shared the same mission. They built what they called the Central Team of ten people, half foreigners (including Larry and Nicole) and half Indians. "The ten of us hid nothing," Larry said. "We had gone well beyond official relationships to deep friendships."

Larry became deeply immersed in ending smallpox, and his wife, Girija, was always right there with him. Together, they visited nearly every district in India. Alongside them was Zafar Hussain, a paramedical assistant born in poverty in India, who dedicated his life to eradicating smallpox. "No one in the organization reported to Zafar, but it seemed like everyone worked for him," Larry said. Zafar was supposed to be his assistant; in reality he was Larry's tutor.

Together, Zafar, Larry, and the rest of the central team of ten eventually built a deeply committed collective of over 180,000 people. Community health workers went village to village, house to house, giving vaccinations, identifying cases of smallpox, and then separating out the sufferers to avoid spreading the disease. "Indian workers made the program a success, and that is why smallpox could be eradicated," Zafar noted humbly in a PBS interview. "Everybody worked together. It was a time when—from the lowest to the highest position—everyone was busy with the eradication program. . . . We were all equal . . . I believe that everyone made it into a miracle."

As for his dear friend Zafar, Larry said, "He risked his life many times because he realized the campaign to eradicate smallpox was something he could help with, something that he could do. He eradicated smallpox. It's ordinary people who become the heroes."

The eradication of smallpox mirrored the approach of the ozone community: an intoxicating purpose, unlikely partnerships, committed friends who were in service to others, relational scaffolding to encourage distributed efforts across thousands of people—and, of course, a handful of Deep Connections at the center, the central team of ten.

Every time I think about the closing of the ozone hole, or the ending of smallpox, or companies like Natura, I'm filled with hope and the realization that collectively we truly can do anything. We simply need the will, the determination, the right Deep Connections, and a focus on meaningful measures of success.

CHAPTER EIGHT

Interconnected

My humanity is bound up in yours, for we
can only be human together.

—Archbishop Desmond Tutu

I t was seven a.m. on January 23, 2015. As I awkwardly scrambled across icy roads at the World Economic Forum in Davos, Switzerland, I hoped I would catch the launch of Professor Johan Rockström's book *Big World, Small Planet*.

I had met Johan a few years earlier for a conversation that would spark my interest in the ozone success story. He is cofounder of the esteemed Stockholm Resilience Centre and an internationally recognized leader on issues related to Earth resilience. I was intrigued by a new interconnected planetary framework he had co-created in 2009.

Inspired by ozone pioneers Sherry, Mario, and Paul, Johan and fellow scientists Will Steffen, a professor at the Australian National University, and Katherine Richardson, a professor at the University of Copenhagen, collaborated with more than two dozen of the world's best Earth System scientists to identify the Planetary Boundaries, a framework based on nine interconnected biophysical processes that regulate the stability of the Earth System. Breach these boundaries and humanity could face catastrophic and irreversible environmental damage.

This era of Earth System science recognizes that the planet has entered a new geological epoch, the Anthropocene (coined by Paul Crutzen), in which human dominance over nature is destabilizing and destroying the interconnected planetary systems that keep us alive. The scientists' hope is that by understanding this Anthropocene reality, human beings will step up to the responsibility and opportunity to change their relationship with nature to be positive Earth stewards. "Living up to the Anthropocene means building a culture that grows with Earth's biological wealth instead of depleting it," wrote Paul and coauthor Christian Schwägerl in a January 2011 article for Yale. "Remember, in this new era, nature is us."

Among the Planetary Boundaries described in the framework is the ozone layer, a great collective success story (as you've seen throughout this book) in which humanity collaborated to halt a looming disaster of its own making. The other eight boundaries, including land use, chemical pollution, biodiversity, and climate change, are not such shining stories of collective success—yet.

With the Planetary Boundaries as their guide, proof of collective success with the ozone layer, and Sherry, Mario, and Paul as a model, a new genre of Earth System scientists is emerging to collaborate across disciplines and borders to solve a global crisis that will determine the future of many generations to come. At the epicenter of this global movement are the Deep Connections between Johan, Will,

Katherine, and a growing community of other renowned scientists, like Kevin Noone (whom you met briefly in chapter five).

For Johan, Will, and Katherine, deep trust, scientific rigor, and respect inform every aspect of their work together, allowing them to be completely frank with one another. Much like the partnership of Sherry and Mario, there's no competition for prestige among them, no displays of ego or jealousy. "We are completely free from that," Johan said. "It's just a seamless, respectful partnership that makes it so easy." Through their close work together they can see beyond their own limitations and gain a fuller understanding of the problem. "I don't like to work on my own because it's much more fun to get multiple ideas, try to synthesize them," said Will. "That's how you generate new knowledge."

The Planetary Boundaries framework scientifically identifies the Earth System processes and systems that contribute to regulating the functioning and ultimately the state of the entire Earth System. An attempt was made by some of the world's best scientists to quantify a scientific range of key control variables for each boundary process and system. Stay within this boundary range and we remain in a "safe operating space." Go beyond the safe boundary and we enter first the scientific uncertainty zone, where things can start to go wrong, and then a very high-risk zone. Currently science estimates that four of the nine boundaries have been transgressed, two into the uncertainty zone (climate change and land-use change), and two into the high-risk zone (loss of biodiversity and overloading of nitrogen and phosphorus).

When ozone depletion crossed the threshold into the danger zone, a courageous collective trusted the science and dedicated their lives to bringing the world together to successfully innovate and bring us back into a safe operating space.

With four boundaries already transgressed and others at risk, our inaction is a direct threat to the future of generations to come. Now is the moment to stand on the shoulders of the ozone community and join forces in the greatest challenge and opportunity of our lives.

This analysis and tool set a scientific challenge for the world to come together across sectors to innovate and create solutions, just as the ozone community did. It's a challenge that requires looking at the world and the Planetary Boundaries as inherently interconnected. "Modern science tends to take a complex system and break it down and focus on disciplinary areas of expertise," said Will. "People like to run off with their favorite boundary, work on it at great depth, and forget that they're actually connected."

The Planetary Boundaries framework helps us understand the interconnectedness not just of Earth's many subsystems, but those of all humanity. "Natural science has always been about describing objects and things," Katherine said. "We're beginning to realize, in many contexts, it's interactions that life is really all about."

Back in Davos at the *Big World, Small Planet* book launch, I pushed through the snow and made it to the cozy Swiss restaurant just in time to sneak into the back of the room, where I joined a handful of earnest systems geeks like me. Since that moment, I've reflected on how we get the world to collaborate on a scale larger than we've ever imagined to tackle complex, interconnected issues.

One place we can start is celebrating partners like Sherry, Mario, Paul, Mostafa, Stephen, Jonathan, Joe, Brian, Johan, Katherine, and Will—and so many others who dedicate their lives to the collective good. It seems odd to me that the ozone success story and the Planetary Boundaries are not talked about in every school, university, and conversation about collaborating at scale. Perhaps we are so programmed to applaud individual superheroes that we shy away from celebrating collectives of leaders who are driving the systemic change that we so desperately need.

Imagine what a different world we would live in if these collaborators became the role models for the future of leadership.

I'm convinced that the only way we are ever going to tackle the complexities of our shared challenges is by collaborating on a global scale, as we saw in the previous chapter. And the only way to do that is to build the Deep Connections that allow us to move forward together without becoming overwhelmed by fear.

This movement toward cooperation will demand a revolution of social virtues.

As I'm writing this book, the world is more divided than ever before, stoked by a culture of fear and self-interest. We've ripped apart much of the cultural fabric that was keeping humanity connected, and we've lost touch with the natural world. In the 2017 Edelman Trust Barometer, 53 percent of respondents felt that government, business, and media systems were failing them, and out of that group, 83 percent feared the erosion of social values.

In 2020, COVID-19 ignored our man-made borders, took advantage of our selfish individualism, and showed the world just how interconnected we all are. It also shone a spotlight on how unprepared humanity is to collectively respond to crises that scoff at national and global borders. As the virus ripped through the world, I was reminded of a plea from a young Egyptian man who courageously stood up in an intergenerational leader meeting we were hosting in Cairo in 2012: "When will politicians around the world realize that the only borders left are on old maps?"

Hopefully soon.

This global pandemic brought out the worst and best in humanity. People, companies, and nations hoarded and profiteered from lifesaving medical supplies, fights broke out over frozen food, and people put others' lives at risk through their self-centered actions. Health workers sacrificed themselves for their communities, competitors collaborated on vaccines, and citizens came together to support the most vulnerable in their communities. I watched in awe as a group of African leaders, led by President Cyril Ramaphosa and including others such as Strive Masiyiwa, Dr. John Nkengasong, Donald Kaberuka, Trevor Manuel, and Ngozi Okonjo-Iweala, mobilized financing for Africa, secured vaccines, and built a medical supplies platform to fight the pandemic. A wise continent-wide response to ensure no country and no individual was left behind. Their focus on collective interest put many other global leaders to shame.

Even when everyone seemed to realize that the one thing they missed was human connection, many leaders around the world used the pandemic as a moment to promote divided national and personal agendas.

Part of the issue is that technology is often separating rather than connecting us. An NBC News poll in May 2021 showed that nearly two-thirds of Americans feel that social media platforms are tearing us apart rather than uniting us. I was reminded of this one early morning in New York City when I passed a schoolyard. My heart filled with memories: wild play, a buzzing hive of friends, a sea of gangly legs and arms all trying to kick the same ball amid an ever-increasing chorus of joyous shrieks. Yet the reality in front of me was very different. Uniformed children were sitting all by themselves, backs hunched, huddled over their phones. The stillness stopped me cold. No joyous shrieks, no running, no laughter, no play, no connection with each other. I know this was just one moment in one schoolyard. Nevertheless, this scene struck me as the norm we might be headed toward, the new world order that has grown around us.

As we've seen from the partnership stories in this book, we can choose a future in which we rise above an obsession with individual gain, away from domination and toward a partnership mentality, where technology could become a tool to aid meaningful connection and to create solutions at scale. We could incentivize people and organizations to collaborate for the benefit of humanity and the planet. Or we could take the other path and fall back into our warped measures of success linked to profit, power, meaningless online "friends," and individual achievement.

To choose the right path, we need to be vigilant in shifting society's measure of success from fame and money to the meaningful relationships we've nurtured and how we can use our time wisely to make other people's lives better. Richard Reed, cofounder of Innocent Drinks, explained his measure of a life well lived: "Happiness and success are about collaboration, your relationships, how much you invest in them, how much time you spend with those people that nourish you the most, and how much you help those people."

As we create new measures of success, we must start by constantly asking, "Who is missing from the conversation?" The growing gap in equality and the divides perpetuated by technology's ability to silo information distribution have separated us from the Deep Connections that could help us change the world. Before I conducted some of the interviews in this book, I was hesitant, thinking that my views might be so different that I would never be able to enjoy the discussion and learn something new. How wrong I was. It made me realize how siloed I was in my thinking and how important it is to find Deep Connections that are radically different and that will unsettle me.

We can shift the world from a frame of competition to one of cooperation. When people don't have to be perfect, the door is opened to complementary partnering. "We waste so many cycles on being competitive versus collaborative as human beings," shared Keith Yamashita. "Who's better, who's right, who gets to call the shot, who's in power—if we could just take all of that wasted energy and apply it to what could I bring, what could you bring, then together we could do something extraordinary."

Reimagining the world can begin with nurturing Deep Connections of meaning and love in our lives, and using them as epicenters for collaborations at a scale we cannot yet comprehend. We can leave behind the baggage we've accumulated through self-interested individualism—material things, misguided notions of fame, and the absence of justice in our communities. We can build strong ecosystems of trust, respect, and belief in each other that serve as beacons for a positive revolution of love.

The wisdom from the partnerships who generously shared their stories in this book is a bright light of hope. They've demonstrated that the Six Degrees of Connection can lead to meaningful relationships for a better life, businesses, and world. They've also shown us how to use these Deep Connections as a foundation for large-scale collaborations.

We already know we can do it. We have closed the ozone hole, we've stopped smallpox, we've built successful businesses on trust and community, and we've learned how to fly with the sun's energy. We've felt the kindness and compassion of meaningful relationships.

The time I've spent with these great partnerships over the past decade has been some of the most rewarding of my life. Each of their interviews was bursting with curiosity, joy, and love. It was (a good) contagious.

One of the moments I will treasure forever is spending two days with Anthony Ray Hinton and Lester Bailey (whom you met in chapter four) at their homes in Quinton, Alabama. My dear friend Shannon Sedgwick Davis joined us for the interview, and afterward, we shared a lovely meal and then walked about thirty feet to the very tiny church that sits sandwiched between Ray's and Lester's homes. Entering the church, we could almost feel the walls reverberating with song from that week's worship service.

As we walked down the rickety staircase of this well-loved church onto the peaceful dirt road among the towering pine trees, Ray gently said, "My wish for everyone is to have a friend like Lester."

There is nothing more important than the partnerships that make you who you are in this world.

Who and what will you
love into being?

Gratitude

An invisible red thread connects those
destined to meet, regardless of time, place,
or circumstances. The thread may stretch or
tangle, but never break.

—Chinese Proverb

Writing this book and building the not-for-profit it supports, Plus Wonder, has been a humbling, wondrous experience. A perfect example of the power of partnership and the collective effort of so many brilliant people. There is absolutely no way I could have done this on my own. This fifteen-year collaborative effort has nurtured so many friendships who have shaped this book and shaped me in the process. It has made me even more certain that nothing is more important than investing in the relationships that shape who we are in this world, and in turn shape the individual and collective change we can make in the world.

I can never express my overwhelming gratitude to so many of you on a couple of pages, but here goes an attempt at starting the process. . . .

To the sixty-plus partnerships and collectives (see page 219) who generously shared their wisdom and personal experiences—none of this would exist without you. Every interview was like a master class in how to be a great partner and a good human being. Filled with laughter, love, tears, and a renewed sense of wonder in the world. Thank you for giving so much of yourself. We are all in debt to you. An extra note of thanks to The Elders. I feel so privileged to have learned from your relationships over the last seventeen years. Your Deep Connections sparked the idea for Plus Wonder and changed the course of my life.

To the core Plus Wonder Collective—Andrea Brenninkmeijer, Joann (Jo) McPike, Ellie Kanner, Kelly Hallman, John Stares, Shannon Sedgwick Davis, Cindy Mercer, Todd Holcomb, Keith Yamashita, Mich Ahern, and Lisa Weeks Valiant. This book and Plus Wonder are here because of you. Thanks for standing together during the many ups and downs, for your all-in support, your laughter, your wisdom, and your belief that partnering and collaborating will change the world. I feel blessed to be on this exciting journey with you and can't wait to share this wisdom as widely as possible.

Thanks to Adrian Zackheim and Simon Sinek for taking the risk on this book when so many others thought it was a crazy idea. Your wisdom, belief, and thoughtful direction have made this a far, far better book and movement. Thanks for spending the time with me to shape a much bigger idea that will hopefully spark many Deep Connections and meaningful collaborations in the world. Thanks to the entire Optimism Press and Portfolio teams, especially Merry Sun whose patience and calm intelligence have guided this book every step of the way. I so appreciate you wading through many weeds with me to create the clarity to do justice to the wisdom from the sixty-plus partnerships. Thanks to Megan McCormack, DeQuan Foster, Mary Kate Skehan, Jessica Regione, Brian Lemus, and Mike Brown for your enthusiasm and hard work—you are a brilliant team!

This book is filled with the ideas, hard work, love, and critical insights from so many people. A very special thanks to Laurie Flynn for your enthusiasm, your comforting heart, and your help in shaping a core thread in this book, the ozone story and other collaboration stories. Laurie and the wonderful Lisa Weeks Valiant gave this book your all and I will forever be thankful for your hard work on many long nights, weekends, and last-minute rushes. Special thanks also to Sara Grace; your ability to step back, see the bigger picture, cut through the clutter, ask the right questions, and tighten story lines is second to none. Laurie, Sara, and Lisa, your positive energy and partnership have made the creation of this book a joy. To David Moldawer for your patience, your expert writing skills, and your invaluable challenges to ensure this book was the best it could be. You were a critical force in transforming this from a bundle of ideas to a far more interesting book.

Andrea, Greg, and Eric Alan, our "kitchen table" discussions breathed life into the idea and grounded it in Deep Connection. I'll forever be thankful to all of you for the time, love, and insight you brought to this, including the brainstorm standing by your fridge where "The Six Degrees of Connection" phrase was born!

To Ajaz Ahmed and Johnny Budden from AKQA—your generosity, brilliant creative skills, and open-hearted collaboration with the wonderful Portfolio design team created an elegant, compelling, and beautiful cover. Thanks also Ajaz for the many years of friendship. To Martin Hill and Philippa Jones for your stunning environmental sculptures that added the magic of Mother Nature to the book. To

Milos Perovic, Ian Brewer, Jo, and the whole team from NoFormat, thanks so much for helping us bring the Six Degrees of Connection and Plus Wonder to life in the book and online. And to the wonderful, committed education team, Breanna Morsadi, Ashley Silver, Nicholas Martino, and Jo—your wisdom, insights, and passion helped view this wisdom from the perspective of students and teachers. Can't wait to realize our dream to have the wisdom from these partnerships and collectives in every school! A big thanks to Mel Agace for all your hard work and creative brilliance in producing the initial videos, and to Steven Sawalich and David Alexander for taking the baton and producing hundreds of beautiful videos. And, of course, Ellie Kanner, you've put so much love and personal time into shaping hundreds of hours of footage into captivating story lines—we've been so lucky to have you leading this! And to Les Copland whose design expertise has transformed many a complex idea into something simple and captivating.

Thanks to Richard Branson for a wonderful partnership over the past twenty-plus years. Your commitment to positive impact and your consistent approach to collaborating has given me the opportunity to listen and learn from some of the best collaborators in the world. I will forever be thankful to you for your belief in me, and your belief that absolutely anything is possible. What an enormous privilege it has been to work with you and our partners to create so many meaningful collectives. Thanks to the rest of the Branson family, Joan, Holly, and Sam, for your love and support over the years. And, of course, to the wonderful Vanessa Branson and Flo Devereux, what an adventure it has been!

Great gratitude to Peter Gabriel, who is a beacon of cooperation. Thanks for creating the name Plus Wonder (in an afternoon) and believing in the power of partnerships to change the world. Your steadfast encouragement (along with your water fights with Richard) kept me smiling over the years.

To Johan Rockström who got me obsessed with the success of the Montreal Protocol and the community who committed their lives to protecting the ozone layer. Your vision with Planetary Boundaries is one of the most important collective efforts we need to get behind for the survival of humanity and the planet.

To the Virgin Unite family—so many magic moments from our adventures are captured in this book. I feel so fortunate every day to have the chance to work with so many wonderful people. A special thanks to Sue Hale, Nicola Elliot, and Helen Clarke, who have shared many magnetic (and often crazy) moments as we built collectives like The Elders and The B Team.

And, of course, thanks to my amazing husband, Chris Waddell, for your enduring kindness, for your unconditional love, and simply for always being there. I'm so lucky to have you as my life partner. Thanks also to the whole Waddell and Oelwang clans for all your love and patience with my crazy ideas and relentless work hours.

So many of you have been part of this collective to inspire and bring to life *Partnering* and Plus Wonder. . . . I will be forever grateful to all of you. . . .

Kathy Calvin, José María Figueres, George Polk, Jochen Zeitz, Joanna Rees, Sharon Johnson, Robin Bowman, Chandra Jesse, Peter Beikmanis, Nathan Rosenberg, Alexander Grashow, Anna Gowdridge, Van Jones, Anthony Ray Hinton, Lester Bailey, Pat Mitchell, Jane Tewson, Kaushik Viswanath, Chantel Hamilton, Adam Grant, Casey Gerald, Gregory David Roberts, Bill Meyers, Jane Cavolina, Steve Goodey, Kym Walton, Paul O'Sullivan, Sanjeev Gandhi, Kumi Naidoo, Angela

Dower, Megan DeNew Wussow, Tom Bonney, Kathleen Romley, Noemi Weiss, Charlotte Goodman, Su Lee, Bill Place, Betsy Coyle, Leonide Delgatto, Heerad Sabeti, Jim Courtney, Nane Annan, Emily Sayer, Geraldine Corbett, Jackie McQuillan, Paul Polman, Bob Collymore, Sharan Burrow, Mark Gilmour, Christine Choi, Arianna Huffington, Greg Rose, Halla Tomasdottir, Radek & Helen Sali, Phil Weiner, Roma Khanna, Jules Kortenhorst, Marty Pickett, Holly Peppe, Maria Eitel, Gina Murdock, Deneen Howell, Jennifer Aaker, Yanik Silver, Charlie Garcia, Naomi Bagdonas, Lelia Akahloun, Graça Machel, Strive & Tsitsi Masiyiwa, Alexia Hargrave, Susan Goldsmith, Morley Kamen, Amber Kelleher, the Price family, Tobi, Ruby, Basha, Knobbe Martens, Perlman & Perlman, Julianne Holt-Lunstad, SD Squared, Wondros, Mpho Tutu . . . and many more . . .

Plus Wonder Partnerships

Two country boys that never had anything,
yet we were the richest of all. We had each
other. We had the whole world.

—Anthony Ray Hinton

With great gratitude to the enduring partnerships who shared their wisdom through their honest and profound stories to inspire Deep Connections of purpose in the world.

All proceeds from this book will be donated to select partner charities and the not-for-profit Plus Wonder. Please join our community at www.pluswonder.org.

1. Stephen O. Andersen, Mario Molina, Sherwood Rowland, and Mostafa Tolba, friends, economists, and scientists, partners in closing the ozone hole

2. Phil Aroneanu, Will Bates, Kelly Blynn, May Boeve, Jamie Henn, Bill McKibben, Jeremy Osborn, and Jon Warnow, friends, cofounders of 350.org

3. Paul Bennett and Jim Cooper, spouses, partners in designing a better world

4. David Blankenhorn and John Wood Jr., friends, partners in depolarizing America

5. Erika Boyd and Kirsten Ussery, cofounders of Detroit
    Vegan Soul

6. Stewart Brand and Ryan Phelan, spouses, cofounders
    of Revive & Restore

7. Richard Branson and Peter Gabriel, friends, partners in
    peace and human rights

8. Larry and Girija Brilliant, spouses, partners in the
    collective that eradicated smallpox

9. Tim and Gaynor Brown, spouses, partners in designing
    better lives

10. Gro and Arne Brundtland, spouses, partners in global
    health, international development, and life

11. Penelope Canan and Nancy Reichman, colleagues,
    friends, partners in protecting the ozone layer

12. Jimmy and Rosalynn Carter, thirty-ninth president
    and first lady of the United States of America,
    cofounders of the Carter Center

13. Ray Chambers and Peter Chernin, friends, cofounders
    of Malaria No More

14. Robin Chase and Cameron Russell, family, activists for
    climate change and the new economy

15. Lawrence Chickering and Jim Turner, friends,
    cofounders of *The Transpartisan Review*

16. Ben Cohen and Jerry Greenfield, friends, cofounders
    of Ben & Jerry's

17. Andrea and Barry Coleman, spouses, cofounders of Riders for Health

18. Jo Confino and Paz Perlman, spouses, partners inspiring harmony with Earth and life

19. Severn and Sarika Cullis-Suzuki, sisters, environmental activists, executive director and member, David Suzuki Foundation

20. Wade Davis and Carroll Dunham, friends, partners in the beauty, wisdom, and spirituality of Indigenous cultures

21. Bill Draper, Robin Richards Donohoe, Rob Kaplan, Jim Bildner, and Christy Chin, partners and change makers, the DRK Foundation

22. Sylvia Earle and the ocean, friend, marine biologist, National Geographic Explorer-in-Residence, and founder of Mission Blue

23. Mick and Caskey Ebeling, spouses, cofounders of Not Impossible Labs and Not Impossible Foundation

24. Sangu, Edmund, and Banguu Delle, brothers, cofounders of Golden Palm Investments

25. Eve Ellis and Annette Niemtzow, spouses, partners in empowering women

26. Joseph Farman, Brian G. Gardiner, and Jonathan Shanklin—friends, scientists, partners in discovering the ozone hole

27. Christiana and José María Figueres, siblings, humanitarians, climate change leaders

28. Joe Gebbia, Brian Chesky, and Nathan Blecharczyk, friends, cofounders of Airbnb

29. Robert P. George and Cornel West, brothers, friends, fellow citizens, partners in truth-seeking

30. Lord Hastings of Scarisbrick CBE and Gloria Abramoff FRSA, friends, House of Lords, BBC Media and social engagement, partners in empowering better global social conditions

31. Tony and Pat Hawk, siblings, partners in enriching the lives of youth through skateboarding

32. Martin Hill and Philippa Jones, partners in life, art, and nature

33. Anthony Ray Hinton and Lester Bailey, best friends for life, partners in advocating for ending the death penalty

34. Bert and John Jacobs, brothers, cofounders of Life is Good

35. Dereck and Beverly Joubert, spouses, National Geographic Explorers, founders of Big Cats Initiative, cofounders of Great Plains Conservation

36. Sarah Kay and Phil Kaye, friends, codirectors of Project VOICE

37. Mark Kelly and Gabby Giffords, spouses, advocates, public servants

38. Azim Khamisa and Ples Felix, friends, partners in the Tariq Khamisa Foundation

39. Andy Kuper and Jim Roth, friends, founder and cofounder of LeapFrog Investments

40. Lindsay and David Levin, spouses, change makers in education and leadership

41. Amory and Judy Lovins, spouses, partners in creating the new energy future

42. Andrew Maxwell Mangino and Kanya Balakrishna, life partners, cofounders of the Future Project

43. Cindy Mercer and Addison Fischer, friends, cofounders of Planet Heritage

44. Pat Mitchell and Scott Seydel, spouses, media innovator and environmental business champion

45. Jacqueline Novogratz and Chris Anderson, spouses, partners in social entrepreneurship

46. Ngozi Okonjo-Iweala and Uzodinma Iweala, family, director-general of the World Trade Organization; author, doctor, and film producer; partners for a fairer world

47. Bertrand Piccard and André Borschberg, friends, cofounders of Solar Impulse

48. Alex Rappaport and Blake Harrison, friends, cofounders of Flocabulary

49. Donna Red Wing and Bob Vander Plaats, friends, social justice activist and president and CEO of the Family Leader

50. Chris Redlitz and Beverly Parenti, spouses, cofounders of the Last Mile

51. Richard Reed, Adam Balon, and Jon Wright, friends, cofounders of Innocent Drinks and JamJar Investments

52. Katherine Richardson, Johan Rockström, and Will Steffen, friends, Earth System scientists, and co-creators of the Planetary Boundaries

53. Robbie Schingler and Will Marshall, friends, cofounders of Planet

54. Luiz Seabra, Pedros Passos, and Guilherme Leal, friends, cofounders of Natura

55. Kevin Starr and Henry Arnhold, friends, cofounders of the Mulago Foundation

56. Jane Tewson and Charles Lane, spouses, partners in working for a fair and just world

57. Jagdish D. Thakkar, Ashish J. Thakkar, Ahuti Chug, and Rona Kotecha, family, partners in Mara Foundation and Mara Group

58. Ned Tozun and Sam Goldman, friends, cofounders of d.light

59. Desmond and Leah Tutu, spouses, partners in peace, human rights, freedom, and life

60. Deborah Willis and Hank Willis Thomas, family, artists united by love and art to change the world

61. Sheryl WuDunn and Nicholas Kristof, spouses, Pulitzer Prize–winning journalists, coauthors of *Half the Sky*, *A Path Appears*, and *Tightrope*

62. Keith Yamashita and Todd Holcomb, spouses, partners in using creativity as a catalyst for societal change

63. Jacki and Greg Zehner, spouses, cofounders of the Jacquelyn and Gregory Zehner Foundation

Six Degrees of Connection Shorthand

A guide for building connections that matter. From the collective wisdom of over sixty of some of the greatest partnerships of our time.

 First Degree: Something Bigger—Lift your purpose through meaningful partnerships. Deepen your connection by becoming part of something bigger.

 Second Degree: All-In—Feel safe in the relationship and know you 100 percent have each other's backs for the long run. This gives you the freedom and confidence to do something bigger.

 Third Degree: The Ecosystem—Stay all-in through a moral ecosystem, alive with the daily practice of six essential virtues. These are Enduring Trust, Unshakable Mutual Respect, United Belief, Shared Humility, Nurturing Generosity, and Compassionate

Empathy. Over time, they become reflexive responses, creating an environment of kindness, grace, and unconditional love.

Fourth Degree: Magnetic Moments—Stay connected and strengthen your ecosystem through intentional practices, rituals, and traditions that keep curiosity and wonder alive, create space for honest communication, spark unlimited joy, and build a wider supportive community.

Fifth Degree: Celebrate Friction—Take the heat out of conflict and turn it into a learning opportunity. Ignite sparks of creative combustion for shared solutions and greater connection, staying all-in and focused on something bigger.

Sixth Degree: Collective Connections—A framework of design principles to scale collaborations, with Deep Connections at the center as role models, hubs of momentum, and connective tissue.

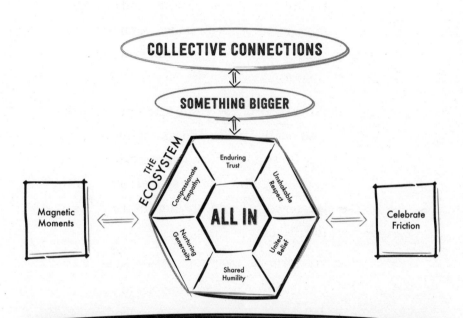

COLLECTIVE CONNECTIONS

SOMETHING BIGGER

THE ECOSYSTEM

Enduring Trust

Compassionate Empathy

Unshakable Respect

ALL IN

Nurturing Generosity

United Belief

Shared Humility

Magnetic Moments

Celebrate Friction

SIX DEGREES OF CONNECTION™ FRAMEWORK FOR DEEP CONNECTIONS

Words of Wisdom and Collaborative Resources

The Six Degrees of Connection framework is a combination of the collective wisdom of over sixty enduring partnerships of purpose. Practicing these six consistent characteristics of great partnerships will change your relationships, your companies, and your life for the better. Most important, it will change other people's lives for the better, and it just might lead to collaborations that will change the world.

Here are some words of wisdom from the Plus Wonder partners, videos for further insights, and places to go to learn more about the Six Degrees of Connection:

First Degree: Something Bigger

Lift your purpose through your meaningful partnerships. Deepen your connection by becoming part of something bigger.

Words of Wisdom

- *"We had an end purpose that was so wonderful that if we could make it become a reality, we were going to give it everything."* —Richard Branson

- *"One plus one can equal a thousand—you are not going to do that on your own! One thing we aligned on was the idea that making a lot of money didn't really turn us on in and of itself, or the idea of just building a business didn't really turn us on. It was the idea that maybe the business could be utilized for something bigger."* —Bert Jacobs

- *"We felt we could do this together and I had one set of skills, Barry had another set of skills, but we had a united mission, purpose, and a belief that we could actually do this."* —Andrea Coleman

- *"We have a secret weapon and it's not just the two of us but we have a common goal, and our third partner in this is nature and conservation, so we have a higher goal and it's a shared one and it's mutual."* —Dereck Joubert

- *"If it's a big mission, it's outside of reach, and that can be your North Star, that can help you in the tumultuous waters of highs and lows . . . and so you don't lose your path. So having a big mission that's worthy of all of the energy and all the sacrifices that you need to do if you're creating something in this world."* —Robbie Schingler

Explore Something Bigger:

Additional Resources

- Simon Sinek wrote the book *Start with Why* (New York: Portfolio, 2009). Also watch his TED Talk, "How Great Leaders Inspire Action," https://www.ted.com/talks /simon_sinek_how_great_leaders_inspire_action.

- Researchers from University College London, Princeton University, and Stony Brook University found that people who have a sense of purpose and meaning tend to live longer (Andrew Steptoe, Angus Deaton, and Arthur A. Stone, "Subjective Wellbeing, Health, and Ageing," *Lancet* 385, no. 9968 [2015]: 640–48). A recent study (Daryl R. Van Tongeren et al., "Prosociality Enhances Meaning in Life," *Journal of Positive Psychology* 11, no. 3 [2016]: 225–36) reported strong relationships as a key feature for enhancing meaning in life.

- An overview of the neuroscience study on the importance of Purpose in Life (PIL): Adam Kaplin and

Laura Anzaldi, "New Movement in Neuroscience: A Purpose-Driven Life," *Cerebrum* 7 (May–June 2015): 7.

- Investigate the links between purpose and health with National Public Radio's "What's Your Purpose? Finding a Sense of Meaning in Life Is Linked to Health," by Mara Gordin (May 25, 2019), https://www.npr.org/sections /health-shots/2019/05/25/726695968/whats-your -purpose-finding-a-sense-of-meaning-in-life-is-linked -to-health.

Second Degree: All-In

Feel safe in the relationship and know you 100 percent have each other's back for the long run. This gives you the freedom and confidence to do something bigger.

Words of Wisdom

- *"I know Scott supports me 100 percent, that he's my best friend."* —Pat Mitchell

- *"That's the essence of it, really be there. Zen master Thich Nhat Hanh always says the best present you can give to your partner is just to be there. Just so simple."* —Paz Perlman

- *"It's making a commitment to the commitment."*
  —Jacqueline Novogratz

- *"Looking out for long-term well-being—when so many others are focused on short-term gain."* —Robin Chase

- *"Deep inside you become a different person by intimately knowing someone else."* —Charles Lane

- *"If you can get over the fear of the leap of loving before being loved, I think that's the start of it all. And that goes for friendships, and it goes for business partnerships. And it goes for people you have only recently met. It's, are you okay showing up as the most loving version of yourself with the thought there may be no return? But, when you do it, it always returns."* —Keith Yamashita

- *"The thing I most value is I have this certain North Star that I know I can come back to that just lays out: this is reality— this is truth. This is a touchstone that I can go to at any point, and Lindsay just gives that to me, every day."*
  —David Levin

Explore All-In:

Additional Resources

- Dan Buettner, author of *The Blue Zones* (Washington, DC: National Geographic, 2012), spent years studying the longest-living communities in the world to find out their secrets to longevity, which include enduring all-in relationships.

- Harvard's Grant Study ("Study of Adult Development," https://www.adultdevelopmentstudy.org /grantandglueckstudy) has followed 268 people over eighty years of their lives. George Vaillant, the director of the study for three decades, says, "When the study began, nobody cared about empathy or attachment, but the key to healthy aging is relationships, relationships, relationships."

- Dr. Brené Brown, from the University of Houston Graduate College of Social Work, has spent years studying vulnerability, courage, worthiness, and shame. Her TED Talk, "The Power of Vulnerability"

(June 2010, https://www.ted.com/talks/brene_brown
_the_power_of_vulnerability?language=en), helps to
explain how embracing vulnerability can assist us in
being more all-in.

- In 2019, the American Psychological Association
  published a meta-analysis of more than two decades of
  research revealing how positive relationships boost
  self-esteem, and vice versa. This longitudinal study
  shows us how the quality of our relationships and the
  type of feedback we receive from our Deep Connections
  directly links to who we become and what we believe
  we can achieve in this world. See Michelle A. Harris and
  Ulrich Orth, "The Link Between Self-Esteem and Social
  Relationships: A Meta-Analysis of Longitudinal
  Studies," *Journal of Personality and Social Psychology* 119,
  no. 6 (2020): 1459–77, https://www.apa.org/pubs
  /journals/releases/psp-pspp0000265.pdf.

Third Degree: The Ecosystem

Stay all-in through a moral ecosystem, alive with the daily practice of
six essential virtues.

Words of Wisdom

- *"Well, we have shared values, without a shadow of doubt."* —Barry Coleman

- *"I think that it is important in any partnership that it has to transcend cognitive and even emotional connection. It has to get to that deep spiritual connection for you to sustain, for you to be trusting, for you to be respectful, for you to be able to look at conflict as an opportunity to be able to create love and unity."* —Azim Khamisa

- *"Values are extremely important and have been, in large part, the most important thing . . . it's how people construct their characters and how they behave in the world."* —Uzodinma Iweala

- *"When your partner speaks, the world stops."* —Paul Bennett

Explore the Ecosystem:

Additional Resources

- The John Templeton Foundation currently hosts a number of studies around the importance of virtues in its Character Virtue Development program (https://www.templeton.org/funding-areas/character-virtue-development).

- Dave Phillips is a leadership mentor who also works on virtues for teams and leaders—https://www.dphillips.com.

- The Foundation for a Better Life (https://www.passiton.com/who-we-are) focuses on promoting values and virtues.

- The School of Life (https://www.theschooloflife.com) is an education company for emotional learning that explores many of the six virtues.

- Learn more about relationship expert John Gottman's Four Horsemen and the role they play in predicting the health of a relationship ecosystem. See Ellie Lisitsa, "The Four Horsemen: Criticism, Contempt, Defensiveness, and Stonewalling," Gottman Institute, April 23, 2013, https://www.gottman.com/blog/the-four-horsemen-recognizing-criticism-contempt-defensiveness-and-stonewalling/.

- According to Noam Wasserman, author of *The Founder's Dilemmas* (Princeton, NJ: Princeton University Press, 2012) and *Life Is a Startup* (Stanford, CA: Stanford University Press, 2019), nearly two-thirds of start-ups fail because the founding team or partnership doesn't build the close relationship and values it needs to succeed.

Words of Wisdom: Enduring Trust

- *"Trust. You can't really have a relationship unless you have trust."* —Jim Cooper

- *"Trust is the most efficient thing going in a business."* —Richard Reed

- *"There were lots of times that we have tried things and not succeeded, but there's always been this fundamental trust that we are aligned around the ultimate purpose, and that gives us space as individuals to try things, and grow, and fail . . . just knowing the other person always has our back."* —Kanya Balakrishna

- *"I think that trust develops . . . trust is vital to any relationship. There is a joyfulness in companionship built* on trust. *Relationships evolve if nurtured, each thriving with the other's support, but the bedrock is always going to be trust.*" —Dereck Joubert

- "*Profound trust is incremental in steps. With a quantum jump over time.*" —Kevin Starr

Explore Enduring Trust:

Additional Resources

- The Edelman Trust Barometer (https://www.edelman .com/trust/2021-trust-barometer) tracks global trust across a range of institutions in over thirty-three countries.

- Trust researcher Rachel Botsman recently wrote a beautiful book, *Who Can You Trust?* (New York: Portfolio, 2017), articulating the close relationship between trust and risk. Her talks on trust and collaboration in the digital realm can be found on the TED website (https://www.ted.com/speakers/rachel _botsman).

- Gottman redefines trust as an action. Read about the Gottman Institute's ATTUNE Model (Zach Brittle, "How to Build Trust in Your Relationship," July 17, 2015, Gottman Institute, https://www.gottman.com/blog /trust/).

- Check out this great breakdown of "The Neuroscience of Trust" from the *Harvard Business Review* that outlines ways to build a culture of trust in a company (Paul J. Zak, January–February 2017, https://hbr.org/2017/01 /the-neuroscience-of-trust).

- Harvard University political scientist and author Robert Putnam wrote the classic book on social capital, *Bowling Alone* (New York: Simon & Schuster, 2000), which documents the dramatic decline of trust and community in the United States over the past fifty years.

- Penn State's Center for Economic and Community Development shared "The Role and Importance of Building Trust" in 2008 (https://aese.psu.edu/research /centers/cecd/engagement-toolbox/role-importance-of -building-trust).

Words of Wisdom: Unshakable Mutual Respect

- *"He learned to respect what I could do, and I learned to respect what he could do. I think this made a huge difference, as I was very insecure about what I was capable of and*

Jimmy believed that I could do anything." —Rosalynn
Carter

- *"I think, first of all, it's the very simplest thing which is deep listening, I think a profound respect, a flexibility, or a willingness to hear something that you may not agree with and try that on for a moment, see what it feels like, step into that other person's shoes."* —Carroll Dunham

- *"In a partnership that works really well, and you have a lot of respect for the other person, you leave a lot of room for potential. So you know what the other person's good at, but you are ready to support and cheer on that other potential."* —Cameron Russell

- *"When we got a chance to just revel in each other's humanity, it didn't take too much time for us to see that we had something even deeper than civility, tolerance. We had a deep love and respect for one another that was in no way reducible to politics, that we had a deep brotherhood that is in no way threatened by disagreement on certain public policy."* —Cornel West

Explore Unshakable Mutual Respect:

Additional Resources

- Kristie Rogers of Marquette University, a researcher of respect in the workplace, shares her findings on the difference between earned respect and owed respect in her article "Do Your Employees Feel Respected?" (*Harvard Business Review*, July–August 2018).

- In a recent survey of nearly twenty thousand employees worldwide by Georgetown University's Christine Porath, respondents ranked respect as the most important leadership behavior. Check out her TEDx Talk, "Why Being Respectful to Your Coworkers Is Good for Business" (https://www.ted.com/talks/christine _porath_why_being_respectful_to_your_coworkers_is _good_for_business?language=en).

- Jim Taylor, PhD, shares his concerns about feeling the "onslaught of disrespect" in his article in *Psychology Today*, "Parenting: Respect Starts at Home" (January 5, 2010, https://www.psychologytoday.com/us/blog

/the-power-prime/201001/parenting-respect-starts
-home).

- "The Price of Incivility," by Christine Porath and
  Christine Pearson (*Harvard Business Review*, January–
  February 2013, https://hbr.org/2013/01/the-price-of
  -incivility), supports this assertion, finding that 80
  percent of employees treated uncivilly spend significant
  work time ruminating on the bad behavior, and 48
  percent deliberately reduce their effort.

Words of Wisdom: United Belief

- *"Each time you're starting something it's so painful, sort of
  giving birth to these organizations. Many times I've said,
  can I quit now, can I just give up, and Stewart has always
  been there to say, absolutely don't give up, you know you can
  do this."* —Ryan Phelan

- *"Together we go places that we wouldn't individually have
  the fortitude or the insight to go to."* —Caskey Ebeling

- *"There's this centerpiece that I think is more the DNA of our
  relationship, where it is about that sense of possibility in the
  world."* —Todd Holcomb

- *"Would we take as many risks if we were not partners? I
  would say no. I would say, I'm sure, no. I wouldn't have even
  thought about it. I wouldn't have had the level of curiosity.
  And I don't think I would have had the confidence."* —Eve
  Ellis

- *"And we've forgotten that belief and metaphor is what's always driven the human spirit. In other words the measure of a culture is not just what they do but the quality of their aspirations, the metaphors that propel them forward."*
—Wade Davis

Explore United Belief:

Additional Resources

- The *New York Times* bestselling author Daniel Coyle's book *The Culture Code* (New York: Bantam Books, 2018) shows how groups can create great things through cultures of cohesion and cooperation.

- Jennifer Michael Hecht, poet, philosopher, and historian, teaches us how "we believe each other into being," emphasizing that "sometimes when you can't see what's important about you, other people can." Listen to her poignant interview with Krista Tippett on the podcast *Becoming Wise* ("We Believe Each Other into Being," On Being, last updated April 1, 2019, https://onbeing.org/programs/we-believe

-each-other-into-being-jennifer-michael-hecht/)
or enjoy her wisdom on our need for one
another in an extended version of the interview on the
podcast *On Being with Krista Tippett* (https://onbeing
.org/programs/jennifer-michael-hecht-we-believe-each
-other-into-being-on-being/). Please note: Both
interviews touch on suicide.

- Superteacher Rita Pierson shares in her TED Talk that
  "every kid needs a champion" (May 2013, https://www
  .ted.com/talks/rita_pierson_every_kid_needs_a
  _champion). Check out this compelling speech to learn
  more about the power of united belief in schools.

- Eric Van den Steen, "On the Origin of Shared Beliefs
  (and Corporate Culture)," *RAND Journal of Economics* 41,
  no. 4 (2010): 617–48, http://web.mit.edu/evds/www
  /research/pdf/VandenSteenEric_shared_beliefs.pdf.

Words of Wisdom: Shared Humility

- *"I think one of the best by-products of our relationship is
  that my ego has gone in a very healthy way. I feel like I'm in
  service in this relationship. I feel like I'm in service in my
  work."* —Paul Bennett

- *"I think one of the things that an incredibly broad and bold
  vision of profit with purpose does is it casts a bright light on
  anything that doesn't fit well with the partnering mentality.
  With a humility mentality. With a meritocracy mentality.
  With a change-orientated mentality. The vision says [narrow*

and potentially selfish concern] doesn't belong here. It's not appropriate against the scale of this vision." —Andy Kuper

- *"How do we encourage people to look outside of themselves for support and additional skills and complementary skills, not be so proud to think that you can do everything. That's probably the ticket."* —Alex Rappaport

- *"I think we don't take ourselves too seriously, which I think is important. We take the issues very seriously, but we don't take ourselves too seriously. We've had a lot of fun together over the years and we've had a lot to smile about."* —Richard Branson

- *"I think good partnerships probably value equality so that there's not competition and I think it allows for that ebb and flow."* —Blake Harrison

Explore Shared Humility:

Additional Resources

- Jennifer Cole Wright et al., "The Psychological Significance of Humility," *Journal of Positive Psychology*

12, no. 1 (2017): 3–12, https://www.tandfonline.com /doi/abs/10.1080/17439760.2016.1167940?journalCode =rpos20.

- Dr. Brad Owens, an assistant professor of business ethics at Brigham Young University, specializes in the role humility plays in our lives, specifically in leadership. Read his article "The Reign of Humility Within" (BYU Wheatley Institution, March 6, 2019, https://wheatley .byu.edu/the-reign-of-humility-within/) and listen to his interview on the podcast *Moral Impact* (https://www .youtube.com/watch?v=-WTJwdC3Hp8).

- Boston University's Danielsen Institute specializes in research around humility in their desire to understand this virtue within the human experience. For further reading, check out *The Brink*'s article highlighting Boston University's work on the benefits of humility: Rich Barlow, "Studying the Benefits of Humility," March 27, 2017 (http://www.bu.edu/articles/2017/studying -the-benefits-of-humility/).

- Humility Science (http://humilityscience.com) is the hub for those interested in learning more about the science of this virtue. Take their diagnostic survey to see how humble you are and learn more on humility from their book *Cultural Humility* (Washington, DC: American Psychological Association, 2017).

- The Templeton Foundation offers excellent resources and ongoing research on what is newly termed

"intellectual humility" (https://www.templeton.org
/discoveries/intellectual-humility). Check out their
video "The Joy of Being Wrong" (https://www.youtube
.com/watch?v=mRXNUx4cua0&t=42s), and their
episode on the podcast *Philosophy Talk*, "How to
Humbly Disagree" (https://www.kalw.org/arts-culture
/2020-09-25/philosophy-talk-how-to-humbly
-disagree#stream/0).

- Find more on humility and the power of meditation in
  Matthieu Ricard's book *Altruism: The Power of
  Compassion to Change Yourself and the World* (New York:
  Little, Brown, 2015).

Words of Wisdom: Nurturing Generosity

- *"I believe the way to build a relationship as well as a
  partnership is to have deep respect for each other. That
  respect allows you to share, and encourage creativity,
  accolades, and all without jealousy because when one
  succeeds, we both succeed."* —Beverly Joubert

- *"My tip for someone who's going to build a relationship with
  someone else, whether it be personal or business, is you need
  to look out for the other person's best interest, not your
  own."* —Pat Hawk

- *"If you're going to be co-purposeful and co-generous, you
  can't be egomaniacs. You can't be pushing your position,
  your agenda, your thoughts. . . . You're about a bigger*

purpose so you've got to be generous with releasing what you think and be really willing to go with somebody else's thoughts." —Lord Hastings

- *"Reciprocity is the norm in most societies. Most ritual beliefs, when it comes down to it, certainly in relation to the landscape, are always expressions of reciprocity. The earth gives to me, I must protect the earth. It's not rocket science."* —Wade Davis

- *"We have tried not to keep score in our relationship. We try to live in a place of gratitude with a lot of thank-yous."* —Jacki Zehner

Explore Nurturing Generosity:

Additional Resources

- Wharton Professor, organizational psychologist, and bestselling author Adam Grant explores the world of takers, matchers, and givers. Check out his book *Give and Take* (New York: Viking, 2013), watch his TED Talk "Are You a Giver or a Taker?" (https://www.youtube

.com/watch?v=YyXRYgjQXX0), and take his give-and
-take quiz (https://www.adamgrant.net/quizzes
/give-and-take-quiz/) to see your reciprocity style.

- A comprehensive white paper from the John Templeton
  Foundation, "The Science of Generosity" (May 2018,
  https://ggsc.berkeley.edu/images/uploads/GGSC-JTF
  _White_Paper-Generosity-FINAL.pdf), produced by the
  Greater Good Science Center at UC Berkeley, tackles
  questions linked to generosity.

- The article "Giving Thanks Can Make You Happier," by
  Harvard Health Publishing (November 22, 2011,
  https://www.health.harvard.edu/healthbeat/giving
  -thanks-can-make-you-happier), cited a study of
  couples that found that "individuals who took time to
  express gratitude for their partner not only felt more
  positive toward the other person but also felt more
  comfortable expressing concerns about their
  relationship."

- Check out Dr. Robert A. Emmons's lecture "Four Lessons
  I've Learned About Gratitude" (https://www.youtube
  .com/watch?v=3vGk6USZsVc) and Dr. Michael E.
  McCullough and Arthur Zajonc's interview, "Mind and
  Morality: A Dialogue," on the podcast *On Being with
  Krista Tippett*.

- An intriguing 2019 study, "It Pays to Be Generous"
  (https://www.fool.com/the-ascent/research/study-it
  -pays-be-generous/), by the Ascent (a division of the

Motley Fool), compared generous and less generous people.

Words of Wisdom: Compassionate Empathy

- *"You always have to put yourself in the shoes of the other person. If you don't understand where they are coming from, if you don't have an appreciation for their arguments and how they are seeing things, it's very, very challenging to put a meaningful partnership together."* —José María Figueres

- *"That's the part about having a good friendship, having a mutual friendship, is understanding each other. That is one of the greatest gifts there is."* —Lester Bailey

- *"For us, I think one of the keys to our survival, and I think it's something that would work for other people, is the ability to deploy empathy to a greater degree. So if Beverly is struggling with something, even not communicating it, I try as much as I can to put myself into her situation and the minute I'm there I can see why she's thoroughly pissed off with me, for example, although that never happens, right? No. But the minute I've got empathy and I can understand where she . . . what her problems or what her situation is, that makes it a lot easier for us to deal with it. And I think that, again, it's something that the more we look down and we get wound up in our lack of time today in our society, the less time we've got to be empathetic to other people."* —Dereck Joubert

- *"Understanding is love."* —Jo Confino

Explore Compassionate Empathy:

Additional Resources

- Check out Stanford University professor of psychology and director of the Stanford Social Neuroscience Lab Jamil Zaki's new book, *War for Kindness: Building Empathy in a Fractured World* (New York: Broadway Books, 2019). Also check out his Kindness Challenges (https://www.warforkindness.com/challenges) and start building your empathy muscles.

- Justin Bariso, author of *EQ Applied* (Germany: Borough Hall, 2018), further explains the breakdown of empathy in his article "There Are Actually 3 Types of Empathy. Here's How They Differ—and How You Can Develop Them All" (*Inc.*, September 19, 2018, https://www.inc.com/justin-bariso /there-are-actually-3-types-of-empathy-heres -how-they-differ-and-how-you-can-develop-them-all .html).

- For a simple and fun explanation of empathy, watch this short clip from actor Mark Ruffalo on *Sesame Street* (https://www.youtube.com/watch?v=9 _1Rt1R4xbM).

Fourth Degree: Magnetic Moments

Keep connected and strengthen your ecosystem through intentional practices, rituals, and traditions that keep curiosity and wonder alive, create space for honest communication, spark unlimited joy, and build a wider supportive community.

- *"Open, trusting communication at all times and on all issues. We had a continuous dialogue, about every issue under the sun! It included commenting on nuances, pluses, and minuses in each other's approaches and performances. The trust we built made this possible, without hurting each other's feelings. It really helped us both in our daily lives, at work and at home."* —Gro Brundtland

- *"I can't finish her sentences, and I hope she can't finish mine, at least not most of them. And then we take that curiosity that we're able to maintain in each other and point it at the world."* —Stewart Brand

- *"Even if you have a foundation of trust and a foundation of respect you can't take it for granted. You need to make sure that you nurture the partnership; to me the food of partnership is communication. You always have to be open, transparent, and communicate."* —Sangu Delle

- *"Joy is central and also the only kind of unlimited resource. Which doesn't mean it's easy to come by, but I think it is a fuel that is completely renewable."* —Phil Kaye

- *"One of the things that I think has connected the two of us, but also I would say all of our family members, is the love of community and love of building community. That everyone was always welcome within the doors of my grandmother's house, my parents' house, my cousins' and family's house."* —Hank Willis Thomas

- *"And time is really the investment of the journey of friendship and a relationship and being willing to track on to get it done. Take time. Be purposeful."* —Lord Hastings

Ten Examples of Magnetic Moments

1. President and Mrs. Carter used to meet on the Truman Balcony at the White House every afternoon to debrief each other on the day.

2. José María and Christiana Figueres had coffee and cake with their grandfather every Sunday until he was 105.

3. The cofounders of the Future Project, Andrew Maxwell Mangino and Kanya Balakrishna, have a wonderful affirmation ritual they call "awesome ceremonies," where they highlight something brilliant about the other person each day. They also hold a forty-eight-hour intensive Dream Summit weekend designed to create a new sense of possibility—and to reimagine the path when there is a breakdown on the way to their vision.

4. Robbie Schingler and Will Marshall make their New Year's resolutions together with their team to increase their audacity and hold each other accountable.

5. Lindsay and David Levin host Friday night (Shabbat) dinners where everyone shares their personal view on something important to them in the world.

6. Ray Hinton and Lester Bailey have a wonderful Saturday ritual. After church they head to lunch, with a stop at the barbershop to get their hair cut—even though they joke that Lester has no hair left to cut. It doesn't matter. What matters to both of them is simply being together.

7. Gabby Giffords and Mark Kelly have breakfast together. Gabby has ordered the same thing for four years: scrambled eggs with basil, spinach, and cheddar cheese, and raisin toast with no butter and a side of fruit.

8. Keith Yamashita and Todd Holcomb shout, "Go be a rock star!" before either of them goes to do something challenging.

9. Joe Gebbia, Nathan Blecharczyk, and Brian Chesky, cofounders of Airbnb, meet every Sunday night from six to nine o'clock to hold each other accountable for the previous week and make a plan for the coming week.

10. Bert and John Jacobs's mother created a gratitude ritual every night at dinner by saying, "Tell me something good that happened today."

Explore Magnetic Moments:

Additional Resources

- Check out "The Restorative Power of Ritual," by Scott Berinato (*Harvard Business Review*, April 2, 2020, https://hbr.org/2020/04/the-restorative-power-of -ritual).

- Casper ter Kuile recently published a book called *The Power of Ritual* (New York: HarperOne, 2020).

- Check out Priya Parker's book, *The Art of Gathering* (New York: Riverhead, 2018).

- Learn more about *Flow*, by Mihaly Csikszentmihalyi (New York: HarperPerennial, 1991), considered one of the cofounders of positive psychology.

- Ingrid Fetell Lee researches joy and how we can find more of it. Check out her TED Talk, "Where Joy Hides and How to Find It" (April 2018, https://www.ted.com /talks/ingrid_fetell_lee_where_joy_hides_and_how_to _find_it), and her many books, including *Joyful* (New York: Little, Brown, 2018).

- Spencer Harrison, a professor at INSEAD, Erin Pinkus, and Jon Cohen wrote an article in the *Harvard Business Review* on curiosity in the workplace, "Research: 83% of Executives Say They Encourage Curiosity. Just 52% of Employees Agree" (September 20, 2018, https://hbr.org /2018/09/research-83-of-executives-say-they -encourage-curiosity-just-52-of-employees-agree%27). Also check out Spencer and Jon's TEDx Talk, "Curiosity Is Your Superpower" (October 22, 2018, https://www .youtube.com/watch?v=xZJwMYeE9Ak).

- Check out neuroscientist Beau Lotto's TED Talk "How We Experience Awe—and Why It Matters" (April 2019, https://www.ted.com/talks/beau_lotto_and_cirque_du _soleil_how_we_experience_awe_and_why_it_matters? language=en).

- Professor Evan Imber-Black wrote an article examining how the pandemic of 2020 changed our rituals, "Rituals in the Time of COVID-19: Imagination, Responsiveness, and the Human Spirit" (*Family Process* 59, no. 3 [2020]: 912–21).

- Also check out Dan Buettner's Blue Zone research to learn more about moais, groups of five friends who commit to come together and support one another for the rest of their lives. See Aislinn Kotifani, "Moai— This Tradition Is Why Okinawan People Live Longer, Better" (https://www.bluezones.com/2018/08/moai -this-tradition-is-why-okinawan-people-live-longer -better/).

Fifth Degree: Celebrate Friction

Take the heat out of conflict and turn it into learning opportunities. Ignite sparks of creative combustion for shared solutions and greater connection, staying all-in and focused on something bigger.

Words of Wisdom

- *"[We believe in] giving a little space for the person to shine in their area and not focusing on the one part that may bug you. Instead, how about the other ninety-nine things this person does great? Just let those thrive and not focus on the points of tension as much. It's like our mother taught us, you know, tell me something good; let's start the meeting with what's working together right now." —John Jacobs*

- *"[Our purpose] allows us to disagree without being disagreeable. To argue loudly but persuade one another. And I think it's those things, in my mind, that keep the partnership together. That sense of empathy. That sense of trust. That sense of we're doing something for a higher purpose, fundamentally." —Jim Roth*

- *"Disagree—never disrespect. The shared values are love, respect and trust. And communication. We don't always agree on everything, but we always agree to discuss, and I think that's really important. I think that's important for anyone, that you can have debates and discuss and disagree, but never disrespect." —Chris Redlitz*

- *"Deal with things as they come, deal with them quickly, and move on, so that you can get back to enjoying life with one another." —Erika Boyd*

- *"If you run into a bump, know that that's normal and anybody who's ever worked in partnership has hit a bump and it's okay to do that and you'll recover. I think that a more concrete tool to focus on is just being direct and honest about what the issue was. . . . Find the person who you had an issue with and ask them what the issue was about and resolve it." —May Boeve*

Explore Celebrate Friction:

Additional Resources

- *Harvard Business Review* featured an article, "How to Mend a Work Relationship" (Brianna Barker Caza, Mara Olekalns, and Timothy J. Vogus, February 14, 2020, https://hbr.org/2020/02/how-to-mend-a-work-relationship), based on a review of over three hundred studies that focused on workplace relationships, relationship transgressions, and relationship repair.

- Leadership expert and bestselling author Robin Sharma discusses the importance of celebrating friction in three short and insightful articles: "Celebrate Conflict" (https://www.robinsharma.com/article/celebrate-conflict), "The Four Riders of Conflict" (https://www.robinsharma.com/article/the-four-riders-of-conflict), and "Pick Fights Fast" (https://www.robinsharma.com/article/pick-fights-fast).

- Edutopia's "What Brain Science Teaches Us About Conflict Resolution" (Sarah Gonser, February 5,

2020, https://www.edutopia.org/article/what
-brain-science-teaches-us-about-conflict-resolution)
provides us with an educator's insight into the
challenging emotions that accompany disagreements
among our youth.

- Sheila Heen is a professor of negotiation at Harvard Law
  School and a bestselling coauthor of two books, *Difficult
  Conversations: How to Discuss What Matters Most* (New
  York: Penguin Books, 1999) and *Thanks for the Feedback:
  The Science and Art of Receiving Feedback Well* (New York:
  Viking Press, 2014). Check out her online course on
  difficult conversations (Acumen Academy, https://www
  .acumenacademy.org/course/sheila-heen-on-difficult
  -conversations.

- Bestselling author, professor of management science
  and engineering, and professor of organizational
  behavior Dr. Bob Sutton is an expert in organizational
  friction. His latest book, *The Asshole Survival Guide: How
  to Deal with People Who Treat You Like Dirt* (New York:
  Houghton Mifflin Harcourt, 2017), and his newest
  project with Huggy Rao, the Friction Project (https://
  www.bobsutton.net/friction-project), speak to "the
  causes and cures for destructive organizational
  friction—and when it is wise to make things harder
  to do."

- Rebecca Zucker from Next Step Partners reviews the
  SHARED feedback model on her leadership blog, in

"Getting Under Your Skin: How to Respond?" (June 27, 2016, https://nextsteppartners.com/respond-vs-react/). She describes how self-awareness is a leader's superpower, especially when managing conflict. Continue on her blog with "How Not to Be Defensive" (October 14, 2019, https://nextsteppartners.com /how-to-not-be-defensive/).

Sixth Degree: Collective Connections

A framework of design principles to scale collaborations, with Deep Connections at the center as role models, as hubs of momentum, and as connective tissue.

Words of Wisdom

- *"We first must make peace with nature. We've no hope for making peace among humankind, our fellow humans . . . if we fail to take care of the systems of the natural world. It is the underpinning of everything."* —Sylvia Earle

- *"I think, at its deepest level, it's about shared purpose and it's about what originally drew us together, which is being part of a movement to confront climate change."* —May Boeve

- *"The ten of us and our families, our wives and our extended families, we formed a partnership where we deeply respected each other, hid nothing . . . it was the primacy of what we called the central committee or the central team [focused on ending smallpox in India]. And it was magical, and it still is."* —Larry Brilliant

- *"There was no one [in the ozone community] worried about losing their own personal identity because they were strong, strong characters in and of themselves. . . . These partnerships [in the ozone community] are successful because they combine strong personalities with the will to collaborate."* —Nancy Reichman

- *"I think the role of sharing stories has always been important, and part of the value of working in a network is that you're connected to so many more people. . . . The secret sauce is a high level of activity done jointly. And I think that's more than anything why we've trusted each other and been able to build a community of staff and volunteers that includes more than 160 staff and hundreds of thousands of people who're active around the world."* —May Boeve

- *"What they would implement, and how, has been based on a circle of friends, an ever-growing circle of friends, that has worked tirelessly under conditions of personal trust."* —Mostafa Tolba

Explore Collective Connections:

Additional Resources

- David Price, author of *The Power of Us: How We Connect, Act and Innovate Together* (London: Thread Books, 2020), shares his wisdom on what it looks like to harness the power of collaboration and diverse thinking.

- Robert Greenleaf is credited with founding the powerful movement called "servant-leadership." His Center for Servant Leadership (https://www.greenleaf .org) reminds us that true leadership must start with the intention to serve others.

- Read Larry Brilliant's book, *Sometimes Brilliant* (New York: HarperOne, 2016), to learn more about the collective that ended smallpox in India.

- Nancy Reichman and Penelope Canan, authors of the book *Ozone Connections: Expert Networks in Global Environmental Governance* (New York: Routledge, 2017), argue that "we need to understand how the implementation of complex global environmental agreements depends on the construction and exploitation of social connections among experts who act collectively to define solutions to environmental problems."

- Three other great books on protecting the ozone layer are *Ozone Diplomacy* by Richard Benedick (Cambridge, MA: Harvard University Press, 1991), *Protecting the Ozone Layer* by Stephen O. Andersen and K. Madhava Sarma (New York: Routledge, 2002), and *Ozone Crisis* by Sharon L. Roan (New York: Wiley Science Editions, 1989).

- Watch the PBS documentary *Ozone Hole: How We Saved the Planet* (2019, https://www.pbs.org/show/ozone-hole-how-we-saved-planet/).

- Read the following books either authored or coauthored by Johan Rockström: *Breaking Boundaries: The Science of Our Planet* (New York: DK, 2021); *Big World, Small Planet* (New Haven, CT: Yale University Press, 2015); *The Human Quest: Prospering Within Planetary Boundaries* (Stockholm, Sweden: Langenskiölds, 2012); and *Bankrupting Nature: Denying Our Planetary Boundaries* (New York: Routledge, 2012).

- Watch the Netflix documentary *Breaking Boundaries: The Science of Our Planet* (directed by Jon Clay, 2021).

- In *Together: The Healing Power of Human Connection in a Sometimes Lonely World* (New York: Harper Wave, 2020),

US Surgeon General Vivek Murthy writes about our innate desire to connect and the value of community.

- Marissa King's *Social Chemistry: Decoding the Patterns of Human Connection* (New York: Dutton, 2021) can help you build more meaningful and impactful relationships.

- David Bradford and Carole Robin's *Connect: Building Exceptional Relationships with Family, Friends, and Colleagues* (New York: Currency, 2021) is based on the landmark course on relationships at the Stanford Graduate School of Business.

Six Degrees of Connection Images

Martin Hill and Philippa Jones,
partners in life, art, and nature

The remarkable environmental sculptures representing each of the Six Degrees of Connection were created by one of the Plus Wonder partnerships, Martin Hill and Philippa Jones, who have been creative partners since 1994.

For over two decades, these New Zealand–based artists have traveled to remote locations to create environmental sculptures. They share a deep love of rock climbing and a respect for the natural world. They've won numerous awards and just launched a new project about our interconnected world called Fine Line, a global environmental art and science endeavor consisting of twelve ephemeral sculptures made on high points connected by a line that encircles the earth, a symbol of natural systems that connect us all in the web of life. Each sculpture is made from natural materials found at the site that return to nature. You can learn more about their work at https://martin-hill.com/projects/the-fine-line/.

Here are a few nuggets of wisdom from their partnership. . . .

- *"Joy is the essential glue. Joy in each other, joy in each other's achievements, even joy in each other's mistakes—we learn more from our mistakes."* —Martin Hill

- *"I can say without hesitation that the combination of our similarities and complementary skills and approaches to life make our partnership work."* —Philippa Jones

- *"Our partnership with the earth is based on our understanding that we are part of nature, not apart from nature. We keep our partnership strong by living and working close to nature and honoring ecological processes."* —Martin Hill

- *"Climbing together we are totally reliant on each other for the safety of our lives. This level of vulnerability is not generally recognized in daily life, although we all risk our lives just driving and flying. In our lives together and in our collaborative art practice we take risks all the time; pushing each other's boundaries is essential."* —Martin and Philippa

Notes

We cannot live only for ourselves. A thousand fibers connect us with our fellow men; and among those fibers, as sympathetic threads, our actions run as causes, and they come back as effects.

—Herman Melville

xi **"Who has loved"**: Wenxian Zhang, "The Enduring Legacy of Fred Rogers at Rollins College," *From the Rollins Archives* (blog), https://blogs.rollins.edu/libraryarchives/2020/03/02/the-enduring-legacy-of-fred-rogers-at-rollins-college/?utm_source=rss&utm_medium=rss&utm_campaign=the-enduring-legacy-of-fred-rogers-at-rollins-college.

xii **the rich biographies**: With gratitude to Scilla Elworthy, Oxford Research Group, for leading the curation of the precious content in these binders.

xii **set of partners**: With gratitude to Andrea Brenninkmeijer and Scilla Elworthy for helping to lovingly build this community. And to all The Elders Advisory Council members, who have been a joy to work with over the past fifteen years.

xiv *The Art of War*: Sun Tzu, *The Art of War* (New York: Penguin, 2009).

xiv *The Joy of Cooking*: Irma S. Rombauer, Marion Rombauer Becker, and Ethan Becker, *The Joy of Cooking* (New York: Scribner, 2006).

xvi **the 40 percent of employees**: Emily Wetherell and Sangeeta Agrawal, "What Engaged Employees Say About Your Brand," Gallup, November 16, 2020, https://www.gallup.com/workplace/324287/engaged-employees-say-brand.aspx. See also Jim Harter, "U.S. Employee Engagement Holds Steady in First Half of 2021," Gallup, July 29, 2021, https://www.gallup.com/workplace/352949/employee-engagement-holds-steady-first-half-2021.aspx.

xvi **2020 study from the Pew:** Lee Rainie and Andrew Perrin, "The State of Americans' Trust in Each Other amid the COVID-19 Pandemic," Pew Research Center, April 6, 2020, https://www.pewresearch.org /fact-tank/2020/04/06/the-state-of-americans-trust-in-each-other -amid-the-covid-19-pandemic/.

xx **When Warren Buffett:** Marcel Schwantes, "Bill Gates Said Warren Buffett Helped Him Define Success in a New Way. Here It Is in a Few Words," *Inc.*, June 10, 2019, https://www.inc.com/marcel-schwantes/bill-gates-said-warren-buffett-helped-him-define-success-in-a-new-way-here -it-is-in-a-few-words.html; Bill Gates, "What I Learned at Work This Year," *GatesNotes* (blog), December 29, 2018, https://www.gatesnotes .com/About-Bill-Gates/Year-in-Review-2018.

xxi **"We can honor him":** Mary Robinson, "Nelson Mandela: 'The Most Inspiring Individual I Have Ever Met,'" The Elders, December 5, 2013, https://theelders.org/news/nelson-mandela-most-inspiring-individual -i-have-ever-met.

Chapter One: Six Degrees of Connection

1 **André was alone:** See Alan Taylor, "Flying Around the World in a Solar Powered Plane," *Atlantic*, July 26, 2016, https://www.theatlantic .com/photo/2016/07/flying-around-the-world-in-a-solar-powered -plane/493085/; "Record-Breaking Flight from Nagoya to Hawaii," Logbook, SolarImpulse Foundation, https://aroundtheworld.solarimpulse .com/leg-8-from-Nagoya-to-Hawaii.

Chapter Two: Something Bigger

13 **"The only trouble is":** *Ozone Hole: How We Saved the Planet*, PBS video, 55:51, 2019, https://www.pbs.org/show/ozone-hole-how-we-saved -planet/.

14 **British chemist James Lovelock:** Barbara J. Finlayson-Pitts, "F. Sherwood Rowland: A Man of Science, Vision, Integrity, and Kindness," *Proceedings of the National Academy of Sciences* 109, no. 35 (2012): 13881–82, https://www.pnas.org/content/109/35/13881.

15 **the scientific journal *Nature*:** Mario J. Molina and F. S. Rowland, "Stratospheric Sink for Chlorofluoromethanes: Chlorine Atom-Catalysed Destruction of Ozone," *Nature* 249 (1974): 810–12, https:// www.nature.com/articles/249810a0.

15 **What they did not expect:** Lanie Jones, "Ozone Warning: He Sounded Alarm, Paid Heavy Price," *Los Angeles Times*, July 14, 1988, https://www .latimes.com/archives/la-xpm-1988-07-14-mn-8873-story.html.

16 **"What's the use"**: Sharon L. Roan, *Ozone Crisis* (New York: Wiley Science Editions, 1989), 121.

18 **the Rivonia Trial**: "Trials and Prisons Chronology," Nelson Mandela Foundation, https://www.nelsonmandela.org/content/page/trials-and -prison-chronology.

18 **"If it needs be"**: "I am prepared to die," April 20, 2011, Nelson Mandela Foundation, https://www.nelsonmandela.org/news/entry/i-am-prepared -to-die.

19 **Truth and Reconciliation Commission**: *The Truth and Reconciliation Commission (TRC)*, permanent exhibition, Apartheid Museum, https:// www.apartheidmuseum.org/exhibitions/the-truth-and-reconciliation -commission-trc.

25 **"Anything or anyone"**: David Whyte, *The House of Belonging* (Langley, WA: Many Rivers Press, 1997).

29 **on Saturday, January 8, 2011**: Marc Lacey and David M. Herszenhorn, "In Attack's Wake, Political Repercussions," *New York Times*, January 8, 2011, https://www.nytimes.com/2011/01/09/us/politics/09giffords.html.

29 **In August 2020**: "'He'll Be There for You, Too,' Gabrielle Giffords Says of Joe Biden," *New York Times* video, 2:29, August 19, 2020, https://www.ny times.com/video/us/elections/100000007297620/gabrielle-giffords- speaks-dnc.html.

30 **"Our nation's gun violence"**: Joe Biden (@JoeBiden), Twitter, August 19, 2020, https://twitter.com/joebiden/status/1296253868901142529?lang=en.

30 **"It becomes pretty obvious"**: Captain Mark Kelly (@CaptMarkKelly), Twitter video, February 12, 2019, https://twitter.com/CaptMarkKelly /status/1095301632093433864.

30 **"I couldn't stop thinking"**: Gabrielle Giffords (@GabbyGiffords), Twit- ter, January 6, 2021, https://twitter.com/gabbygiffords/status/13469845 03248474112?lang=en.

Chapter Three: All-In

37 **"That really hurt"**: *Ozone Hole: How We Saved the Planet,* PBS video, 55:51, 2019, https://www.pbs.org/show/ozone-hole-how-we-saved- planet/.

38 **$8 billion**: Wendy Becktold, "'Ozone Hole' Shows That We Avoided Plan- etary Disaster Before," *Sierra*, April 20, 2019, https://www.sierraclub.org /sierra/ozone-hole-shows-we-avoided-planetary-disaster-before-pbs -documentary; "Evidence at Last," Understanding Science, University of California, Berkeley, https://undsci.berkeley.edu/article/0_0_0/ozone _depletion_06.

38 **DuPont took out:** Cheryl Mahaffy, "Press Coverage of the Fluorocarbon Controversy: The Rise and Decline of a 'Hot' Scientific Issue" (paper presented at the 62nd Annual Meeting of the Association for Education in Journalism, Houston, August 5–8, 1979), https://files.eric.ed.gov/fulltext/ED177595.pdf.

38 **A chemical trade magazine:** Felicity Barringer, "F. Sherwood Rowland, Cited Aerosols' Danger, Is Dead at 84," *New York Times*, March 12, 2012, https://www.nytimes.com/2012/03/13/science/earth/f-sherwood-rowland-84-dies-raised-alarm-over-aerosols.html.

39 **Only 4 supported restrictions:** Sharon L. Roan, *Ozone Crisis* (New York: Wiley Science Editions, 1989), 103.

39 **"It looks and sounds like science fiction":** Roan, *Ozone Crisis*, 56.

40 **"Rowland invented a new kind":** "In Memoriam: Frank Sherwood Rowland," University of California, Irvine, https://senate.universityof california.edu/_files/inmemoriam/html/franksherwoodrowland.html.

41 **"she has been":** F. Sherwood Rowland, "F. Sherwood Rowland Biographical," The Nobel Prize, https://www.nobelprize.org/prizes/chemistry/1995/rowland/biographical/.

41 **Sherry was asked:** Barbara J.Finlayson-Pitts, "F. Sherwood Rowland: A Man of Science, Vision, Integrity, and Kindness," *Proceedings of the National Academy of Sciences* 109, no 35 (2012): 13881–82, https://www.pnas.org/content/109/35/13881.

44 *Everything to Gain*: Jimmy Carter and Rosalynn Carter, *Everything to Gain* (Fayetteville: University of Arkansas Press, 1995).

54 **"95% of people":** Jo Confino, "Changing Yourself, Changing the World," *Guardian*, April 10, 2012, https://www.theguardian.com/sus tainable-business/coping-methods-work-burnout-business-values.

56 **malaria, a deadly disease:** "Malaria," World Health Organization, April 1, 2021, https://www.who.int/news-room/fact-sheets/detail/malaria.

59 **"There are two kinds":** Esther Perel, "Cultivating Desire," *The Knowledge Project*, episode #71, https://fs.blog/knowledge-project/esther-perel/.

59 **"bids for attention":** Zach Brittle, "Turn Towards Instead of Away," Gottman Institute, April 1, 2015, https://www.gottman.com/blog/turn -toward-instead-of-away/.

Chapter Four: The Ecosystem

67 **geophysicist Joseph Farman:** Fiona Harvey, "Joe Farman Obituary," *Guardian*, May 16, 2013, https://www.theguardian.com/environment /2013/may/16/joe-farman.

68 **"possibly destroy the ozone layer"**: Steve Norton, "Oral History Interviews: Jon Shanklin," American Institute of Physics, October 7, 1999, https://www.aip.org/history-programs/niels-bohr-library/oral-histories /32994.

68 **"our planet can change"**: Jonathan Shanklin, "Reflections on the Ozone Hole," *Nature* 465 (2010): 34–35, https://www.nature.com /articles/465034a.

69 **findings in a paper in *Nature***: J. C. Farman, B. G. Gardiner, and J. D. Shanklin, "Large Losses of Total Ozone in Antarctica Reveal Seasonal ClO_x/NO_x Interaction," *Nature* 315 (1985): 207–10, https://www.nature .com/articles/315207a0.

69 **National Ozone Expedition:** "Susan Solomon: Pioneering Atmospheric Scientist," NOAA, https://celebrating200years.noaa.gov/historymakers /solomon/welcome.html.

71 **the Montreal Protocol was adopted:** "About Montreal Protocol," UN Environment Programme, https://www.unep.org/ozonaction/who-we -are/about-montreal-protocol.

72 **"suspending disbelief and cynicism"**: Penelope Canan and Nancy Reichman, *Ozone Connections* (London: Routledge, 2017), 172.

72 **letters of gratitude:** Canan and Reichman, *Ozone Connections*, 177.

72 **member of the Solvents Committee:** Canan and Reichman, *Ozone Connections*, 159.

72 **"What they would implement"**: Canan and Reichman, *Ozone Connections*, 61.

74 **a colony of aspen trees:** "Meet Pando, One of the Oldest Organisms on Earth," Earth.com, June 27, 2019, https://www.earth.com/news /pando-oldest-organisms/.

78 **led by Julia Rozovsky:** Massey Morris, "This Google Manager Shares His Secrets for Building an Effective Team," *Fast Company*, August 15, 2018, https://www.fastcompany.com/90218743/this-google-manager -shares-his-secrets-for-building-an-effective-team.

79 **The Edelman Trust Barometer study:** Richard Edelman, "20 Years of Trust," Edelman, https://www.edelman.com/20yearsoftrust/.

82 **"could have been better partners"**: "A Message to Our Hosts from CEO Brian Chesky," Airbnb, https://www.airbnb.com/d/host-message.

83 **One software company:** "Buffer Transparency," Buffer, https://buffer .com/transparency.

83 **"elephants, dead fish and vomit"**: Blake Morgan, "How to Build the Most Customer-Focused Culture in the World," *Forbes*, December 11, 2017, https://www.forbes.com/sites/blakemorgan/2017/12/11/how-to

-build-the-most-customer-focused-culture-in-the-world/?sh=6ce64e5 556d6.

86   **Robert was raised:** J. I. Merritt, "Heretic in the Temple," *Princeton Alumni Weekly*, October 8, 2003, https://www.princeton.edu/~paw /archive_new/PAW03-04/02-1008/features1.html.

92   **we and so many others:** With great thanks to the many partners who have helped incubate and support The Elders over the years.

101 **named after George Bizos:** "George Bizos: Anti-Apartheid Lawyer Who Defended Mandela Dies Aged 92," BBC, September 10, 2020, https:// www.bbc.com/news/world-africa-54094248.

101 **Adam Grant showed:** Adam Grant, https://www.adamgrant.net /book/give-and-take/.

102 **Dereck Joubert and his wife:** Selene Brophy, "SA NatGeo Explorers Dereck and Beverly Joubert Share Intimate Details of Near-Fatal Buffalo Charge," *News24*, April 14, 2017, https://www.news24.com/news24/ travel/sa-natgeo-explorer-dereck-and-beverly-joubert-share-intimate-details-of-near-fatal-buffalo-charge-20170414; "Beverly Joubert," Academy of Achievement, https://achievement.org/achiever/beverly-joubert/.

107 **"improve others' well-being":** Amy Emmert, "Empathy: The Glue We Need to Fix a Fractured World," *Strategy+Business*, October 20, 2020, https://www.strategy-business.com/article/Empathy-The-glue-we-need -to-fix-a-fractured-world?gko=56f1f.

107 **"He made quite an impression":** Anthony Ray Hinton with Lara Love Hardin, *The Sun Does Shine* (New York: St. Martin's Press, 2018), x.

108 **Ray and Henry first met:** Hinton and Hardin, *The Sun Does Shine*, 145.

108 **"Everybody knew Henry had shame":** Hinton and Hardin, *The Sun Does Shine*, 155.

109 **"All his life he was taught hate":** Ron Wagner, "There Is No Feeling Like Being Free," Furman University, March 1, 2019, https://news.fur man.edu/2019/03/01/there-is-no-feeling-like-being-free/.

Chapter Five: Magnetic Moments

117 **"informal social relations formed":** Penelope Canan and Nancy Reichman, *Ozone Connections: Expert Networks in Global Environmental Governance* (London: Routledge, 2017), 47.

122 **They created a very successful business:** Learn more about the project at https://www.innocentdrinks.co.uk/.

122 **Jon was the "operations guru":** "Our Story," JamJar Investments, https://www.jamjarinvestments.com/about.

125 **"The joy of connection":** Susan Piver, *The Four Noble Truths of Love* (Somerville, MA: Lionheart Press, 2018).

128 **The poet Ross Gay:** Ross Gay, "Joy Is Such a Human Madness," The On Being Project, July 25, 2019, https://onbeing.org/blog/joy-is-such -a-human-madness/.

128 **Stephen Hawking wrote:** "Stephen Hawking," Goodreads, https://www .goodreads.com/quotes/9725596-but-it-would-be-an-empty-universe -indeed-if-it.

131 **he led a campaign:** "The Whole Earth Disk: An Iconic Image of the Space Age," Smithsonian National Air and Space Museum, December 23, 2009, https://airandspace.si.edu/stories/editorial/whole-earth-disk -iconic-image-space-age.

137 **Dan Buettner found:** Aislinn Kotifani, "Moai—This Tradition Is Why Okinawan People Live Longer, Better," https://www.bluezones .com/2018/08/moai-this-tradition-is-why-okinawan-people-live -longer-better/.

137 **YPO:** "YPO Forum," YPO, https://www.ypo.org/profile/ypo-forum/.

140 **a few IDEO rituals:** "Tim Brown on Nudging Your Company Culture To- ward Creativity," IDEO U, https://www.ideou.com/blogs/inspiration /creative-confidence-series-tim-brown-on-nudging-your-company -culture-towards-creativity.

141 **"the most dangerous woman":** Luke Nozicka, "Donna Red Wing, 'a Force to Be Reckoned with' in Fight for LGBTQ Rights, Dies After Battle with Cancer," *Des Moines Register*, April 16, 2018, https://www .desmoinesregister.com/story/news/2018/04/16/donna-red-wing -des-moines-lgbtq-advocate-civil-rights-activist-dies-cancer-one -iowa/522936002/.

143 **"You're buying coffee":** Robert Samuels, "He Saw Her Marriage as 'Unnat- ural.' She Called Him 'Bigoted.' Now, They Hug," *Washington Post*, July 4, 2015, https://www.washingtonpost.com/politics/he-saw-her-marriage- as-unnatural-she-called-him-bigoted-now-theyre-friends/2015/07/04 /9e44e7c6-1a90-11e5-bd7f-4611a60dd8e5_story.html.

145 **"story of us":** Kyle Benson, "Love Quiz: How Do You Tell the Story of Your Relationship?," Gottman Institute, December 12, 2016, https:// www.gottman.com/blog/tell-story-relationship/.

Chapter Six: Celebrate Friction

149 **Lee Thomas, the head of:** "Interview with Lee Thomas," EPA Alumni As- sociation, April 19, 2012, https://www.epaalumni.org/userdata/pdf /60740780F5ACB3D5.pdf.

151 **"You are welcome"**: Penelope Canan and Nancy Reichman, *Ozone Connections: Expert Networks in Global Environmental Governance* (London: Routledge, 2017), 163, 172.

151 **To mobilize a wider collective**: Stephen O. Andersen originated the insights in this section.

152 **"They gradually become"**: Stephen O. Andersen and K. Madhava Sarma, *Protecting the Ozone Layer* (New York: Routledge, 2002), 305.

154 **the Four Horsemen**: Ellie Lisitsa, "The Four Horsemen: Criticism, Contempt, Defensiveness, and Stonewalling," Gottman Institute, April 23, 2013, https://www.gottman.com/blog/the-four-horsemen -recognizing-criticism-contempt-defensiveness-and-stonewalling/.

155 **"We examined couples"**: Author interview with John Gottman, March 4, 2020; see https://www.gottman.com/love-lab/.

155 **rise in perfectionism**: Thomas Curran and Andrew P. Hill, "Perfectionism Is Increasing, and That's Not Good News," *Harvard Business Review*, January 26, 2018, https://hbr.org/2018/01/perfectionism-is-increasing -and-thats-not-good-news?registration=success.

155 **increasingly divided and fearful**: Alexa Lardieri, "Survey: Majority of People Around the World Feel Divided," *U.S. News & World Report*, April 25, 2018, https://www.usnews.com/news/politics/articles/2018 -04-25/survey-majority-of-people-around-the-world-feel-divided.

166 **"Resentment is like"**: David Horsey, "Nelson Mandela Transformed Himself and Then His Nation," *Los Angeles Times*, December 6, 2013, https://www.latimes.com/opinion/topoftheticket/la-xpm-2013-dec -06-la-na-tt-nelson-mandela-20131206-story.html.

Chapter Seven: Collective Connections

173 **British prime minister**: Stephen O. Andersen and K. Madhava Sarma, *Protecting the Ozone Layer* (New York: Routledge, 2002), 101.

174 **"We need to go further"**: Andersen and Sarma, *Protecting the Ozone Layer*, 305.

174 **"Clearly it would be intolerable"**: Andersen and Sarma, *Protecting the Ozone Layer*, 101.

174 **effectively used the media**: Andersen and Sarma, *Protecting the Ozone Layer*, 102.

174 **"Actually, Prime Minister"**: Andersen and Sarma, *Protecting the Ozone Layer*, 102; Craig R. Whitney, "20 Nations Agree to Join Ozone Pact," *New York Times*, March 8, 1989, https://www.nytimes.com/1989/03/08/world /20-nations-agree-to-join-ozone-pact.html.

175 **"Politicians from every bloc"**: Whitney, "20 Nations Agree to Join Ozone Pact."

178 **"to keep the machine in good order"**: R. Buckminster Fuller, *Operating Manual for Spaceship Earth* (Zurich: Lars Müller, 2008).

178 **"For centuries mankind"**: Margaret Thatcher, speech concluding Saving the Ozone Layer Conference (London, March 7, 1989), Margaret Thatcher Foundation, https://www.margaretthatcher.org/document /107595.

180 **"They inspire others"**: Penelope Canan and Nancy Reichman, *Ozone Connections: Expert Networks in Global Environmental Governance* (London: Routledge, 2017), 37.

184 **"The 'spirit of the protocol'"**: Richard E. Benedick, *Ozone Diplomacy: New Directions in Safeguarding the Planet* (Cambridge, MA: Harvard University Press, 1991), 332.

185 **His straightforward demeanor**: Canan and Reichman, *Ozone Connections*.

185 **For Jay Baker**: Canan and Reichman, *Ozone Connections*, 23.

186 **Industrialized nations used 88 percent**: Jorgen Wettestad, *Designing Effective Environmental Regimes: The Key Conditions* (Cheltenham, UK: E. Elgar, 1999), 139.

189 **"At the moment"**: Richard C. J. Somerville, *The Forgiving Air* (Los Angeles and Berkeley: University of California Press, 1996), https://publishing .cdlib.org/ucpressebooks/view?docId=ft6290079d&chunk.id =d0e524&toc.depth=1&toc.id=0&brand=ucpress&query=afraid.

191 **Natura's mission from the start**: "Our Reason for Being," Natura, https://www.naturabrasil.com/pages/about-us.

193 **"Du Pont's policy has always been"**: William Glaberson, "Behind Du Pont's Shift on Loss of Ozone Layer," *New York Times*, March 26, 1988, https://www.nytimes.com/1988/03/26/business/behind-du-pont-s -shift-on-loss-of-ozone-layer.html.

194 **"Their decision is welcome"**: Sharon L. Roan, *Ozone Crisis* (New York: Wiley Science Editions, 1989), 245.

194 **"They said, 'Dad, that's fantastic'"**: Glaberson, "Behind Du Pont's Shift."

195 **The EPA estimates**: Stephen Leahy, "Without the Ozone Treaty You'd Get Sunburned in 5 Minutes," *National Geographic*, September 24, 2017, https://www.nationalgeographic.com/news/2017/09/montreal-protocol -ozone-treaty-30-climate-change-hcfs-hfcs/.

198 **killed at least 300 million people**: American Museum of Natural History, "Smallpox," https://www.amnh.org/explore/science-topics/disease -eradication/countdown-to-zero/smallpox.

198 **a brash young American doctor:** Larry Brilliant, *Sometimes Brilliant* (New York: HarperOne, 2016).

Chapter Eight: Interconnected

203 *Big World, Small Planet*: Johan Rockström and Mattias Klum, *Big World, Small Planet* (New Haven, CT: Yale University Press, 2015).

204 **"Living up to the Anthropocene":** Paul J. Crutzen and Christian Schwägerl, "Living in the Anthropocene: Toward a New Global Ethos," *Yale Environment 360*, January 24, 2011, https://e360.yale.edu/features/living_in_the_anthropocene_toward_a_new_global_ethos.

208 **technology is often separating:** Mark Murray, "Poll: Nearly Two-Thirds of Americans Say Social Media Platforms Are Tearing Us Apart," NBC News, May 9, 2021, https://www.nbcnews.com/politics/meet-the-press/poll-nearly-two-thirds-americans-say-social-media-platforms-are-n1266773.

Photo Credits

Inside jacket collage design by Les Copland/DoubleTake Creative

TOP ROW: Jim Cooper and Paul Bennett (Photo courtesy Plus Wonder); Hank Willis Thomas and Deborah Willis (Photo courtesy Plus Wonder); Adam Balon, Richard Reed, and Jon Wright (Photo courtesy JamJar Investments); Girija and Larry Brilliant (Photo courtesy Larry and Girija Brilliant); Jane Tewson and Charles Lane (Photo courtesy Jane Tewson and Charles Lane); Gro and Arne Brundtland (Photo credit Bernt Sønvisen); Bill Draper, Robin Richards Donohoe, and Rob Kaplan (Photo courtesy Draper Richards Kaplan Foundation); Lord Dr. Michael Hastings of Scarisbrick CBE and Gloria Abramoff (Photo credit Ben Cantopher); Lawrence Chickering and Jim Turner (Photos courtesy The Transpartisan Review); Tim and Gaynor Brown (Photo courtesy Plus Wonder)

ROW TWO: Mostafa Tolba and Stephen O. Andersen (Photos courtesy Stephen O. Andersen); Sherwood Rowland and Mario Molina (Photo courtesy University of California, Irvine); Sherwood and Joan Rowland (Photo courtesy Rowland Family); Paz Perlman and Jo Confino (Photo courtesy Plus Wonder); André Borschberg and Bertrand Piccard (Photo courtesy Solar Impulse); Carroll Dunham and Wade Davis (Photo courtesy Plus Wonder); Eve Ellis and Annette Niemtzow (Photo courtesy Plus Wonder); Ngozi Okonjo-Iweala and Uzodinma Iweala (Photo courtesy Uzodinma Iweala); Ray Chambers and Peter Chernin (Photo courtesy Malaria No More); Joseph Farman, Brian G. Gardiner, and Jonathan Shanklin (Photo courtesy British Antarctic Survey)

ROW THREE: Alex Rappaport and Blake Harrison (Photo courtesy Plus Wonder); Sylvia Earle (Photo credit Kip Evans); Kelly Blynn, Jamie Henn, Will Bates, Phil Aroneanu, May Boeve, Jeremy Osborn, and Matt Fitzgerald (Photo credit Jon Warnow); Bert and John Jacobs (Photo credit Aimee Corrigan); Peter Gabriel and Richard Branson (Photo courtesy The Elders); Ryan Phelan and Stewart Brand (Photo credit Mark Alan Lovewell/Vineyard Gazette); Nancy Reichman (Photo courtesy Nancy Reichman) and Penelope Canan (Photo courtesy University of Central Florida); Guilherme Leal, Luiz Seabra, and Pedros Passos (Photo courtesy Natura)

ROW FOUR: Caskey and Mick Ebeling (Photo courtesy Plus Wonder); Anthony Ray Hinton and Lester Bailey (Photo courtesy Plus Wonder); Phil Kaye and Sarah Kay (Photo credit Taylor Lenci); Dereck and Beverly Joubert (Photo copyright Beverly Joubert); Erika Boyd and Kirsten Ussery (Photo courtesy Detroit Vegan Soul); Chris Redlitz and Beverly Parenti (Photo courtesy Chris Redlitz and Beverly Parenti); Keith Yamashita and Todd Holcomb (Photo courtesy Plus Wonder); Robert P. George and Cornel West (Photo courtesy Robert P. George); Robin Chase and Cameron Russell (Photo courtesy Plus Wonder); Andrea and Barry Coleman (Photo credit Tom Oldham)

ROW FIVE: Jim Roth and Andy Kuper (Photo courtesy Plus Wonder); David Blankenhorn (Photo courtesy Braver Angels) and John Wood Jr. (Photo courtesy John Wood Jr.); José María and Christiana Figueres (Photo courtesy Plus Wonder); Jimmy and Rosalynn Carter (Photo courtesy Plus Wonder); Desmond and Leah Tutu (Photo credit Michel Bega/The Citizen); Ben Cohen and Jerry Greenfield (Photo credit David Seaver Photography); Andrew Maxwell Mangino and Kanya Balakrishna (Photo courtesy Plus Wonder); Addison Fischer and Cindy Mercer (Photo courtesy Plus Wonder); Scott Seydel and Pat Mitchell (Photo courtesy Plus Wonder)

ROW SIX: Banguu, Sangu, and Edmund Delle (Photo courtesy Delle Family); Pat and Tony Hawk (Photo courtesy Tony Hawk, Inc/The Skatepark Project); Chris Anderson and Jacqueline Novogratz (Photo courtesy Jacqueline Novogratz and Chris Anderson); Amory and Judy Lovins (Photo courtesy Amory and Judy Lovins); Greg and Jacki Zehner (Photo courtesy Plus Wonder); Sam Goldman and Ned Tozun (Photo courtesy d.light); Johan Rockström (Photo credit M. Axelsson/Azote), Katherine Richardson (Photo courtesy Katherine Richardson), and Will Steffen (Photo courtesy Will Steffen); Nathan Blecharczyk, Joe Gebbia, and Brian Chesky (Photo courtesy Airbnb)

BOTTOM ROW: Donna Red Wing and Bob Vander Plaats (Photo © Rodney White—USA TODAY NETWORK); Henry Arnhold and Kevin Starr (Photo courtesy Plus Wonder); David and Lindsay Levin (Photo courtesy Lindsay and David Levin); Sheryl WuDunn and Nicholas Kristof (Photo courtesy Plus Wonder); Azim Khamisa and Ples Felix (Photo courtesy Tariq Khamisa Foundation); Severn and Sarika Cullis-Suzuki (Photo courtesy Plus Wonder); Martin Hill and Philippa Jones (Photo credit Ian McDonald); Ashish J. Thakkar, Ahuti Chug, Jagdish D. Thakkar, and Rona Kotecha (Photo courtesy Mara Group); Robbie Schingler and Will Marshall (Photo courtesy Planet Labs, Inc.)

Index

Note: Page numbers in *italics* refer to diagrams.

Abramoff, Gloria, 101
absence in relationships, 8, 59
action, taking loving, 106–9
affirmations that build respect, 105
African American community, 138–39
African National Congress, 101
Airbnb, 80–82, 83–84
All-In (Second Degree of Connection),
    37–64
  about, 4, 5
  as act of generosity, 105
  barriers to being, 58–59
  and the Carters, 43–46
  and commitment to the commitment,
    42–43
  examining your commitment to being,
    62–63
  finding strength in differences, 46–49
  and friends before partners, 49–51
  and letting go of fear, 60–61
  and mutual hard work, 52–54
  and taking the long view in
    relationships, 54–58
all-or-nothing language, 165
altruism, extreme, 105
amnesia, positive, 165–66
Andersen, Stephen O.
  collaborative leadership of, 180–81
  and distributed leadership, 190
  and ecosystem of virtues, 70–72
  efforts at recognizing others, 115–16

family atmosphere built by, 119
and Kigali Amendment, 196
and Lee-Bapty, 152–53
and managing friction/conflict,
    150–51, 163
and personal/collective purpose, 183
recruitment of collaborators, 187
and Thatcher, 174
thoughtful gifts from, 115–16
and unlikely connections, 187–88
Anderson, Chris, 26–28, 61
anger and resentment, 166
Annan, Kofi, xii, 119
Anthropocene geological epoch, 204
"applied hope" concept of Lovins, 25
Arnhold, Henry, 79
The Art of War (Sun Tzu), xiv
assumptions, avoiding, 99
attention, bids for, 59
audacity
  shared, 28–30
  and understanding your limitations, 99
Australian Conservation Foundation, 189
authentic selves, space to be, 61

Bailey, Lester, 25, 106–8, 112, 120, 211
Baker, Jay, 185
Balakrishna, Kanya, 129
Balon, Adam, 121–24
bearers of truth, 63
Beginning Anew practice, 132–33

belief, united
 four ways to sustain, 94–96
 as key virtue, 5, 75–76, *78*, 90–96
 and shared humility, 96–97
Ben & Jerry's, xiii. *See also* Cohen, Ben;
  Greenfield, Jerry
Benedick, Richard, 175, 184
Bennett, Paul, 62–63, 88–89, 100
Biden, Joe, 30
bids for attention, 59
Biko, Steve, 119
Bildner, Jim, 97
Bizos, George, 101
Blake, Donald, 38–39, 41
Blecharczyk, Nate, 80–82
Blue Zone research, 137
body language, 84
borders, national, 207–8
Borschberg, André
 and competition between partners, 96
 and considering the other's
  perspective, 160
 and constructing a third way, 161
 and learning in moments of friction,
  154, 155–58
 partnership with Bertrand, 1–3
 and Solar Impulse's historic flight, 1–3
Borschberg, Yasemin, 1
Boyd, Erika, 25, 31–32, 105
Brand, Stewart, 131–32
Branson, Richard
 and The Elders initiative, xii, 91, 92, 126
 and humor, 164
 joy and play embraced by, 120,
  126–27
 meeting with Mandela, xi
 and positive amnesia, 165–66
Brenninkmeijer, Andrea, 92, 195
Brilliant, Girija, 199
Brilliant, Larry, 198–200
Brinkhorst, Laurens Jan, 149–50
British Antarctic Survey, 67
Brown, Gaynor, 140–41
Brown, Tim, 140
Brundtland, Arne, 168, 170
Brundtland, Gro, 168, 170
B Team, xiii, 188
Buettner, Dan, 137
Buffer software company, 83
Buffett, Warren, xx
Burrow, Sharan, 188

Canan, Penelope, 179–81, 188
Carter, Jimmy
 all-in commitment to relationship,
  43–46
 author's interview with, 43–44
 book co-authored with Rosalynn, 6, 45
 childhood origins of relationship, 9
 confidence in Rosalynn, 95
 and The Elders, 92, 93–94, 119
 and Mandela, xii
 partnership with Rosalynn, 43–46
 and shared rituals, 128
 struggles of, 6, 44–45
Carter, Rosalynn
 all-in commitment to relationship,
  43–46
 author's interview with, 43–44
 book co-authored with Jimmy, 6, 45
 childhood origins of relationship, 9
 credited as most important person in
  White House, 44, 95
 Jimmy's confidence in, 95
 partnership with Jimmy, 43–46
 and shared rituals, 128
 struggles of, 6, 44–45
Carter Center, 46
Celebrating Friction (Fifth Degree of
  Connection), 149–71
 about, 5, *5*
 in Borschberg and Piccard's
  relationship, 155–58
 considering other perspectives in,
  160–61
 creating a safe space for, 162–63
 and finding common ground, 169–70
 and finding/constructing a third
  way, 161
 and getting help/support, 167–68
 harnessing friction gracefully, 153–55
 and keeping perspective, 165
 learning moments in friction, 154
 and the long game, 170–71
 and positive amnesia, 165–66
 and understanding the why, 158–59
 and understanding your triggers,
  166–67
 and value of humor, 164–65
 and veto powers, 163–64
centenarians of Okinawa, Japan, 137
Chambers, Ray, 55–58
Chase, Robin, 54–55

Chernin, Peter, 55–58
Chesky, Brian, 80–82
Chickering, Lawrence (Lawry), 169–70
children, 52–53
Chin, Christy, 97
chlorofluorocarbons (CFCs)
    crisis averted by halting use of, 195
    DuPont's reversal on, 193–94
    impact on ozone layer, 15, 67–68, 69
    and less industrialized countries,
        186–87
    Montreal Protocol's ban on, 70–72
    and ozone hole discovery, 41–42, 67–68
    phasing out of, 179, 190
    and pushback against Rowland and
        Molina's research, 15–16, 37–40
    Sherwood and Molina's research on,
        14–16
    See also ozone community
choices, daily, 32–35
Christian Coalition of America, 141
Cicerone, Ralph, 39
civility, xvi, 88
climate change, xvi. See also ozone
        community
"cloak of authority," putting aside, 151
Cohen, Ben
    on being all-in, 50
    differences with Jerry, 49–50
    "friends before partners" mantra of, 51
    on managing potential conflict, 159
    partnership with Jerry, xiii, 49–51
    trust in partnership of, 84
    and united belief, 94–95
    and veto powers, 163
collaboration. See Collective Connections
Collective Connections (Sixth Degree of
        Connection), 173–200
    about, 5, 5
    and collective purpose, 183–84
    and culture of service/friendship, 193–94
    importance of, 176
    and open-tent ethic, 186–87
    in ozone community, 173–75, 178–82,
        197–99
    and relational scaffolding, 190–93
    role of group composition/dynamics in,
        177–78
    at scale, 179, 197–98
    and smallpox eradication in India,
        198–200

and starting with manageable goals,
        185–86
and unlikely connections, 187–89
commitment to relationships, imbalance
        in, 8, 59
common ground
    finding, 169–70
    mutual awareness of, 91
communication/conversations
    collective practice of, 123–24
    and deep listening, 132–33
    defusing conflict through, 158–59
    in digital mediums, xvi, 135–36, 155
    Friday Talk practice of Confino and
        Perlman, 132–33, 158, 162
    at Innocent Drinks, 123–24
    making hard conversations the norm,
        83–84
    making space for, 47, 59, 63, 120,
        132–36, 146, 162–63
    rituals in, 128–29, 132–33, 134–35,
        142–43, 162
community
    magnetic moments that build, 120,
        136–41, 146
    "moais" of Okinawan centenarians, 137
    role of respect in, 90
company cultures, strengthened by
        rituals, 140–41
compassion
    Andersen's application of, 71, 72
    empathy rooted in, 5, 59, 76, 78, 106–12
    generosity with time as act of, 105–6
    as outcome of six virtues, 77
    of Tutu, 19
    universal, 77
competition
    in Borschberg and Piccard's
        relationship, 158
    and culture at DRK, 98
    between partners, 57, 62
    with yourself, 95–96
compromise, 52
confidence, 95, 97
Confino, Jo
    on change starting with oneself, 54
    on community, 105
    everyday living rituals of, 132–34
    Friday Talk practice of, 132–33,
        158, 162
    on joy, 125–26

Confino, Jo (*cont.*)
  on knowing your triggers, 166
  on respect, 88
  on understanding, 109
  on vulnerability, 110–11
conflict
  making a space for managing, 63
  as opportunity to love and
      unify, 49
  ozone community's approaches to
      managing, 149–53
  roller coaster of, 8
  sparking innovation with, 157
  See also Celebrating Friction
connection, the joy of, 125
contempt, 155
control, letting go of complete, 100
Cooper, Jim, 88–89, 100
Corona, Jorge, 72
coronavirus pandemic of 2020
  Airbnb's response to crisis, 81–82
  and digital communication, 135–36
  impact on human connection, xx
  and need for more global
      cooperation, 182
  and political borders, 207–8
criticism, managing, 37–40, 154
Crutzen, Paul, 39, 40, 196, 204, 206
Cullis, Tara Elizabeth, 130
Cullis-Suzuki, Sarika, 130–31
Cullis-Suzuki, Severn, 130–31
curiosity, magnetic moments that spark,
      120, 128–32, 146

Davis, Shannon Sedgwick, 211
Davis, Wade, xvi–xvii, 73–77
decision making practices, 123–24,
      150–52
Deep Connections
  about, xii–xiii
  dearth of time devoted to, xvii
  fundamental importance of, xiv
  number of, 10
  pitfalls that inhibit, 8–9
  and quest for success, xv
  See also Six Degrees of Connection
defensiveness, 154
Delle, Banguu, 134–35, 160, 163
Delle, Edmund, 134–35, 160, 163
Delle, Sangu, 25, 104, 134–35, 160, 163
depth of relationships, 17

Detroit Vegan Soul, 25, 31–32, 104–5. *See
      also* Boyd, Erika; Ussery, Kirsten
differences
  celebrating, 61, 75
  finding strength in, 46–49
  honoring and respecting, 88, 141–43
  and respect for others' opinions,
      86–88
  and unlikely connections, 187–89
digital communication, xvi, 135–36, 155
dignity, 26
disagreements
  considering other perspectives in,
      160–61
  creating spaces for, 192
  without disrespect, 89
disappointments, dealing with, 20–21
disengagement, xvi, 59
disrespect, 89
diverse thinking, importance of Deep
      Connections to, 10
diversity, valuing, 100
Donohoe, Robin Richards, 97–98, 99
drama, 8, 153–54
Draper, Bill, 97–98, 99
Draper Richards Kaplan (DRK), 97–99
Dunham, Carroll, 73–77
DuPont, 38, 189, 193–94

Earth System science, 204–5
Ebeling, Caskey, 26, 127, 128–29
Ebeling, Mick, 127, 128–29
Ecosystem (Third Degree of Connection),
      67–112
  about, 4, *5*
  for collective good, 73–77
  daily practice of virtues, 73
  interconnectedness of virtues in, 77, *78*
  loss of moral ecosystem, 74
  virtue of compassionate empathy, 76,
      78, 106–12
  virtue of enduring trust, 75, *78*, 79–85
  virtue of mutual respect, 75, *78*, 85–90
  virtue of nurturing generosity, 76, *78*,
      101–6
  virtue of shared humility, 76, *78*,
      96–101
  virtue of united belief, 75–76, *78*,
      90–96
Edelman Trust Barometer study, 79, 207
ego, taming, 96–101, 157

The Elders
    author's interviews with, xvii–xviii
    collective purpose of, 184
    and Deep Connections, xiii
    early meetings to organize, xi–xii
    as independent initiative, 186
    launching of, 118–19
    and Mandela's ninetieth birthday
        celebration, xxi
    Mandela's speech to, 93, 184
    origins of, 91–94
    at Robben Island, 112
elephants, altruism among, 105
Elliott, Nicola, xi
Elworthy, Scilla, 92
empathy
    about, 76
    and bids for attention, 59
    five ways to strengthen, 109–12
    and generosity with one's time, 106
    promoted by Tariq Khamisa
        Foundation, 48
    rooted in compassion, 5, 59, 76, 78,
        106–12
    in Six Degrees of Connection
        framework, 5
    of Stephen, 71–72
    and taking loving action, 106–9
    and Thatcher's work on Montreal
        Protocol, 174
    three types of, 107
    of Tolba, 70
Environmental Protection Agency (EPA),
    39, 195
Equal Justice Initiative, 106
Everything to Gain: Making the Most of the
    Rest of Your Life (Carter and
    Carter), 6, 45

failure, fear of, 155
fake news, 79
fallibility, acknowledging, 87, 160
families, service prioritized in, 23, 27–28
Farman, Joseph, 67–69, 136, 160–61,
    173, 206
fear, letting go of, 60–61, 75
Felix, Ples, 47–49, 120, 162
fighting, 59
Figueres, Christina, xiii, 23, 196–97
Figueres, José María, xiii, 23, 197
Find Your Why (Sinek), 24

Fischer, Addison, 161
Flocabulary, 94. See also Harrison, Blake;
    Rappaport, Alex
forgiveness
    Khamisa's forgiveness of son's killer, 47,
        109–10, 162, 166
    and managing friction/conflict, 154
    and positive amnesia, 166
freedom through shared
    understanding, 112
friction. See Celebrating Friction
Friday Talk practice of Confino and
    Perlman, 132–33, 158, 162
friendships
    before business partnerships, 49–51
    conventional advice on, 7
    creating a culture that supports, 193–95
    in ozone community, 117–18, 179–80,
        194–95, 200
    that unsettle you, 88
Fuller, Buckminster, 177–78
Future Project, 129

Gabriel, Peter
    "Biko" performed by, 119
    and The Elders initiative, xii, 91, 92
    on importance of communication, 132
    joy and play embraced by, 120, 126–27
    and positive amnesia, 165–66
    on value of humor, 164
Gandhi, Mohandas, 145
gang violence, 46–47, 49
Gardiner, Brian G., 67–69, 136, 160–61,
    173, 206
Gay, Ross, 128
Gebbia, Joe, 80–82
generational divide, unlikely partnerships
    across, 189
generosity
    and abundant love, 77
    Andersen's exercising of, 115–17
    and being all-in, 105
    five ways to engage, 103–6
    nurturing, 5, 76, 78, 101–6
George, Robert P., 86–88, 91, 160
Giffords, Gabby, 28–30
Give and Take (Grant), 101–2
givers and takers, 101–2
Glas, Joseph, 194
global disengagement, sense of, xvi
globalism, 40

glory, sharing, 104–5
goals. *See* purpose
"go fast/go far" proverb, xxii
good fortune, sharing, 104
Google's Project Aristotle, 78
Gottman, John, 26, 59, 154–55
Grant, Adam, 101–2
Grasset, Nicole, 199
gratitude
  daily practice of, 144–45
  scorecards for, 103–4
Greenfield, Jerry
  on being all-in, 50
  differences with Ben, 49–50
  "friends before partners" mantra
    of, 51
  on managing potential conflict, 159
  partnership with Ben, xiii, 49–51
  trust in partnership of, 84
  and united belief, 94–95
  and veto powers, 163
Greenpeace, 189
growing apart, two categories of, 59
gun violence, 29–30, 46–47

hard work, mutual, 52–54
Harrison, Blake, 94, 160
Hastings, Lord, 1, 100–101
Hawk, Tony, 115, 139
Hawking, Stephen, 128
Hays, Henry Francis, 108–9
help, asking for, 48, 167–68
Hicks, Tony, 46–47, 109–10
Hinton, Anthony Ray, 25, 106–9, 112,
    120, 211
Holcomb, Todd, 60–61
human trafficking, 143
humility
  and Airbnb's pandemic response, 82
  and confidence, 97
  five principles to cultivate, 99–101
  and managing friction/conflict,
    155, 161
  shared humility, 76, *78*, 96–101
  in Six Degrees of Connection
    framework, 5
  and sparking innovation in
    conflict, 157
  and united belief, 96–97
Hussain, Zafar, 199–200
hydrofluorocarbons (HFCs), 196

ideas differing from your own, opening
    up to, 75
IDEO, 139–41
impact, bias toward, 16
Imperial Chemical Industries
    (ICI), 38
India, smallpox eradication in,
    198–200, 210
indifference, 59
Indigenous wisdom, 76
individualism
  and coronavirus pandemic of
    2020, 207
  and decline of generosity, 105
  and loneliness crisis, xvi
  and loss of moral ecosystem, 74
  and quest for success, xiv–xv
individuality, respecting, 146
inequality, xvi
Innocent Drinks, 121–24, 132, 145. *See
    also* Balon, Adam; Reed, Richard;
    Wright, Jon
intentions, assuming good, 82–83
interest, lack of, 59
interpersonal skills, 63
Iweala, Ikemba, 23
Iweala, Ngozi, 23
Iweala, Uzodinma (Uzo), 23, 67, 89

Jacobs, Bert, 25, 104, 144
Jacobs, John, 25, 104, 144
JamJar investment firm, 124
Johnson, Harold, 39
John Templeton Foundation, 105
Joubert, Beverly, 9, 102–3, 105, 165
Joubert, Dereck, 102–3, 105, 165
joy, magnetic moments that inspire, 120,
    125–28, 146
"Joy Is Such a Human Madness"
    (Gay), 128
The Joy of Cooking (Rombauer, Becker, and
    Becker), xiv
judgment, letting go of, 109–10

Kaberuka, Donald, 208
Kaplan, Rob, 97, 98, 99
Kathrada, Ahmed, 18
Kay, Sarah, 162–63, 166
Kaye, Phil, 162–63, 166
Kelley, David, 139–40
Kelly, Mark, 28–30

Khamisa, Azim
    and compassionate empathy, 109–10
    forgiveness exercised by, 47, 109–10,
        162, 166
    and strength in opposing forces, 46–49
    trees planted by, 120
Khamisa, Tariq, 46–47, 109–10
Khamisa, Tasreen, 110
Knowledge Project podcast (Perel), 59
Kristof, Nicholas, 52–54
Kuper, Andy, 26, 99, 100, 159, 164

Lane, Charles, 137
language choices, 165
leadership, distributed, 190
Leal, Guilherme, 191
LeapFrog Investment, 26, 99. *See also*
        Kuper, Andy; Roth, Jim
Lee-Bapty, Steve, 152–53
LGBTQ rights, 141–43
Life is Good mission statement, 25
lift, sustaining united belief with, 96
limitations, understanding your, 99–100
listening
    and compassionate empathy, 109
    deep listening, 88–89, 132–33
    defusing conflict through, 158–59
    and practicing curiosity, 128
    practicing respectful, 75
    See also communication/conversations
loneliness crisis, xvi
longevity of relationships, 17
long game/long view taking the, 54–58,
        170–71
Long Now Foundation, 131
love
    being all-in on, 42–43
    between Cohen and Greenfield, 51
    focusing on giving, 63
    and generosity of spirit, 77
    holding back on, 42–43
    as outcome of six virtues, 77
Lovelock, James, 14
loving action, 106–9
Lovins, Amory, 24–25, 100

Mabaso, Thulani, 112
Machel, Graça
    background of, xi
    and The Elders, xi–xii, 91, 118–19
    meeting with, xi–xii, xvii

and ninetieth birthday celebration of
        Nelson, xx–xxi
    partnership with Nelson, xii
Magnetic Moments (Fourth Degree of
        Connection), 115–46
    about, 4–5, 5, 119–20
    best practices for creating, 145–46
    and curiosity and wonder, 120,
        128–32, 146
    at Innocent Drinks, 121–25
    and joy and play, 120, 125–28, 146
    power to bridge differences, 141–43
    and space for honest communication,
        120, 132–36, 146
    and time with supportive community,
        120, 136–41, 146
    traditions, rituals, and practices of,
        118–21
    value of, 121
malaria, mission to end, 55–58
Malaria No More, 56–57
Mandela, Nelson
    and Bizos, 101
    celebration of life honoring, 18–19
    and The Elders, xi–xii, 91, 93, 118, 184
    hopefulness of, xxi
    meeting with, xi–xii, xvii
    ninetieth birthday celebration, xx–xxi
    partnership with Graça, xii
    prison cell of, 112
    on resentment, 166
    Robinson on honoring memory of, xxi
    on trial, 18, 101
Mangino, Andrew Maxwell, 129
Manuel, Trevor, 208
Married to Gro (Brundtland), 170
Marshall, Will, 85
Masiyiwa, Strive, 208
McFarland, Mack, 194
meaning, lack of shared, 8
media, politicized, 79
meetings, managing friction in,
        150–52, 193
Mercer, Cindy, 161
mirrors, partners functioning as, 63, 167
missions. *See* purpose
mission statements, 25–26
mistakes, making, 6, 7–9, 84, 129
Mitchell, Pat, 96
"moais" of Okinawan centenarians, 137
Mody, Russi, 198–99

Molina, Mario
  alliances built by, 39
  background of, 14
  and CFCs research, 14-16
  and DuPont's policy reversal, 193-94
  and Earth System science, 204
  honoring work of, 206
  impact on science field, 40, 69-70
  integrity and character of, 69, 72
  and lived values, 73
  and Nobel Prize, 104, 196
  ozone hole discovery validating work
      of, 41-42, 69
  and personal/collective purpose, 183
  pushback experienced by, 15-16, 37-40
  recognition shared with Sherry, 104
  and Sherry's curiosity, 130
  and Thatcher, 174
  and unlikely connections, 187-88
Montreal Protocol
  collective purpose represented by, 184
  and ecosystem of virtues, 70-72
  importance of, 195
  Kigali Amendment to, 195-96
  and open-tent ethic, 186-87
  recognition of Russia's contributions
      to, 115
  relationships at the core of, 150
  and Thatcher, 174
  and trade restrictions, 190
  unlikely collaborators in, 175, 179
moral ecosystem. See Ecosystem
Music Not Impossible, 129
myopia, cultural, 76

naivete, value of, 128-29
national identity biases, putting
      aside, 151
National Ozone Expedition to
      Antarctica, 69
Natura, 190-92, 200
nature, 100, 130-31, 163
Nature, 15, 37, 69
negativity/negative relationships, 8, 155
Nelson Mandela Foundation in South
      Africa, 18
Nhat Hanh, Thich, 132, 133
Nkengasong, John, 208
Noone, Kevin, 118, 205
Not Impossible Labs, 129
Novogratz, Jacqueline, 26-28, 42, 61

Oelwang, Robert C., 33-35
Okinawan centenarians, 137
Okonjo-Iweala, Ngozi, 208
open-door policies, 139
open-tent ethic, 186-87
Operating Manual for Spaceship Earth
      (Fuller), 177-78
opportunities, sharing, 104
opposing forces, power in, 49
optimism, collective spirit of, 197
ozone community
  and Andersen's cultivation of
      connection, 115-17
  collective purpose of, 184, 195, 200
  and distributed leadership, 190
  and Earth System science, 205-6
  family atmosphere of, 119
  family members integrated into, 117
  friendships and alliances at core of,
      117-18, 179-80, 194-95, 200
  global collaboration in, 173-75, 178-82
  and less industrialized countries, 174,
      186-87
  managing friction/conflict in, 149-53
  and ozone hole discovery, 41-42, 67-68
  success of, 210
  and Thatcher, 173-75, 178-79
  and Tolba's effort to increase
      communication, 117-18
  unlikely collaborators in, 173-75,
      187-89, 200
  See also chlorofluorocarbons; Montreal
      Protocol; specific scientists,
      including Rowland, Frank
      Sherwood "Sherry"
Ozone Connections (Reichman and
      Canan), 179-80
Ozone Hole: How We Saved the Planet (PBS
      documentary), 37

Pando aspen colony, 74
Paris Agreement, 197
passion, and work/life separation, 9
Passos, Pedro, 190-91
patience, urgent, 111-12
pedestal, putting people on, 90
Penan nomadic people of Malaysia, 76
Perel, Esther, 59
perfectionism, rise in, 155
Perlman, Paz, 132-34, 158, 162, 166
Pew Research Center, xvi

Phelan, Ryan, 131–32
photography, ritual of, 138–39
Piccard, Bertrand
    and competition between partners, 96
    and considering the other's
        perspective, 160
    and constructing a third way, 161
    and learning in moments of friction,
        149, 154, 155–58
    partnership with André, 1–3
    and Solar Impulse's historic flight, 1–3
Piccard, Michèle, 156
pitfalls that inhibit Deep Connections,
    8–9
Piver, Susan, 125
Planetary Boundaries framework, 204–7
play
    built into The Elders' schedule, 120
    of Cullis-Suzuki family, 130
    magnetic moments that inspire, 120,
        125–28, 146
Plum Village monastery, 133–34
Plus Wonder (not-for-profit initiative), xviii
Polman, Paul, 188
power over others, 74–75
practices, daily, 119
present, staying, 62–63, 75, 89
Project Aristotle, 78
proximity in experiences, value of, 110
purpose
    and all-in relationships, 53–54
    audacity in, 28–30
    Cohen and Greenfield's commitment
        to shared, 50
    collective, 183–84, 200
    constant evolution of, 25
    daily choice to live with, 32–35
    defining, 9
    as dominant aspect of Deep
        Connections, 16
    as a grounding force, 30–32
    identifying/choosing one's purpose,
        22–24
    language used to describe, 16–17
    lifting, through meaningful
        partnership, 4
    mission statements for, 25–26
    partnerships' reinforcement of, 9
    passion in, 24–26
    and pushback from community, 15–16,
        31–32

relationships' ability to multiply, 16
rituals centered on, 128
and service emphasized in families, 23,
    27–28
shared, 17–22, 24, 54
supporting individuals' separate
    purposes, 26–28
in tragedy, 47–49
See also Something Bigger
pushback, dealing with
    against Boyd and Ussery's Detroit
        Vegan Soul, 31–32
    against Rowland and Molina's research,
        15–16, 37–40

questions
    asking hard questions, 160–61
    placing a premium on, 128–29

racism, xvi
Ramaphosa, Cyril, 208
Rappaport, Alex, 62, 94, 160
Reagan, Ronald, 175, 179
recognition, 104–5, 115–16
Red Wing, Donna, 141–43
Reed, Richard
    on choosing one's relationships, 9, 37
    and company culture, 121–24
    on doing business with friends, 10
    on measure of life well lived, 209
    on respect for others' opinions, 89
Reichman, Nancy, 179–81, 188
relational scaffolding, 190–93
renewable energy, 1–3
renewal, rituals of, 144–45
resentment and anger, 166
respect
    affirmations that build, 105
    between Cohen and Greenfield, 50, 51
    for differing opinions, 86–88, 141–43
    growing, 89–90
    between Kristof and WuDunn, 53
    practicing unshakable mutual, 75, 78,
        85–90
    and putting partners on pedestals, 90
    as related to trust, 85–86
    six common principles that build, 88–90
    in Six Degrees of Connection
        framework, 5
Revive & Restore, 131–32
Richardson, Katherine, 203–5, 206

Ridley, Nicholas, 174
risk taking, 61
rituals
    to address what's not working, 129
    based in nature, 130
    centered on shared experiences/
        purpose, 128
    changing/evolving, 145–46
    in communication, 128–29, 132–33,
        134–35, 142–43, 162
    community based, 136–41
    of everyday living, 132–34
    at Innocent Drinks, 122–23
    of language, 127
    as magnetic moments, 119
    in online/virtual connections,
        135–36
    of play, 120
    of reinvention, 131–32
    of renewal, 144–45
    smoko (smoking break), 136
    in strengthening company culture,
        140–41
    that spark curiosity, 129
    See also Magnetic Moments
Rivett-Carnac, Tom, 197
Rivonia Trial, 18, 101
Roberts, Gregory David, 42
Robinson, Mary, xii, xxi, 119
Rockström, Johan, 203–5, 206
Roth, Jim, 13, 26, 99, 159, 164
Rowland, Frank Sherwood "Sherry"
    background of, 13–14
    and CFCs research, 14–16
    curiosity of, 130
    dedication to family, 41
    and DuPont's policy reversal, 193–94
    and Earth System science, 204
    emphasis on manageable goals,
        185, 186
    honoring work of, 206
    impact on science field, 40, 69–70
    integrity and character of, 69, 72
    and lived values, 73
    nickname of, 13
    and Nobel Prize, 104, 196
    ozone hole discovery validating work
        of, 41–42, 69
    partnership with Joan, 40–41
    and personal/collective purpose, 183
    pushback experienced by, 15–16, 37–40

    recognition shared with Mario, 104
    and Thatcher, 174
    and unlikely connections, 187–88
Rowland, Ingrid, 40, 130, 196
Rowland, Jeffrey, 38, 41, 196
Rowland, Joan, 13, 37, 40–41, 130, 196
Rozovsky, Julia, 78
Russell, Cameron, 54–55
Russian delegation at ozone negotiations
    in Paris, 115–16

Sachs, Jeffrey, 56
sacrifices made for partners, 52
safe harbor, being your partner's, 63
safe space
    for authentic selves, 61
    to grow trust, 83
    for honest/hard conversations, 47,
        84, 156
    and limiting competition, 81
    and managing friction/conflict, 151,
        161, 162–63
    for personal growth, 64
    for vulnerability, 110
safety in relationships, sense of, 4
same-sex marriage, 143
Schwägerl, Christian, 204
Seabra, Luiz, 190–91
Sears, Roebuck and Co., 33–35
segregation in South Africa, 17–19
self-sacrifice, 52, 170
self-scrutiny, 160
separateness, 59
service
    creating a culture of, 193–95
    and culture at DRK, 99
    families dedicated to, 23, 27–28
    Gandhi on value of, 145
    and sense of humility, 100–101
Seydel, Scott, 96
Shanklin, Jonathan, 67–69, 136, 160–61,
    173, 206
shared meaning, lack of, 8
Shatrov, Ya. T., 115
Shultz, George, 175
Sisulu, Albertina, 18
Sisulu, Walter, 18
Six Degrees of Connection
    about, xix
    framework of, 5
    interconnectedness of, 6

summarized, 4–5
See also All-In; Celebrating Friction;
    Collective Connections;
    Ecosystem; Magnetic Moments;
    Something Bigger
skill sets, complementary, 24
skin cancer cases, 195
smallpox eradication in India,
    198–200, 210
"smoko" ritual, 136
social media, 79, 139, 208–9
social structures, state of, xvi–xvii
Solar Impulse's historic flight, 1–3, 96,
    155–58. *See also* Borschberg,
    André; Piccard, Bertrand
Solomon, Susan, 69
Something Bigger (First Degree of
    Connection), 13–35
    about, 4, 5, 16–17
    and all-in relationships, 53–54
    audacity in, 28–30
    and daily choice to live with purpose,
        32–35
    as a grounding force, 30–32
    identifying/choosing one's purpose,
        22–24
    and passion in purpose, 24–26
    shared purpose, 17–22
    supporting separate purposes of
        individuals, 26–28
South Africa, apartheid system in, 17–19
"the sparkles" in conflict management, 157
spiritual connections, 48, 49
Steffen, Will, 203–5, 206
Stevenson, Bryan, 106–8, 110, 112
Stolarski, Richard, 39
stonewalling, 155
strengths, 67–68
success
    author's quest for, xiv–xv
    Buffett on, xx
    celebrating, 193
    conventional advice on achieving, xiv
    desire for collective, 17
    measures of, 209
suffering, helping to alleviate, 107
superhero syndrome, 8–9
Suzuki, David, 130

tailwind, being your partner's, 63
Tambo, Oliver, 18

Tariq Khamisa Foundation, 48, 110
Tata, J. R. D., 199
Tata Group, 198–99
technology, digital, xvi, 135–36, 155
Technology and Economic Assessment
    Panel (TEAP), 71, 72, 181, 185,
    188, 194
Tewson, Jane, 137
Thatcher, Margaret, 173–75, 178–79
third ways, finding/constructing, 161
Thomas, Hank Willis, 138–39
Thomas, Lee, 149–50
Tiananmen Square crackdown, 53
Tolba, Mostafa
    collaborative leadership of, 180
    and collaborators, 177
    and distributed leadership, 190
    and ecosystem of virtues, 70–72
    emphasis on manageable goals, 185
    family atmosphere built by, 119
    honoring work of, 206
    and managing friction/conflict,
        151–52, 163
    and open-tent ethic, 186–87
    and personal/collective purpose, 183
    and spaces for honest communication,
        117–18
    and Thatcher, 174
    and unlikely connections, 187–88
traditions, 119, 123
tragedy, finding purpose in, 47–49
transparency, principle of, 83, 123, 192
trauma, power to unite partnerships, 53
triggers, understanding your, 166–67
Trumbore, Susan, 40
Trump, Donald, 141
trust
    and assuming good intentions, 82–83
    and body language, 84
    between Cohen and Greenfield, 51
    creating a safe space to grow, 83
    defaulting to, 82, 83
    and Edelman Trust Barometer study,
        79, 207
    as key virtue, 5, 75, *78*, 79–85
    in oneself, 84–85
    as related to respect, 85–86
    and taking responsibility for
        mistakes, 84
    between Vander Plaats and Red
        Wing, 142

truth, bearers of, 63
Truth and Reconciliation Commission,
    19, 22
Turner, James (Jim), 169–70
Tutu, Desmond "Arch"
    and apartheid system in South Africa,
        18, 21–22
    and Bizos, 101
    dealing with disappointments, 20–21
    and The Elders, 93–94, 119
    lived virtues of, 77
    and Mandela, xii, xxi
    partnership with Leah, xiii, 19–22
    shared purpose of, 21
    and spirit of ubuntu, 21
    and swimming lessons, 126–27
    and Truth and Reconciliation
        Commission, 19, 22
Tutu, Leah
    and apartheid system in South Africa,
        18, 21–22
    dealing with disappointments, 20–21
    lived virtues of, 77
    partnership with Desmond, xiii, 19–22
    shared purpose of, 21
    and Truth and Reconciliation
        Commission, 22
Twain, Mark, 90

ubuntu, spirit of, 21
understanding
    and compassionate empathy, 109
    freedom through shared, 112
united belief. See belief, united
unsettling friendships, 88
US Environmental Protection Agency
    (EPA), 189
Ussery, Kirsten, 25, 31–32, 105

values
    erosion of, 207
    lived values of Rowland and Molina, 73
    mismatched, 8
    shared, 55

Vander Plaats, Bob, 141–43
veto powers, 163–64
Virgin Group, 35
Virgin Unite, xiii, xv, xviii, 120, 182
virtues
    about, 75–77
    collective, 74
    compassionate empathy, 76, 78, 106–12
    daily practice of, 73
    enduring trust, 75, 78, 79–85
    and forgiveness, 166
    interconnectedness of, 77, 78
    mutual respect, 75, 78, 85–90
    nurturing generosity, 76, 78, 101–6
    shared humility, 76, 78, 96–101
    united belief, 75–76, 78, 90–96
vulnerability
    inability to engage with, 59
    permission to engage in, 110–11

West, Cornel, 86–88, 91, 160
Whyte, David, 25
Willis, Deborah, 138–39
wonder, magnetic moments that inspire,
    120, 128–32, 146
work
    balancing family and purpose with, 33
    disengagement at, xvi
    and personal relationships, 9–10
World Economic Forum, Davos,
    Switzerland, 203, 206
World Trade Organization (WTO), 23
Wright, Jon, 121–24
WuDunn, Sheryl, 52–54

Yamashita, Keith, 60–61, 210
YPO community, 137–38

Zaki, Jamil, 107
Zehner, Greg, 103, 167
Zehner, Jacki, 103
Zen Buddhist practice, 133–34
Zoom calls, 135–36
Zucker, Rebecca, 154